U0424673

材料科学与工程专业英语

（第4版）

主编 刘爱国

哈尔滨工业大学出版社

内 容 提 要

本书是为提高从事材料科学与工程专业学习和研究人员的英语阅读能力而编写的。全书共分六部分:材料科学与工程简介、材料、焊接工艺、铸造工艺、成型工艺、热处理工艺。本书可作为相关专业的专业英语阅读教材,也可供有关人员阅读参考。

图书在版编目(CIP)数据

材料科学与工程专业英语/刘爱国等主编. —4 版. —哈尔滨:哈尔滨工业大学出版社,2007.10(2024.2 重印)

ISBN 978-7-5603-1408-2

Ⅰ. 材… Ⅱ. 刘… Ⅲ. 材料科学–英语 Ⅳ. H31

中国版本图书馆 CIP 数据核字(2007)第 003238 号

责任编辑 孙 杰
封面设计 卞秉利
出版发行 哈尔滨工业大学出版社
社　　址　哈尔滨市南岗区复华四道街 10 号 邮编 150006
传　　真　0451–86414749
网　　址　http://hitpress.hit.edu.cn
印　　刷　哈尔滨市工大节能印刷厂
开　　本　880mm×1230mm 1/32 印张 9.875 字数 340 千字
版　　次　2003 年 8 月第 1 版 2007 年 10 月第 4 版
　　　　　2024 年 2 月第 16 次印刷
书　　号　ISBN 978-7-5603-1408-2
定　　价　36.00 元

(如因印装质量问题影响阅读,我社负责调换)

前言(第4版)

本书是国家"九五"重点图书《材料科学与工程丛书》之一,是为材料科学与工程专业的三、四年级本科生而编写的专业英语教材。

编写本教材的目的是为了让本科生在经历了大学一、二年级的基础英语学习后,通过阅读本书,实现英语教学的不断线,使英语水平再上一个新台阶。

在第一、二、三版的基础上补充了材料科学与工程的总体介绍,材料的基础知识,更新了焊接工艺部分,将焊接领域的新进展融入其中,同时,缩减了科技英语选读部分,强化本书的可读性。

本书选材新颖,覆盖面广,不仅包含了材料科学与工程领域的基础专业而且涉及除此之外的其他各学科的基础知识,从而开阔了学生的视野,丰富了学生的知识。

本书编排独具匠心,把一篇较长的文章分成若干段落,并在每段后提供了几个问题,供学生回答或讨论。这不仅有利于学生及时检查自己对文章的理解情况,还便于教师安排教学。书中用星号(＊)把那些较生僻的词标在每个段落的后面并给出相应的汉语注释,以减少翻字典的次数,提高阅读效率。另外,文中的难句在段后进行了标注,这将更有助于学生对文章的理解。

本书由沈阳理工大学刘爱国编写。因编者水平所限,疏漏之处在所难免,敬请批评指正。

主　编
于沈阳理工大学

CONTENTS

1 Introduction to Materials Science and Engineering

1.1 Definition of Materials Science and Engineering ················· (1)

1.2 Classification of Materials ································· (4)

1.3 Structure of Materials ································· (6)

1.4 Properties and Design ································· (39)

2 Materials

2.1 Ferrous Alloys ································· (69)

2.2 Non-ferrous Alloys ································· (77)

2.3 Advanced Structural Ceramics ································· (80)

2.4 Functional Ceramics ································· (85)

2.5 Polymer ································· (93)

2.6 Semiconductor ································· (103)

2.7 Composites ································· (105)

3 Welding

3.1 Introduction to Welding Processes ································· (115)

3.2 Welding Metallurgy ································· (138)

3.3 Some New Developments in Welding ································· (167)

· 1 ·

4 Casting

4.1 Metal Flow in Die Casting .... (203)

4.2 Optimization of Properties in Aluminum Casting .... (224)

4.3 Precision Casting Process .... (231)

5 Forming

5.1 Fundamentals of Metal Forming .... (249)

5.2 Bulk-metal Forming .... (264)

5.3 Sheet-metal Forming .... (272)

6 Heat Treatment

6.1 Heat Treatment of Steel .... (280)

6.2 Principle of Heat Treatment of Steel .... (282)

Introduction to Materials Science and Engineering

Materials have always been important to the advance of civilization: entire eras are named for them. After evolving from the Stone Age through the Bronze and Iron Ages, now in the modern era we have vast numbers of tailored materials to make use of. We are really living in the Materials Age.

Work and study in the field of materials science and engineering is grounded in an understanding of why materials behave the way they do, and encompasses how materials are made and how new ones can be developed. For example, the way materials are processed is often important. People in the Iron Age discovered this when they learned that soft iron could be heated and then quickly cooled to make a material hard enough to plow the earth; and the same strategy is used today to make high-strength aluminum alloys for jet aircraft. Today we demand more from our materials than mechanical strength, of course—electrical, optical, and magnetic properties, for example, are crucial for many applications. As a result, modern materials science focuses on ceramics, polymers, and semiconductors, as well as on materials, such as metals and glasses, that have a long history of use.

1.1 Definition of Materials Science and Engineering

Material science is the investigation of the relationship among processing, structure*, properties, and performance of materials.[1] The relationship is depicted with a tetrahedron* of materials science and engineering as shown in Figure 1.1.

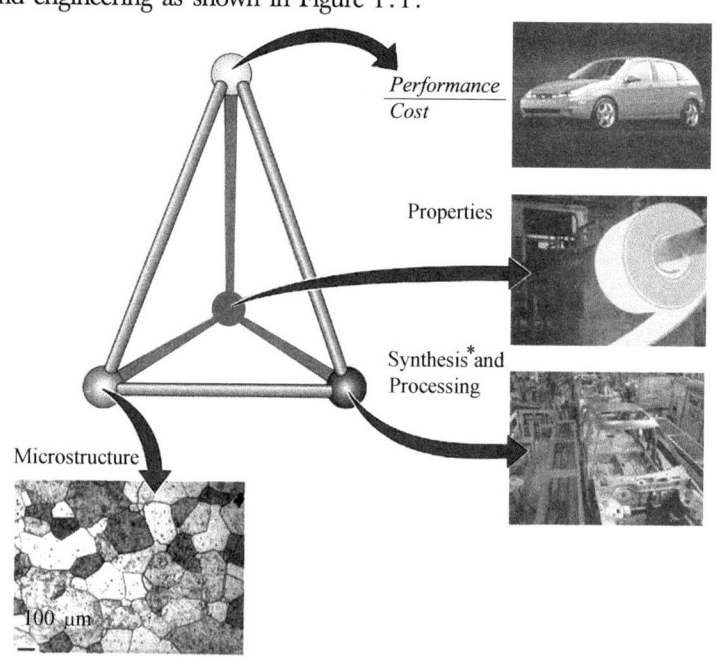

Figure 1.1 Relationship among processing, structure, properties, and performance of materials

The discipline of materials science involves investigating the relationships that exist between the structures and properties of materials. In contrast, materials engineering is, on the basis of these structure-property correlations, designing or engineering the structure of a material to produce a predetermined set of properties. [2]

The structure of a material usually relates to the arrangement of its internal components. Subatomic structure involves electrons within the individual atoms and interactions with their nuclei. On an atomic level, structure encompasses the organization of atoms or molecules relative to one another. The next larger structural realm, which contains large groups of atoms that are normally agglomerated together, is termed "microscopic", meaning that which is subject to direct observation using some type of microscope.[3] Finally, structural elements that may be viewed with the naked eye are termed "macroscopic".

Property is a material trait in terms of the kind and magnitude of response to a specific imposed stimulus. Generally, definitions of properties are made independent of material shape and size. Virtually all important properties of solid materials may be grouped into six different categories: mechanical, electrical, thermal, magnetic, optical, and deteriorative*. For each there is a characteristic type of stimulus capable of provoking* different responses.

In addition to structure and properties, two other important components are involved in the science and engineering of materials. They are "processing" and "performance." With regard to the relationships of these four components, the structure of a material will depend on how it is processed. Furthermore, a material's performance will be a function of its properties.

Key words:
tetrahedron [四面体]   structure [组织]
deteriorative [劣化]   provoke [诱发]
synthesis [合成]

Notes:

[1] 材料科学是研究材料的加工、组织、性能和功能之间关系的科学。

[2] 而材料工程是在组织－性能关系的基础上,对材料的组织进行设计,以获得一系列预定的性能。

[3] 下一级尺寸大一些的组织称为"显微组织",由聚集在一起的大量原子构成,使用某种类型的显微镜可以直接观察。

Questions:

1) What is the relationship of materials science and materials

4   *English in Materials Science and Engineering*

engineering?

2) What is the relationship among processing, structure, properties, and performance of materials?

1.2   Classification of Materials

Materials are classified into five groups: metals, ceramics*, polymers, semiconductors, and composite materials*. Materials in each of these groups possess different structures and properties.

Metals

Metals and alloys generally have the characteristics of good electrical and thermal conductivity, relatively high strength, high stiffness*, ductility* or formability, and shock resistance. They are particularly useful for structural or load-bearing applications. Although pure metals are occasionally used, combinations of metals called alloys provide improvement in a particular desirable property of permit better combinations of properties. [1]

Ceramics

Ceramics are compounds between metallic and nonmetallic elements; they are most frequently oxides, nitrides*, and carbides*. The wide range of materials that falls within this classification includes ceramics that are composed of clay minerals, cement, and glass. These materials have poor electrical and thermal conductivity. Although ceramics may have good strength and hardness, their ductility, formability, and shock resistance are poor. Consequently, ceramics are less often used for structural or load-bearing applications than are metals. However, many ceramics have excellent resistance to high temperatures and certain corrosive media and have a number of unusual and desirable optical, electrical and thermal properties.

Polymers

Polymers include rubber, plastics, and many types of adhesives*. They are produced by creating large molecular structures from organic molecules, obtained from petroleum* or agricultural products, in a process known as polymerization*. [2] Polymers have low electrical and thermal conductivity, have low strengths, and are not suitable for use at high temperatures. Some polymers (thermoplastics*) have excellent ductility, formability, and shock resistance while others (thermosets*) have the opposite properties. Polymers are lightweight and frequently have excellent resistance to corrosion.

Semiconductors

Semiconductors have electrical properties that are intermediate between the electrical conductors and insulators. Furthermore, the electrical characteristics of these materials are extremely sensitive to the presence of minute concentrations of impurity atoms, which concentrations may be controlled over very small spatial regions. The semiconductors have made possible the advent of integrated circuitry that has totally revolutionized the electronics and computer industries.

Composites

Composites are formed from two or more materials, producing properties that cannot be obtained by any single material. Concrete and fiberglass are typical examples of composite materials. A composite is designed to display a combination of the best characteristics of each of the component materials. With composites we can produce lightweight, strong, ductile, high temperature-resistant materials that are otherwise unobtainable, or produce hard yet shock-resistant cutting tools that would otherwise shatter.

Key words:

ceramic [陶瓷]
stiffness [刚度]
nitride [氮化物]
adhesive [胶]
polymerization [聚合]
thermosets [热固性塑料]

composite materials [复合材料]
ductility [塑性]
carbide [碳化物]
petroleum [石油]
thermoplastics [热塑性塑料]

Notes:

[1] 偶尔才使用纯金属,而把金属组合起来可以获得更好的性能组合,可以使需要的某一特定性能获得提高,这种金属组合称为合金。

6　*English in Materials Science and Engineering*

〔2〕它们是用从石油或农产品中获得的有机物分子,通过一个称为聚合的工艺生成大分子结构而制造出来的。

Questions:

1) How are materials classified?
2) What are the differences between metals and ceramics?

1.3　Structure of Materials

The structure of a material can be considered on several levels, all of which influence the final behavior of the product. At the finest level is the structure of the individual atoms that compose the material. The arrangement of the electrons surrounding the nucleus of the atom significantly affects electrical, magnetic, thermal, and optical behavior and may also influence corrosion resistance. Furthermore, the electronic arrangement influences how the atoms are bonded to one another and helps determine the type of material - metal, ceramic, or polymer.

At the next level, the arrangement of the atoms in space is considered. Metals, many ceramics, and some polymers have a very regular atomic arrangement, or crystal structure. The crystal structure influences the mechanical properties of metals such as ductility, strength, and shock resistance. Other ceramic materials and most polymers have no orderly atomic arrangement—these amorphous* or glassy materials behave much differently from crystalline materials. For instance, glassy polyethylene* is transparent while crystalline polyethylene is translucent*. Defects in this atomic arrangement exist and may be controlled to produce profound changes in properties.

A grain* structure is found in most metals, some ceramics, and occasionally in polymers. Between the grains, the atomic arrangement changes its orientation and thus influences properties. The size and shape of the grains play a key role at this level.

Finally, in most materials, more than one phase* is present, with each phase having its unique atomic arrangement and properties. Control of the type, size, distribution and amount of these phases

Introduction to Materials Science and Engineering   7

within the main body of the material provides an additional way to control properties.

Key words:
amorphous [无定形的,非晶的]   polyethylene [聚乙烯]
translucent [半透明的]   grain [晶粒]
phase [相]

1.3.1 Atomic-scale Structures

Atomic structure influences how the atoms are bonded together, which in turn helps us to categorize materials as metals, ceramics, and polymers and permits us to draw some general conclusions concerning the mechanical properties and physical behavior of these three classes of materials.

There are four mechanisms by which atoms are bonded together. In three of the four mechanisms, bonding is achieved when the atoms fill their outer *s* and *p* levels.

1.3.1.1 *Ionic Bonding**

Ionic bonding is always found in compounds that are composed of both metallic and nonmetallic elements, elements that are situated at the horizontal extremities of the periodic table* .[1] A metallic atom easily gives up its valence electrons* to the nonmetallic atom. Both atoms now have filled (or empty) outer energy levels but both have acquired an electrical charge and behave as ions. The atom that contributes the electrons is left with a net positive charge and is a cation* , while the atom that accepts the electrons acquires a net negative charge and is an anion* . The oppositely charged ions are then attracted to one another and produce the ionic bond. For example, attraction between sodium and chloride* ions (Figure 1.2) produces sodium chloride.

When a force is applied to a sodium chloride crystal, the electrical balance between the ions is upset. Partly for this reason, ionically bonded materials behave in a brittle manner. Electrical conductivity is also poor; the electrical charge is transferred by the

8　*English in Materials Science and Engineering*

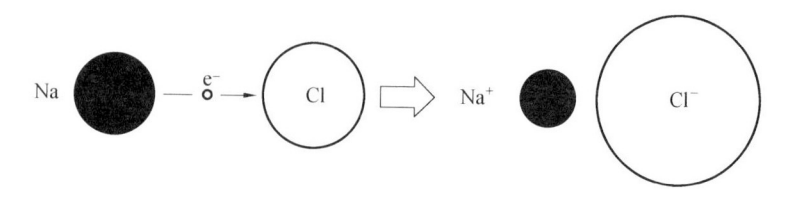

Figure 1.2　Ionic bonding

movement of entire ions, which do not move as easily as electrons. Many ceramic materials and minerals are at least partly bonded by ionic bonds.

1.3.1.2 *Covalent Bonding*[*]

Covalently bonded materials share electrons between two or more atoms. For example, a silicon[*] atom, which has a valence of four, obtains eight electrons in its outer energy shell by sharing its electrons with four surrounding silicon atoms (Figure 1.3). Each instance of sharing represents one covalent bond; thus each silicon atom is bonded to four neighboring atoms by four covalent bonds.

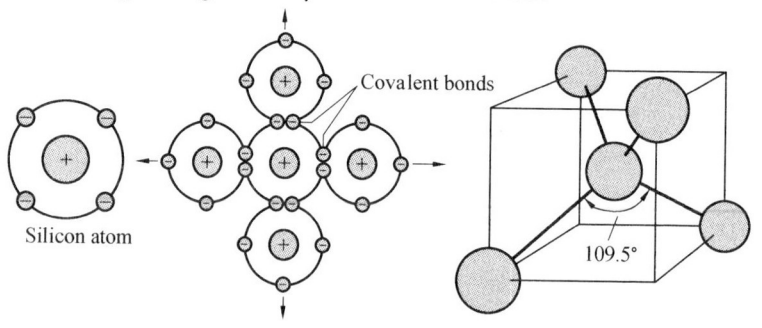

Figure 1.3 Covalent bonding

In order for the covalent bonds to be formed the silicon atoms must be arranged so the bonds have a fixed directional relationship with one another. In the case of silicon, this arrangement produces a tetrahedron, with angles of about 109° between the covalent bonds. Covalent bonds are very strong, and materials bonded in this manner

Introduction to Materials Science and Engineering 9

have poor ductility and poor electrical conductivity. Many ceramic and polymer materials are fully or partly bonded by covalent bonds.

1.3.1.3 *Metallic Bonding*[*]

The metallic elements, which have a low valence, give up their valence electrons to form a "sea" of electrons surrounding the atoms (Figure 1.4). Since negatively charged electrons are missing from the core, the core becomes an ion with a positive charge. The valence electrons, which are no longer associated with any particular atom, move freely within the electron sea and become associated with several atom cores. The positively charged atom cores are held together by mutual attraction to the electron, thus producing the strong metallic bond.

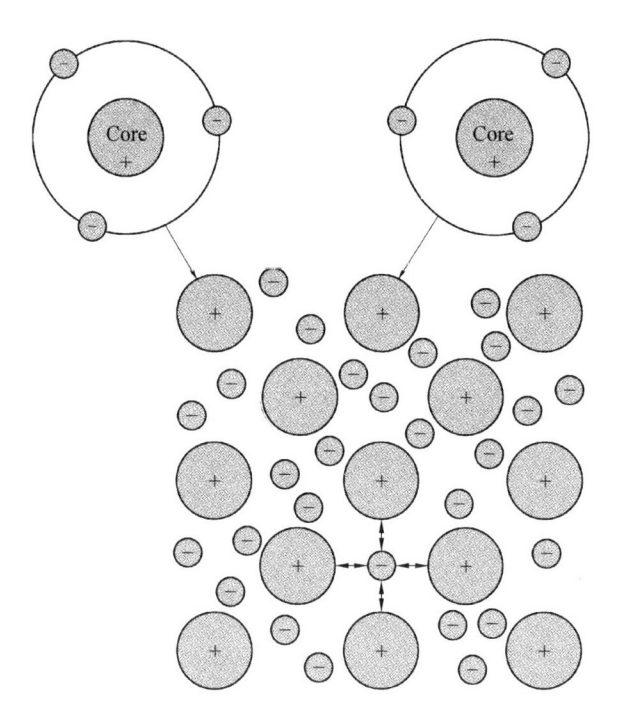

Figure 1.4 Metallic bonding

10　*English in Materials Science and Engineering*

Metallic bonds are nondirectional. The electrons holding the atoms together are not fixed in one position. When a metal is bent and the atoms attempt to change their relationship to one another, the direction of the bond merely shifts, rather than the bond breaking. This permits metal to have good ductility and to be deformed into useful shapes.

The metallic bond also allows metals to be good electrical conductors. Under the influence of an applied voltage, the valence electrons move causing a current to flow if the circuit is complete. Other bonding mechanisms require much higher voltages to free the electrons from the bond.

1.3.1.4 *Van de Waals Bonding* *

Van de Waals bonds join molecules or groups of atoms by weak electrostatic attractions. Many plastics, ceramics, water and other molecules are permanently polarized * ; that is, some portions of the molecule tend to be positively charged, while other portions are negatively charged. [2] The electrostatic attraction between the positively charged regions of one molecule and the negatively charged regions of a second molecule weakly bond the two molecules together. Van de Waals bonding is a secondary bond, and exists between virtually all atoms or molecules.

Key words:

ionic bond [离子键]	periodic table [元素周期表]
valence electron [价电子]	cation [正离子]
anion [负离子]	sodium [钠]
chloride [氯]	covalent bond [共价键]
silicon [硅]	metallic bond [金属键]
Van de Waals bond [范德华键]	polarize [极化]

Notes:

[1] 离子键总是在由金属元素和非金属元素(元素周期表每行最靠两端的元素)组成的化合物中出现。

[2] 多种塑料、陶瓷、水还有其他分子是永久极化的,就是说,分子的某些部分倾向于带正电,而另外一些部分带负电。

Questions:

1) What is the difference between the ionic bonding and covalent bonding?

2) How is the metallic bond produced?

1.3.2 Crystal Structures

Solid materials may be classified according to the regularity with which atoms or ions are arranged with respect to one another. A crystalline material is one in which the atoms are situated in a repeating or periodic array over large atomic distances. The atoms form a regular, repetitive gridlike pattern, or lattice*. The lattice is a collection of points, called lattice points, which are arranged in a periodic pattern so that the surroundings of each point in the lattice are identical.[1] One or more atoms are associated with each lattice point. The lattice differs from material to material in both shape and size, depending on the size of the atoms and the type of bonding between the atoms. The crystal structure* of a material refers to the size, shape, and atomic arrangement within the lattice.

1.3.2.1 *Unit Cells*

The unit cell is a subdivision of the lattice that still retains the overall characteristics of the entire lattice.[2] By stacking identical unit cells, the entire lattice can be constructed. We identify 14 types of unit cells, or Bravais lattices, grouped in seven crystal structures (Figure 1.5). Lattice points are located at the corners of the unit cells and, in some cases, the faces or the center of the unit cell.

1.3.2.2 *Metallic Crystal Structures*

The atomic bonding in this group of materials is metallic, and thus nondirectional in nature. Consequently, there are no restrictions as to the number and position of nearest-neighbor atoms; this leads to relatively large numbers of nearest neighbors and dense atomic packing for most metallic crystal structures. Three relatively simple crystal

12 *English in Materials Science and Engineering*

structures are found for most of the common metals: face-centered cubic, body-centered cubic, and hexagonal close-packed* .

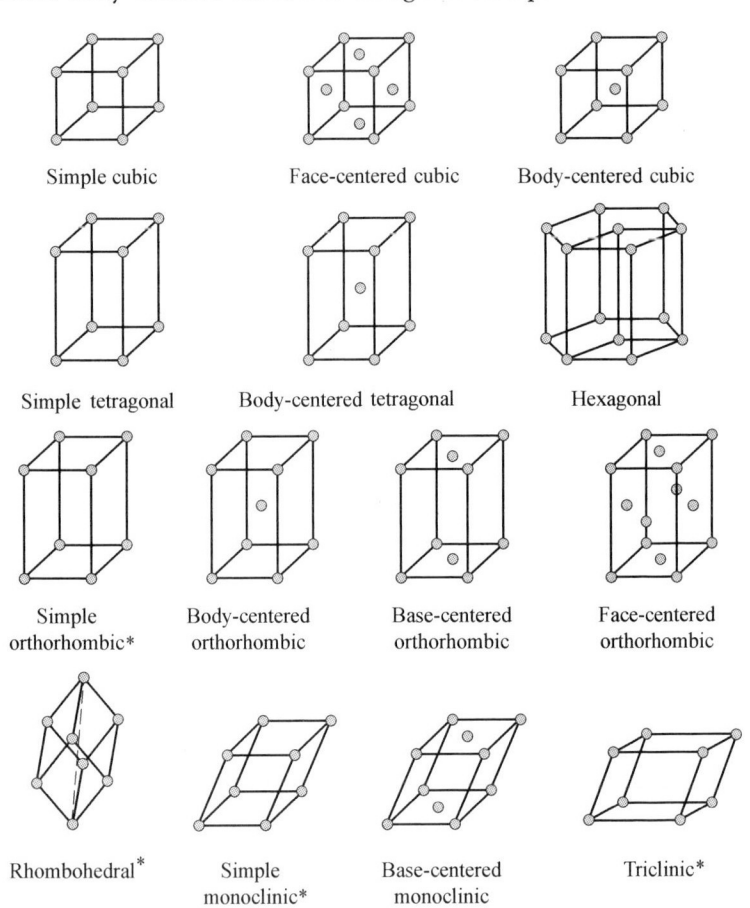

Figure 1.5 The fourteen types of Bravais lattices grouped in seven crystal systems

The Face-centered Cubic Crystal Structure

The crystal structure found for many metals has a unit cell of cubic geometry, with atoms located at each of the corners and the centers of all the cube faces (Figure 1.6). It is aptly* called the face-centered cubic (FCC) crystal structure. Some of the familiar metals

Introduction to Materials Science and Engineering   13

having this crystal structure are copper, aluminum, silver, and gold.

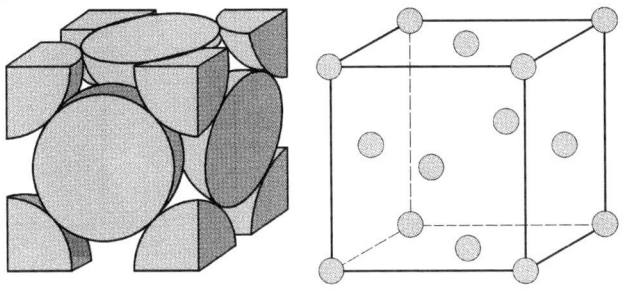

Figure 1.6 Face-centered cubic crystal structure

The Body-centered Cubic Crystal Structure

Another common metallic crystal structure also has a cubic unit cell with atoms located at all eight corners and single atom at the cube center. This is called a body-centered cubic (BCC) crystal structure (Figure 1.7). Chromium*, ion and tungsten exhibit a BCC structure.

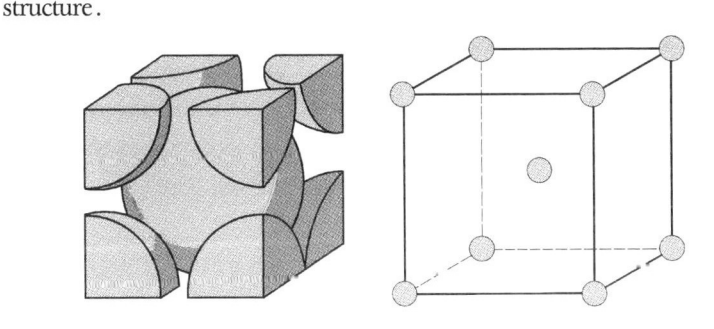

Figure 1.7 Body-centered cubic crystal structure

The Hexagonal Close-packed Crystal Structure

A special form of the hexagonal lattice, the hexagonal close-packed (HCP) structure, is shown in Figure 1.8. The unit cell is the skewed* prism* outlined in the hexagonal lattice. The HCP metals include cadmium*, magnesium, titanium, and zinc.

14 *English in Materials Science and Engineering*

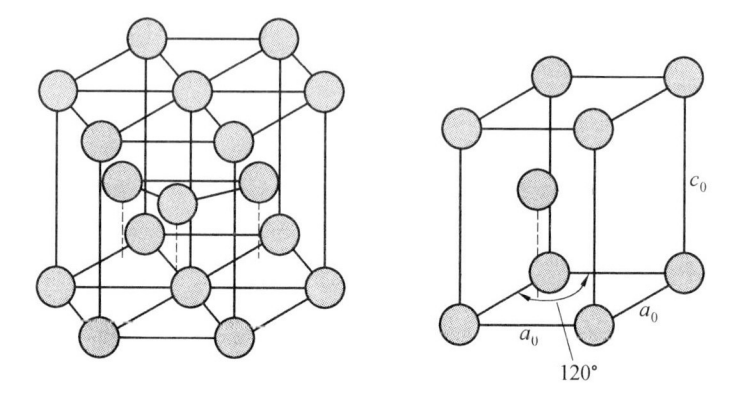

Figure 1.8 Hexagonal close-packed (HCP) structure and its unit cell

1.3.2.3 *Directions and Planes in the Unit Cell*

When dealing with crystalline materials, it often becomes necessary to specify some particular crystallographic plane of atoms or a crystallographic direction. Labeling conventions have been established in which three integers or indices are used to designate directions and planes. [3] The basis for determining index values is the unit cell, with a coordinate system* consisting of three (x, y, and z) axes situated at one of the corners and coinciding with the unit cell edges.

Directions in the Unit Cell

Certain directions in the unit cell are of particular importance. Metals deform, for example, in directions along which atoms are in closest contact. Properties of a material may depend on the direction in the crystal along which the property is measured. Miller indices for directions are the shorthand notation used to describe these directions. The procedure for finding the Miller indices for directions is as follows:

(a) Using a right-hand coordinate system, determine the coordinates of two points that lie on the direction.

(b) Subtract the coordinates of the "tail" point from the coordinates of the "head" point to obtain the number of lattice parameters traveled in the direction of each axis of the coordinate

Introduction to Materials Science and Engineering   15

system.[4]

(c) Clear fractions and/or reduce the results obtained from the subtraction to lowest integers.

(d) Enclose the numbers in square brackets [ ]. If a negative sign is produced, represent the negative sign with a bar over the number.

The [100], [110], and [111] directions are common ones; they are drawn in the unit cell shown in Figure 1.9.

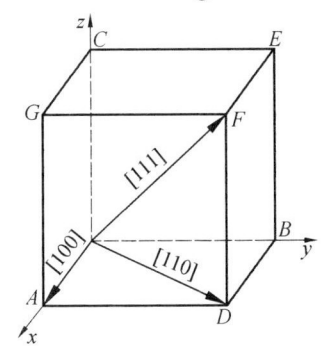

Figure 1.9 The [100], [110], and [111] directions within a unit cell

Planes in the Unit Cell

Certain planes of atoms in a crystal are also significant; for example, metals deform along planes of atoms that are most tightly together. Miller indices can be used as a shorthand notation to identify these important planes, as described in the following procedure.

(a) Identify the points at which the plane intercepts the x, y, and z coordinates in terms of the number of lattice parameters. If the plane passes through the origin, the origin of the coordinate system must be moved.

(b) Take reciprocals of these intercepts.

(c) Clear fractions but do not reduce to lowest integers.

(d) Enclose the resulting numbers in parentheses* ( ). Again, negative numbers should be written with a bar over the number.

Key words:

lattice [空间点阵,晶格]   crystal structure [晶体结构]

16　*English in Materials Science and Engineering*

unit cell [晶胞]　　　　　　　tetragonal [四方的]
hexagonal [六方的]　　　　　orthorhombic [正交的]
rhombohedral [菱方的]　　　　monoclinic [单斜的]
triclinic [三斜的]　　　　　　hexagonal close-packed [密排六方的]
aptly [适当地]　　　　　　　chromium [铬]
skew [歪斜]　　　　　　　　prism [棱镜]
cadmium [镉]　　　　　　　coordinate system [坐标系统]
reciprocal [倒数]　　　　　　parentheses [括弧]

Notes：

[1] 空间点阵就是一些点的集合,这些点称为阵点,阵点呈周期排列,这样每一个阵点周围都是相同的。

[2] 晶胞就是保持整个空间点阵总体性质的最小单元。

[3] 建立了一种采用三个整数,也称为指数,来表示晶向和晶面的方法。

[4] 用终点的坐标减去起点的坐标,以确定在每个坐标轴方向上两点之间的坐标差是几个晶格常数。

Questions：

1）What is the unit cell? Why is the unit cell important?

2）What are the three most common crystal structures for metals?

3）How to find the Miller indices for directions?

1.3.3 Point Defects and Diffusion

1.3.3.1 *Point Defects* *

Point defects are localized disruptions of the lattice involving one or possibly several atoms (Figure 1.10).

A *vacancy* * is produced when an atom is missing from a normal lattice point. Vacancies are introduced into the crystal structure during solidification, at high temperatures, or as a consequence of radiation damage.

An *interstitial defect* is formed when an extra atom is inserted into the lattice structure at a site which is not a normal lattice point. A *substitutional defect* is introduced when an atom is replaced by a different type of atom. The substitutional atom remains at the original normal lattice point. Both interstitial and substitutional defects are present in materials as impurities and may also be intentionally introduced as

Introduction to Materials Science and Engineering 17

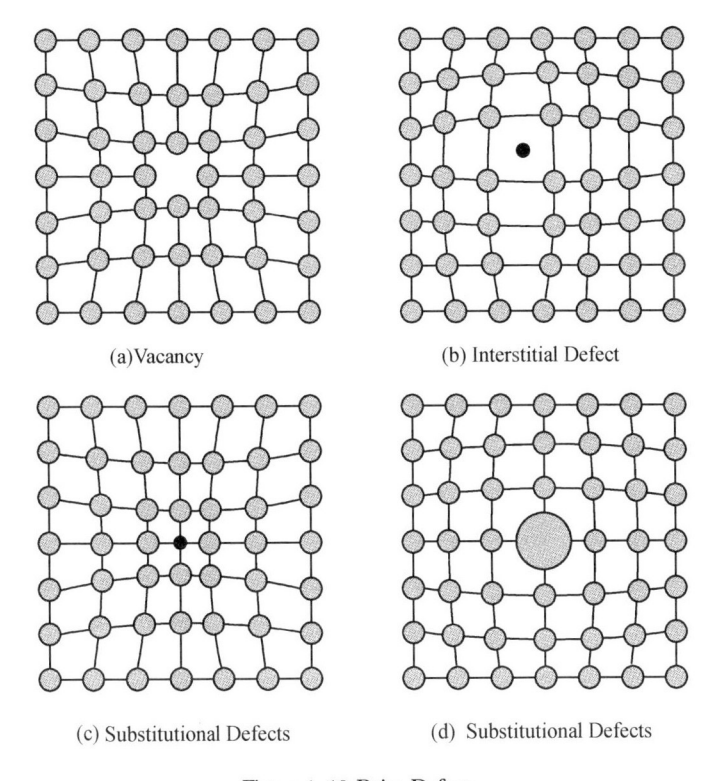

(a)Vacancy

(b) Interstitial Defect

(c) Substitutional Defects

(d) Substitutional Defects

Figure 1.10 Point Defects

alloying elements. The number of these defects is usually independent of temperature.

Point defects disturb the perfect arrangement of the surrounding atoms. When a vacancy or a small substitutional atom is present, the surrounding atoms collapse towards the point defect, stretching the bonds between the surrounding atoms and producing a tensile stress field.[1] An interstitial or large substitutional atom pushes the surrounding atoms together, producing a compressive stress field. In either case the effect is widespread. Intentional addition of interstitial and substitutional atoms into the structure of a material forms the basis for solid solution strengthening* of materials.

18 *English in Materials Science and Engineering*

1.3.3.2 *Diffusion*

Diffusion is the movement of atoms within a material. Atoms move in an orderly fashion to eliminate concentration differences and produce a homogeneous uniform composition. Movement of atoms is required for many of the treatments that we perform on materials. Diffusion is required for the heat treatment of metals, the manufacture of ceramics, the solidification of materials, the manufacture of transistors and solar cells[*], and even the electrical conductivity of many ceramic materials.

1.3.3.3 *Diffusion Mechanisms*[*]

From an atomic perspective, diffusion is just the stepwise migration of atoms from lattice site to lattice site. In fact, the atoms in solid materials are in constant motion, rapidly changing positions. For an atom to make such a move, two conditions must be met: (1) there must be an empty adjacent site, and (2) the atom must have sufficient energy to break bonds with its neighbor atoms and then cause some lattice distortion during the displacement. This energy is vibrational in nature. At a specific temperature some small fraction of the total number of atoms is capable of diffusive motion, by virtue of the magnitudes of their vibrational energies. This fraction increases with rising temperature.

Several different models for this atomic motion have been proposed; of these possibilities, two dominate for metallic diffusion.

Vacancy diffusion. In self-diffusion and diffusion involving substitutional atoms, an atom leaves its lattice site to fill a nearby vacancy (thus creating a new vacancy at the original lattice site). As diffusion continues, we have a countercurrent flow of atoms and vacancies. This mechanism is shown in Figure 1.11.

Interstitial diffusion. When a small interstitial atom is present in the crystal structure, the atom moves from one interstitial site to another. No vacancies are required for this mechanism to work. This mechanism is shown in Figure 1.12.

Introduction to Materials Science and Engineering 19

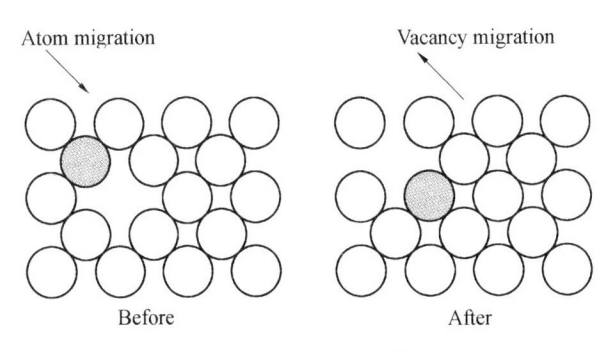

Figure 1.11 Vacancy diffusion

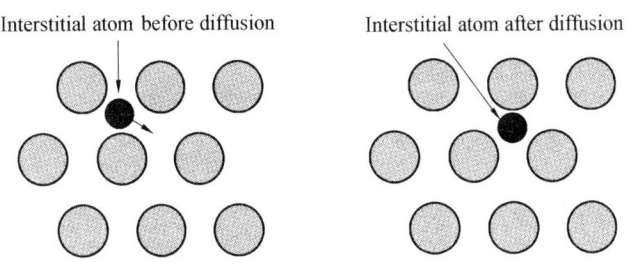

Figure 1.12 Interstitial diffusion

1.3.3.4 *Rate of Diffusion* (*Fick's First Law*)

The rate at which atoms diffuse in a material can be measured by the *flux J*, which is defined as the number of atoms passing through a plane of unit area per unit time. *Fick's first law* explains the net flux of atoms,

$$J = -D \frac{\Delta c}{\Delta x} \tag{1.1}$$

where J is the flux [atoms $(m^2 \cdot s)^{-1}$], D is the diffusivity or diffusion coefficient ($m^2 \cdot s^{-1}$), and $\Delta c/\Delta x$ is the concentration gradient [atoms $(m^3 \cdot m)^{-1}$].

Key words:
point defect [点缺陷]   vacancy [空位]
solid solution strengthening [固溶强化]
solar cell [太阳能电池]

20　*English in Materials Science and Engineering*

Note:

[1] 当存在空位或小置换原子时,周围的原子会向点缺陷靠近,拉伸周围原子之间的键,产生拉应力场。

Question:

What is diffusion? What is the importance of it?

1.3.4 Linear and Planar Defects

1.3.4.1 *Dislocations* * — *Linear Defects*

Dislocations are line imperfections in an otherwise perfect lattice. We can identify two types of dislocations - the screw dislocation* and the edge dislocation*. The screw dislocation (Figure 1.13) can be illustrated by cutting partway through a perfect crystal, then skewing the crystal one atom spacing. If we were to follow a crystallographic plane one revolution around the axis on which the crystal was skewed, traveling equal atom spacings in each direction, we would finish one atom spacing below our starting point.[1] The vector required to complete the loop and return us to our starting point is the Burgers vector* **b**. If we continued our rotation, we would trace out a spiral path. The axis, or line, around which we trace out this path is the screw dislocation. We see that the Burgers vector is parallel to the screw dislocation. An edge dislocation (Figure 1.14) can be illustrated by slicing partway through a perfect crystal, spreading the crystal apart, and partly filling the cut with an extra plane of atoms. The

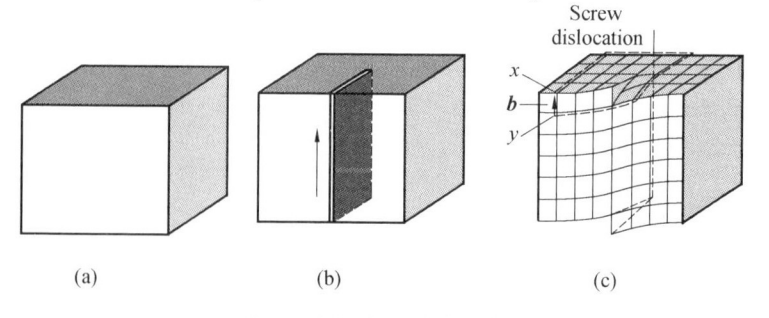

Figure 1.13 Screw dislocation

Introduction to Materials Science and Engineering 21

bottom edge of the inserted plane represents the edge dislocation. If we describe a clockwise loop around the edge dislocation by going an equal number of atom spacings in each direction, we would finish one atom spacing from our starting point. The vector that is required to complete the loop is again the Burgers vector. In this case, the Burgers vector is perpendicular to the edge dislocation.

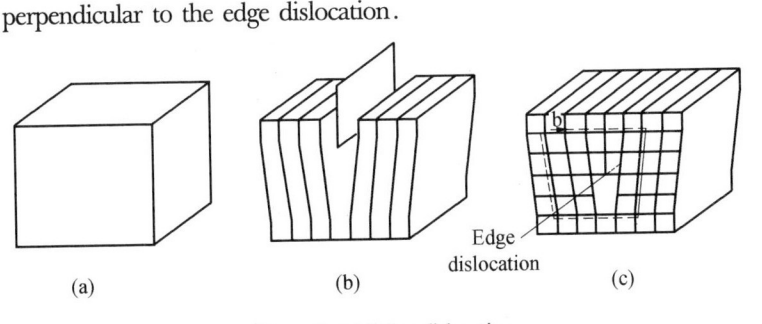

(a)   (b)   (c)

Edge
dislocation

Figure 1.14 Edge dislocation

1.3.4.2 *Surface Defects*

Surface defects are the boundaries that separate a material into regions, each region having the same crystal structure but different orientations.

Grain Boundaries

The microstructure of metals and many other solid materials consists of many grains. A grain is a portion of the material within which the arrangement, or crystal structure, is different for each adjoining grain. A *grain boundary** is the surface that separates the individual grains and is a narrow zone in which the atoms are not properly spaced. A grain boundary is represented schematically from an atomic perspective in Figure 1.15. Within the grain boundary region, which is probably just several atom distances wide, there is some atomic mismatch in a transition from the crystalline orientation of one grain to that of an adjacent one.[2]

Various degrees of crystallographic misalignment between adjacent grains are possible. When this orientation mismatch is slight, on the order of a few degrees , then the term *small* - (or *low* -) *angle grain*

22 *English in Materials Science and Engineering*

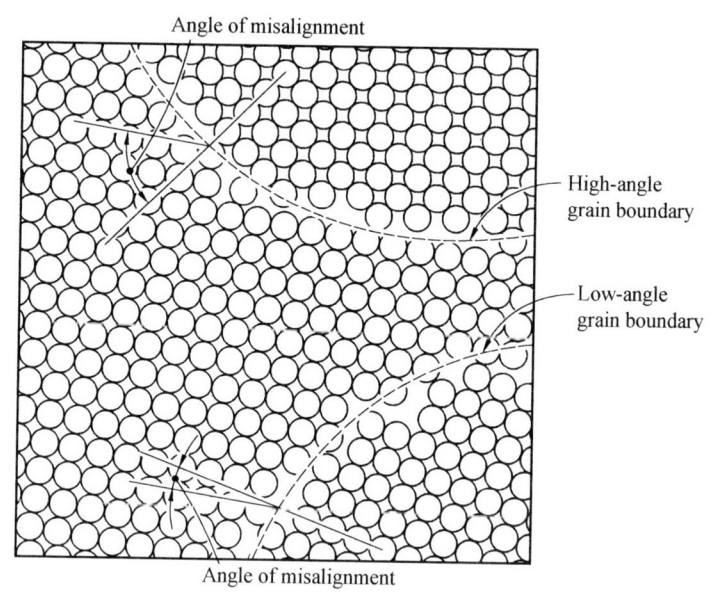

Angle of misalignment

High-angle
grain boundary

Low-angle
grain boundary

Angle of misalignment

Figure 1.15 Grain boundaries

*boundary** is used. These boundaries can be described in terms of dislocation arrays. One simple small-angle grain boundary is formed when edge dislocations are aligned in the manner of Figure 1.16. This type is called a *tilt boundary** .

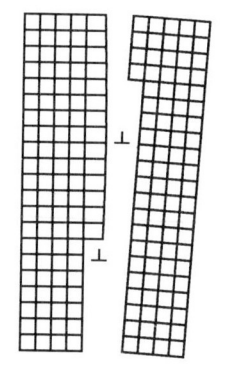

Twin Boundaries*

A twin boundary is a plane across which there is a special mirror image misorientation of the

Figure 1.16 Small-angle grain boundary

lattice structure (Figure 1.17). Twins can be produced when a shear force, acting along the twin boundary, causes the atoms to shift out of position. Twinning occurs during deformation or heat treatment of certain metals. The twin boundaries increase the strength of the metal.

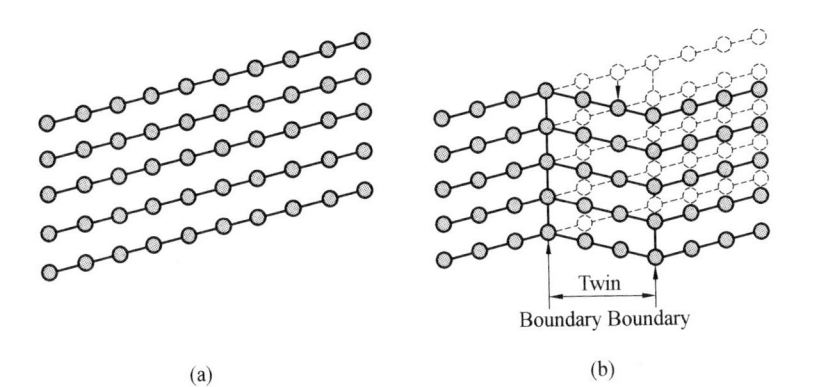

(a)　　　　　　　　　　　　　　(b)

Figure 1.17 Twin boundary

Key words:

dislocation [位错]　　　　　　　　　　screw dislocation [螺形位错]

edge dislocation [刃形位错]　　　　　Burgers vector [柏氏矢量]

spiral [螺旋形的]　　　　　　　　　　grain boundary [晶界]

small- (or low-) angle grain boundary [小角度晶界]

tilt boundary [倾侧晶界]　　　　　　　twin boundary [孪晶界]

Notes:

[1] 如果我们围绕晶体扭曲轴线在同一晶面内走一周,每个方向行走相同晶格数的话,终点会位于起点下方一个晶格的位置。

[2] 晶界区域只有几个原子宽,在这一区域内,从一个晶粒的晶体取向向另一个相邻晶粒的晶体取向过渡,会存在原子错配。

Questions:

1) Is the Burgers vector perpendicular to the screw dislocation?

2) What is a twin boundary?

1.3.5 Non-crystalline* Materials

Non-crystalline solids lack a systematic and regular arrangement of atoms over relatively large atomic distances. Sometimes such materials are also called amorphous, or supercooled liquids, inasmuch as their atomic structure resembles that of a liquid. An amorphous condition may be illustrated by comparison of the crystalline and non-crystalline structures of the ceramic compound silicon dioxide (SiO_2), which may exist in both states. Figure 1.18(a) and 1.18(b) present two-dimensional schematic diagrams for both structures of SiO_2, in which the SiO_4^{4-} tetrahedron is the basic unit. Even though each silicon ion bonds to four oxygen ions for both states, beyond this, the structure is much more disordered and irregular for the non-crystalline structure. Whether a crystalline or amorphous solid forms depends on the ease with which a random atomic structure in the liquid can transform to an ordered state during solidification.[1] Amorphous materials, therefore, are characterized by atomic or molecular structures that are relatively complex and become ordered only with some difficulty. Furthermore, rapidly cooling through the freezing temperature favors the formation of a non-crystalline solid, since little time is allowed for the ordering process. Metals normally form crystalline solids; but some ceramic materials are crystalline, whereas others are amorphous. Polymers may be completely non-crystalline and semi-crystalline consisting of varying degrees of crystallinity*.

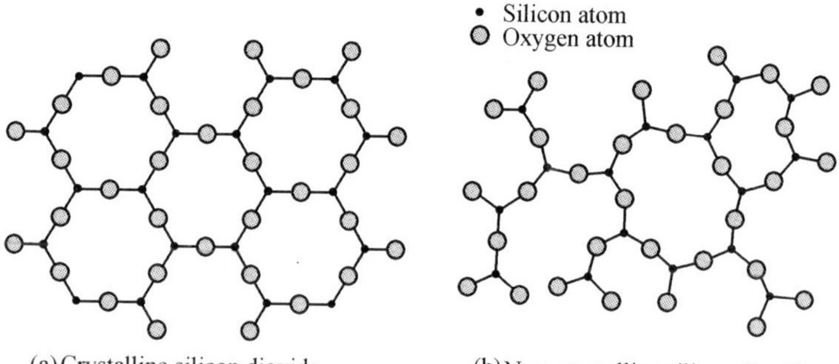

- Silicon atom
- Oxygen atom

(a)Crystalline silicon dioxide   (b)Non-crystalline silicon dioxide

Figure 1.18 Two-dimensional schemes of the structure of silicon dioxide

Key words:

non-crystalline[非晶的]   crystallinity [结晶度]

Note:

[1] 是形成晶体还是形成非晶,取决于液体中的随机原子结构在凝固过程中转变成有序状态是否容易。

1.3.6 Microstructure*

When describing the structure of a material, we make a clear distinction between its crystal structure and its microstructure. The term "crystal structure" is used to describe the average positions of atoms within the unit cell, and is completely specified by the lattice type and the fractional* coordinates of the atoms.[1] In other words, the crystal structure describes the appearance of the material on an atomic length scale. The term "microstructure" is used to describe the appearance of the material on the nm-cm length scale. A reasonable working definition of microstructure is " *the arrangement of phases and defects within a material*."

Many times, the physical properties and, in particular, the mechanical behavior of a material depend on the microstructure. Microstructure is subject to direct microscopic observation, using optical or electron microscopes. In many alloys, microstructure is characterized by the number of phases present, their proportions, and the manner in which they are distributed or arranged. The microstructure of an alloy depends on such variables as the alloying elements present, their concentration, and the heat treatment of the alloy.

1.3.6.1 *Phase Diagrams**

Much of the information about the control of microstructure or phase structure of a particular alloy system is conveniently and concisely displayed in what is called a **phase diagram**, also often termed an *equilibrium or constitutional diagram*. Many microstructures develop from phase transformation, the changes that occur between phases when the temperature is altered (ordinarily upon cooling). This may involve the transition from one phase to another, or the appearance or disappearance of a phase. Phase diagrams are helpful in predicting phase transformations and the resulting microstructures, which may have equilibrium or nonequilibrium character.

26　*English in Materials Science and Engineering*

The understanding of phase diagrams for alloy systems is extremely important because there is a strong correlation between microstructure and mechanical properties, and the development of microstructure of an alloy is related to the characteristics of its phase diagram.[2] In addition, phase diagrams provide valuable information about melting, casting, crystallization, and other phenomena.

◆ Binary Isomorphous Systems *

The easiest type of binary phase diagram to understand and interpret is that which is characterized by the copper-nickel* system (Figure 1.19). Three different phase regions, or fields, appear on the diagram, an alpha (α) field, a liquid (L) field, and a two-phase α + L field. The liquid L is a homogeneous liquid solution composed of both copper and nickel. The α phase is a substitutional solid solution consisting of both Cu and Ni atoms, and having an FCC crystal structure. At temperatures below about 1 080℃, copper and nickel are mutually soluble in each other in the solid state for all compositions. The copper-nickel system is termed **isomorphous** because of this complete liquid and solid solubility of the two components.

For a binary system of known composition and temperature that is at equilibrium*, at least three kinds of information are available:

(1) the phases that are present.

(2) the compositions of these phases.

(3) the percentages or fractions of the phases. The procedures for making these determinations will be demonstrated using the copper-nickel system.

Phases Present

The establishment of what phases are present is relatively simple. One just locates the temperature-composition point on the diagram and notes the phase(s) with which the corresponding phase field is labeled. For example, an alloy of composition (w_{Ni} = 60% ; w_{Cu} = 40%) at 1 100℃ would be located at point A (Figure 1.19). Since this is within the α region, only the single α phase will be present.

Introduction to Materials Science and Engineering   27

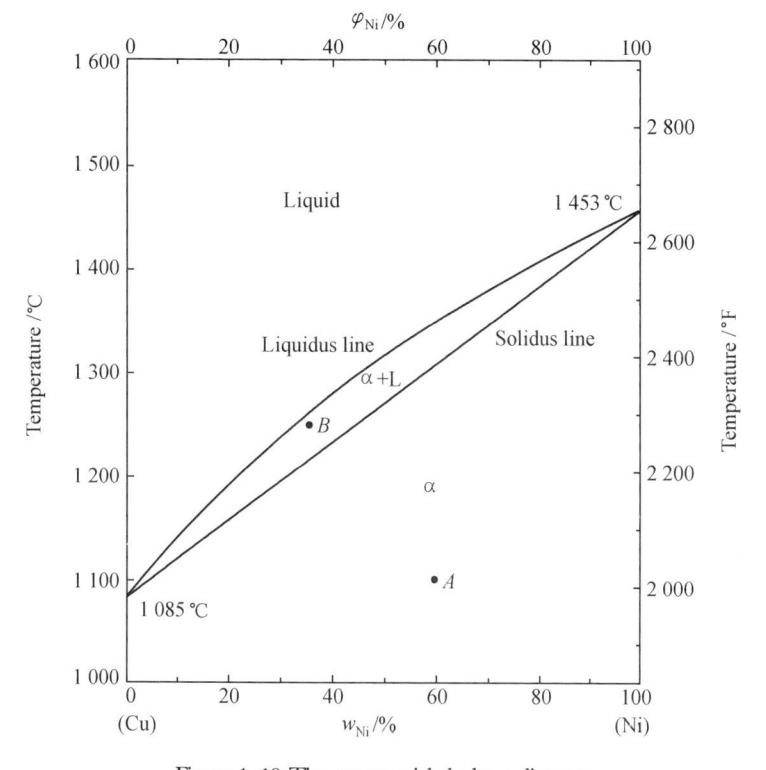

Figure 1.19 The copper-nickel phase diagram

Composition of Each Phase

The first step in the determination of phase compositions is to locate the temperature-composition point on the phase diagram. Different methods are used for single- and two-phase regions. If only one phase is present, the procedure is trivial: the composition of this phase is simply the same as the overall composition of the alloy. For an alloy having composition and temperature located in a two-phase region, the situation is more complicated. In all two-phase regions (and in two-phase regions only), one may imagine a series of horizontal lines, one at every temperature; each of these is known as a **tie line**[*], or sometimes as an isotherm[*]. These tie lines extend across the two-phase region and terminate at the phase boundary lines on

28   *English in Materials Science and Engineering*

either side. To compute the equilibrium concentrations of the two phases, the following procedure is used:

(1) A tie line is constructed across the two-phase region at the temperature of the alloy.

(2) The intersections of the tie line and the phase boundaries on either side are noted.

(3) Perpendiculars are dropped from these intersections to the horizontal composition axis, from which the composition of each of the respective phases is read.

Amount of Each Phase (The Lever Law*)

In single-phase regions, the amount of the single phase is 100%. However, in two-phase regions we must calculate the amount of each phase. If the composition and temperature position is located within a two-phase region, the tie line must be utilized in conjunction with a procedure that is often called the lever law, which is applied as follows:

(1) The tie line is constructed across the two-phase region at the temperature of the alloy.

(2) The overall alloy composition is located on the tie line.

(3) The fraction of one phase is computed by taking the length of the tie line from the overall alloy composition to the phase boundary for the *other* phase, and dividing by the total tie line length. [3]

(4) The fraction of the other phase is determined in the same manner.

◆ Binary Eutectic* Systems

Another type of common and relatively simple phase diagram found for binary alloys is shown in Figure 1.20 for the copper-silver system. This is known as a binary eutectic phase diagram. Three single-phase regions are found on the diagram: α,β, and liquid. The α phase is a solid solution rich in copper; it has silver as the solute component and FCC crystal structure. The β phase solid solution also has an FCC structure, but copper is the solute.

The solubility in each of these solid phases is limited, in that at

Introduction to Materials Science and Engineering 29

any temperature below line *BEG* only a limited concentration of silver will dissolve in copper (for the α phase), and similarly for copper in silver (for the β phase). The solubility limit for the α phase corresponds to the boundary line, labeled *CBA*, between the α/(α + β) and α/(α + L) phase regions; it increases with temperature to a maximum (w_{Ag} = 8.0% at 779℃) at point *B*, and decreases back to zero at the melting temperature of pure copper, point *A* (1 085℃). At temperatures below 779℃, the solid solubility limit line separating the α and α + β phase regions is termed a solvus line[*]; the boundary *AB* between the α and α + L fields is the solidus line. The maximum solubility of copper in the β phase, point *G*, also occurs at 779℃. This horizontal line *BEG*, which is parallel to the composition axis and extends between these maximum solubility positions, may also be considered to be a solidus line; it represents the lowest temperature at which a liquid phase may exist for any copper-silver alloy that is at equilibrium.[4]

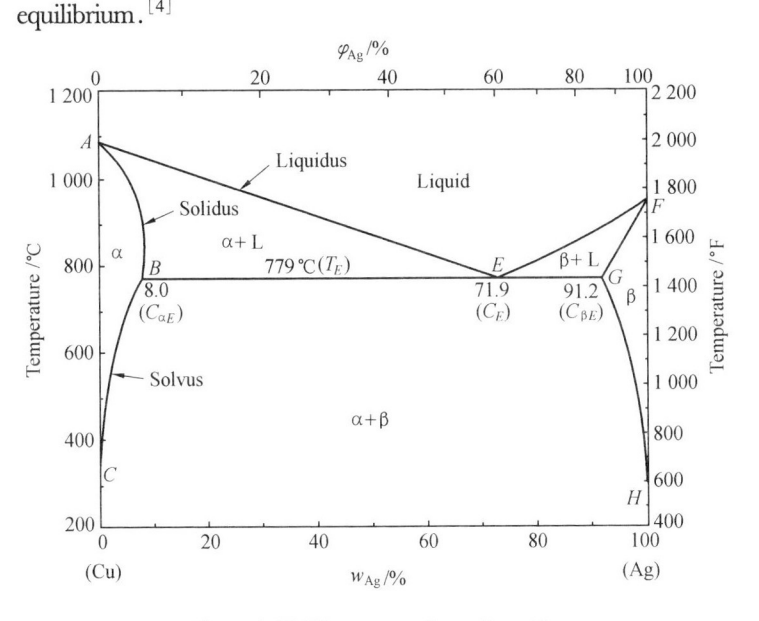

Figure 1.20 The copper-silver phase diagram

30 *English in Materials Science and Engineering*

There are three two-phase regions found for the copper-silver system: $\alpha + L$, $\beta + L$, and $\alpha + \beta$. The α and β phase solid solutions coexist for all compositions and temperatures within the $\alpha + \beta$ phase field; the $\alpha +$ liquid and $\beta +$ liquid phases also coexist in their respective phase regions. Compositions and relative amounts for the phases may be determined using tie lines and the lever law.

The liquidus lines *AE* and *FE* meet at the point *E* on the phase diagram, through which also passes the horizontal isotherm line *BEG*. Point *E* is called an **invariant point**, which is designated by the composition C_E and temperature T_E. An important reaction occurs for an alloy of composition C_E as it changes temperature in passing through T_E. Upon cooling, a liquid phase is transformed into the two solid α and β phases at the temperature T_E; the opposite reaction occurs upon heating. This is called a eutectic reaction, and C_E and T_E represent the eutectic composition and temperature, respectively. $C_{\alpha E}$ and $C_{\beta E}$ are the respective compositions of the α and β phases at T_E. The horizontal solidus line at T_E is called the eutectic isotherm.

◆ The Iron-Iron Carbide (Fe-Fe_3C) Phase Diagram

Of all binary alloy systems, the one that is possibly the most important is that for iron and carbon. Both steels and cast irons[*], primary structural materials in every technologically advanced culture, are essentially iron-carbon alloys.

A portion of the iron-carbon phase diagram is presented in Figure 1.21. Pure iron, upon heating, experiences two changes in crystal structure before it melts. At room temperature the stable form, called ferrite[*], or α iron, has a BCC crystal structure. Ferrite experiences a polymorphic transformation to FCC austenite[*], or γ iron, at 912℃. This austenite persists to 1 394℃, at which temperature the FCC austenite reverts back to a BCC phase known as δ ferrite, which finally melts at 1 538℃. The composition axis in Figure 1.21 extends only to 6.70% (w_C); at this concentration the intermediate compound iron carbide, or cementite[*] (Fe_3C), is formed, which is represented by a vertical line on the phase diagram. Thus, the iron-carbon system may

Introduction to Materials Science and Engineering   31

be divided into two parts: an iron-rich portion, and the other for compositions between 6.70% and 100% (w_C). In practice, all steels and cast irons have carbon contents less than 6.70% (w_C); therefore, we consider only the iron-iron carbide system. Figure 1.21 would be more appropriately labeled the Fe-Fe$_3$C phase diagram.

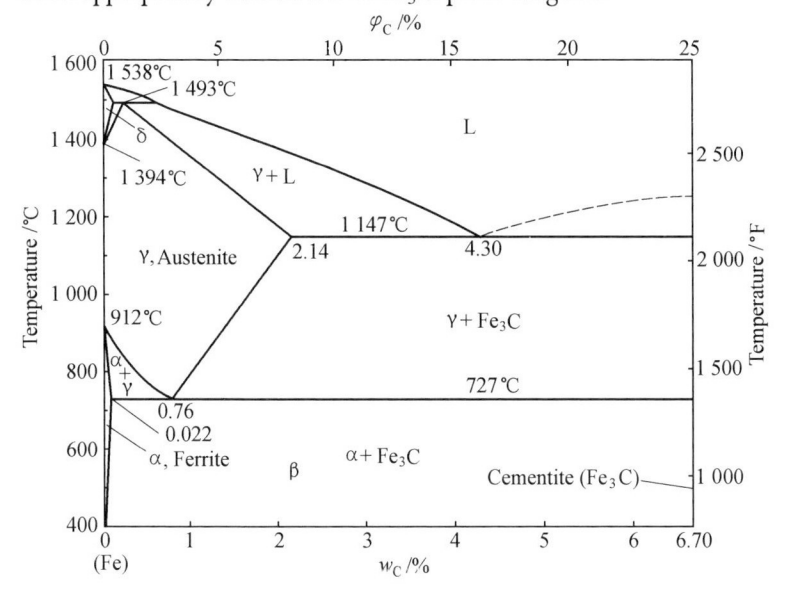

Figure 1.21 The iron-iron carbide phase diagram

Carbon is an interstitial impurity in iron and forms a solid solution with each of α and δ ferrites, and also with austenite. In the BCC α ferrite, only small concentrations of carbon are soluble; the maximum solubility is 0.022% (w) at 727℃. This iron-carbon phase is relatively soft, may be made magnetic at temperatures below 768℃, and has a density of 7.88 g/cm^3.

The austenite, when alloyed with just carbon, is not stable below 727℃. The maximum solubility of carbon in austenite, 2.14% (w), occurs at 1 147℃. This solubility is approximately 100 times greater than the maximum for BCC ferrite. Austenite is nonmagnetic.

The δ ferrite is virtually the same as α ferrite, except for the range

32 *English in Materials Science and Engineering*

of temperatures over which each exists. Since the α ferrite is stable only at relatively high temperatures, it is of no technological importance.

Cementite (Fe_3C) forms when the solubility limit of carbon in α ferrite is exceeded below 727℃. Fe_3C will also coexist with the γ phase between 727 and 1 147℃. Mechanically, cementite is very hard and brittle.

One eutectic exists for the iron-iron carbide system, at 4. 30% (w_C) and 1 147℃. For this eutectic reaction,

$$L \xrightleftharpoons[\text{heating}]{\text{cooling}} \gamma + Fe_3C \qquad (1.2)$$

the liquid solidifies to form austenite and cementite phases. Of course, subsequent cooling to room temperature will promote additional phase changes.

A eutectoid invariant point exists at a composition of 0. 76% (w_C) and a temperature of 727℃. This eutectoid reaction may be represented by

$$\gamma(w_C = 0.76\%) \xrightleftharpoons[\text{heating}]{\text{cooling}} \alpha(w_C = 0.022\%) + Fe_3C(w_C = 6.7\%)$$

$$(1.3)$$

or, upon cooling, the solid γ phase is transformed into α iron and cementite.

1.3.6.2 *Phase transformations* [*]

Mechanical and other properties of many materials depend on their microstructures, which are often produced as a result of phase transformations. These transformations are divided into three classifications. In one group are simple diffusion-dependent transformations in which there is no change in either the number or composition of the phases present. These include solidification of a pure metal, allotropic[*] transformations, and recrystallization[*] and grain growth. In another type of diffusion-dependent transformation, there is some alteration in phase composition and often in the number of phases present; the final microstructure ordinarily consists of two phases. The eutectoid[*] reaction, described by Equation 1.3, is of this type. The third kind of transformation is diffusionless, wherein a metastable phase is produced. A martensitic transformation*, which may be induced in some steel alloys, falls into this category.

Consider again the iron-iron carbide eutectoid reaction, which is fundamental to the development of microstructure in steel alloys. Upon cooling, austenite, having an intermediate carbon content, transforms to a ferrite phase, having a much lower carbon content, and also cementite, with a much higher carbon concentration. Consider an alloy of eutectoid composition ($w_C = 0.76\%$) as it is cooled from a temperature within the γ phase region, say, 800℃, that is, beginning at point a in Figure 1.22 and moving down the vertical line xx'. Initially, the alloy is composed entirely of the austenite phase having a composition of 0.76% (w_C) C and corresponding microstructure. As the alloy is cooled, there will occur no changes until the eutectoid temperature (727℃) is reached. Upon crossing this temperature to point b, the austenite transforms according to Equation 1.3.

The microstructure for this eutectoid steel that is slowly cooled through the eutectoid temperature consists of alternating layers or lamellae* of the two phases (α and Fe_3C) that form simultaneously during the transformation. In this case, the relative layer thickness is approximately 0.8 to 1. This microstructure, represented schematically in Figure 1.22, point b, is called **pearlite*** because it has the appearance of mother of pearl when viewed under the microscope at low magnifications. Mechanically, pearlite has properties intermediate between the soft, ductile ferrite and the hard, brittle cementite.

The alternating α and Fe_3C layers in pearlite form because the composition of the parent phase is different from either of the product phases, and the phase transformation requires that there be a redistribution of the carbon by diffusion.

Consider a composition C_0 to the left of the eutectoid, between 0.022% and 0.76% (w_C); this is termed a **hypoeutectoid*** **alloy.** Cooling an alloy of this composition is represented by moving down the vertical line yy' in Figure 1.23. At about 875℃, point c, the

34　*English in Materials Science and Engineering*

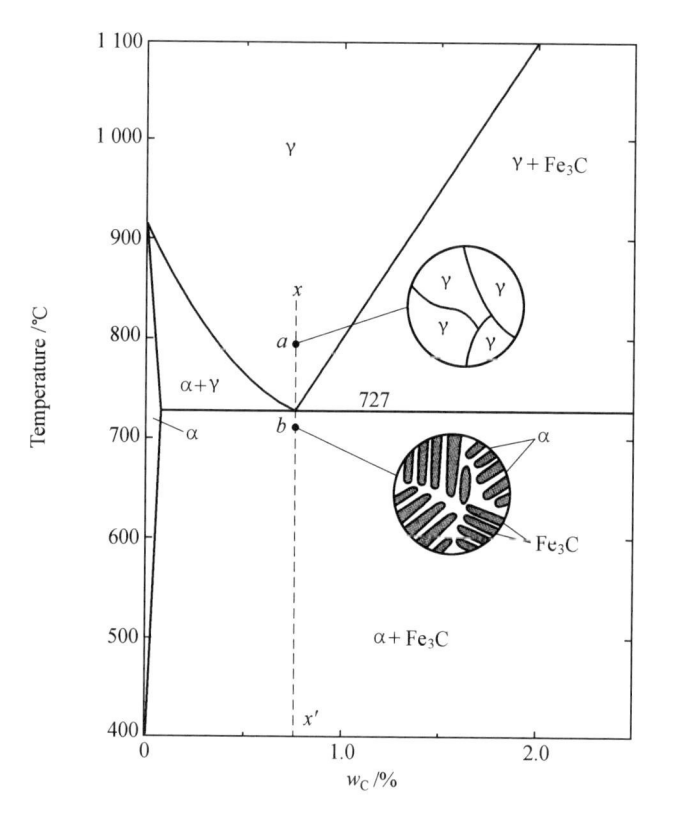

Figure 1.22 Schematic representations of the microstructures for an iron-carbon alloy of eutectoid composition above and below the eutectoid temperature

microstructure will consist entirely of grains of the γ phase. In cooling to point d, about 775℃, which is within the $\alpha + \gamma$ phase region, both these phases will coexist as in the schematic microstructure. Most of the small α particles will form along the original γ grain boundaries. The compositions of both α and γ phases may be determined using the appropriate tie line.

　　While cooling an alloy through the $\alpha + \gamma$ phase region, the composition of the ferrite phase changes with temperature along the $\alpha - (\alpha + \gamma)$ phase boundary, line MN, becoming slightly richer in

Introduction to Materials Science and Engineering 35

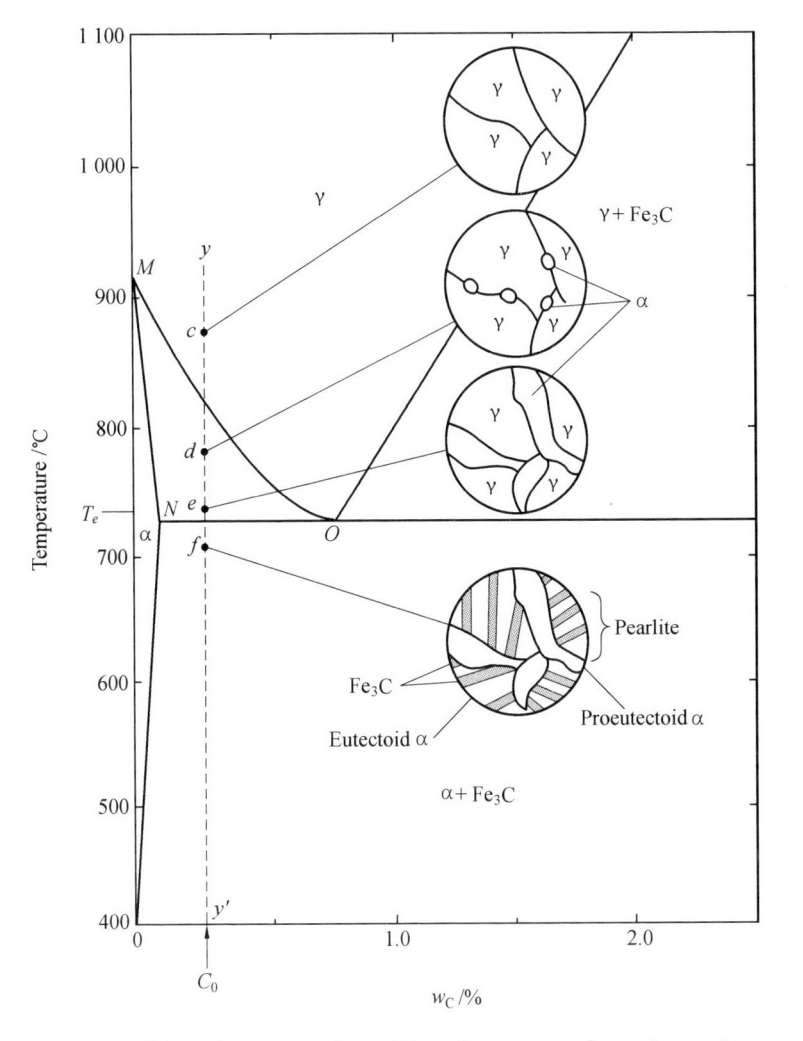

Figure 1.23 Schematic representations of the microstructures for an iron-carbon alloy of hypoeutectoid composition C_0 as it is cooled from within the austenite region to below the eutectoid temperature

carbon. On the other hand, the change in composition of the austenite is more dramatic, proceeding along the $(\alpha + \gamma) - \gamma$ boundary, line MO, as the temperature is reduced. Cooling from point d to e, will

36   *English in Materials Science and Engineering*

produce an increased fraction of the α phase and the α particles will have grown larger.

As the temperature is lowered just below the eutectoid, to point f, all the γ phase that was present at temperature T_e (and having the eutectoid composition) will transform to pearlite, according to the reaction in Equation 1.3. There will be virtually no change in the α phase that existed at point e in crossing the eutectoid temperature—it will normally be present as a continuous matrix phase surrounding the isolated pearlite colonies. Thus the ferrite phase will be present both in the pearlite and also as the phase that formed while cooling through the $\alpha + \gamma$ phase region. The ferrite that is present in the pearlite is called *eutectoid ferrite*, whereas the other, that formed above T_e, is termed **proeutectoid** [*] **ferrite**.

Analogous transformations and microstructures result for hypereutectoid [*] alloys, those containing between 0.76% and 2.14% (w_C) carbon, which are cooled from temperatures within the γ phase field. Consider an alloy of composition C_1 in Figure 1.24 which, upon cooling, moves down the line zz'. At point g only the γ phase will be present with a composition C_1. Upon cooling into the $\gamma + Fe_3C$ phase field, say, to point h, the cementite phase will begin to form along the initial γ grain boundaries. This cementite is called proeutectoid cementite. The cementite composition remains constant as the temperature changes. However, the composition of the austenite phase will move along line PO toward the eutectoid. As the temperature is lowered through the eutectoid to point i, all remaining austenite of eutectoid composition is converted into pearlite. Thus, the resulting microstructure consists of pearlite and proeutectoid cementite as microconstituents.

In addition to pearlite, other microconstituents that are products of the austenitic transformation exist; one of these is called **bainite** [*]. The microstructure of bainite consists of ferrite and cementite phases, and thus diffusional processes are involved in its formation. Bainite forms as needles or plates, depending on the temperature of the

Introduction to Materials Science and Engineering 37

transformation.

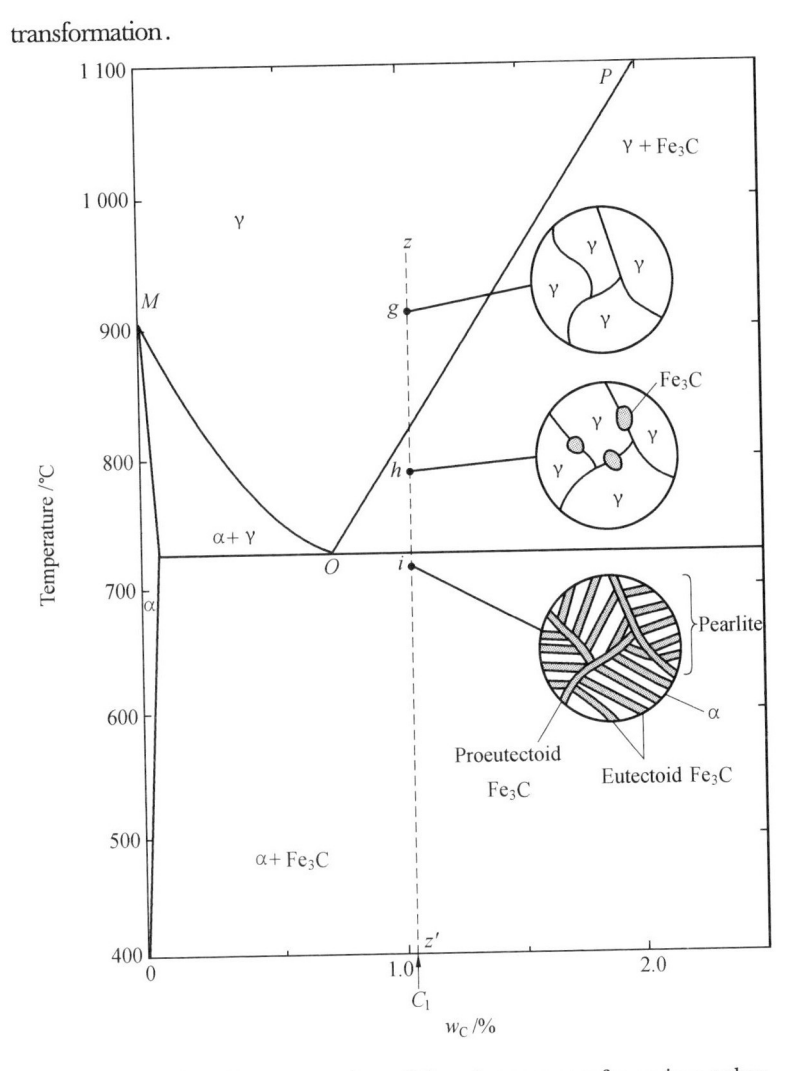

Figure 1.24 Schematic representations of the microstructures for an iron-carbon alloy of hypereutectoid composition C_1 as it is cooled from within the austenite region to below the eutectoid temperature

Another microconstituent or phase called **martensite** is formed when austenitized iron-carbon alloys are rapidly cooled to a relatively low temperature. Martensite is a nonequilibrium single-phase structure that results from a diffusionless transformation of austenite. The martensitic transformation occurs when the quenching rate is rapid enough to prevent carbon diffusion. Any diffusion whatsoever will result in the formation of ferrite and cementite phases.

Key words:

microstructure [显微组织]　　fractional [分数的,部分的,相对的]
bainite [贝氏体]　　　　　　　phase diagram [相图]
nickel [镍]　　　　　　　　　equilibrium [平衡]
tie line [连接线]　　　　　　　isotherm [等温线]
lever law [杠杆定律]　　　　　eutectic [共晶的]
solute [溶质]　　　　　　　　solvus line [溶解度曲线]
solidus line [固相线]　　　　　liquidus line [液相线]
cast iron [铸铁]　　　　　　　ferrite [铁素体]
austenite [奥氏体]　　　　　　cementite [渗碳体]
phase transformation [相变]　　allotropic [同素异形的]
recrystallization [再结晶]　　　martensite [马氏体]
martensitic transformation [马氏体相变]
eutectoid [共析的]　　　　　　lamellae [薄片]
pearlite [珠光体]　　　　　　　hypoeutectic [亚共析]
hypereutectoid [过共析]　　　　proeutectoid [先共析体]
binary isomorphous system [二元匀晶系统]

Notes:

[1]"晶体结构"这个概念用于描述晶胞中原子的平均位置,由晶格类型和原子的相对坐标完全确定。

[2]对合金系统相图的理解非常重要,因为在显微组织和力学性能之间有着非常密切的联系,而对一种合金来说,其显微组织的变化是和它的相图特性有关的。

[3]从整个合金成分点到另外一相的相界之间的连接线长度,除以整个连接线的长度,就是这一相所占的比例。

[4]这一和成分轴平行,处于两个最大溶解度位置之间的水平线 *BEG*,也可以看作是一条固相线,它代表任意一种平衡态的铜银合金中可能存在液态相的最低温度。

Questions:

1) What is a phase diagram? Why it is important?

Introduction to Materials Science and Engineering   39

2) What is the level law?

3) Why only a portion of the iron-carbon diagram is considered in practice?

1.4   Properties and Design

1.4.1 Mechanical Properties

Many materials, when in service, are subjected to forces or loads. In such situations it is necessary to know the characteristics of the material and to design the member from which it is made such that any resulting deformation will not be excessive and fracture will not occur.[1] The mechanical behavior of a material reflects the relationship between its response or deformation to an applied load or force. Important mechanical properties are strength, ductility, hardness, and stiffness.

1.4.1.1 *Yield Strength* *

Most structures are designed to ensure that only elastic deformation will result when a stress is applied. It is therefore desirable to know the stress level at which plastic deformation begins, or where the phenomenon of **yielding** occurs. For metals that experience this gradual elastic-plastic transition, the point of yielding may be determined as the initial departure from linearity of the stress-strain curve.[2] This is sometimes called the **proportional limit** *, as indicated by point P in Figure 1.25. In such cases the position of this point may not be determined precisely. As a consequence, a convention has been established wherein a straight line is constructed parallel to the elastic portion of the stress-strain curve at some specified strain offset, usually 0. 002. The stress corresponding to the intersection of this line and the stress-strain curve as it bends over in the plastic region is defined as the **yield strength** σ_y.

40   *English in Materials Science and Engineering*

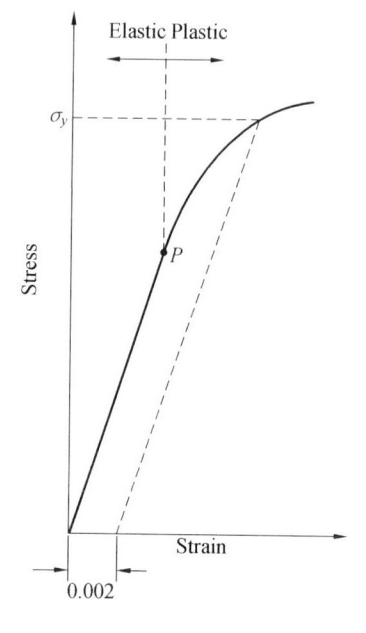

Figure 1.25 Typical stress-strain behavior for a metal showing elastic and plastic deformations

1.4.1.2 *Tensile Strength* [*]

After yielding, the stress necessary to continue plastic deformation in metals increases to a maximum, point M in Figure 1.26, and then decreases to the eventual fracture, point F. The **tensile strength** σ_b is the stress at the maximum on the engineering stress-strain curve. This corresponds to the maximum stress that can be sustained by a structure in tension. If this stress is applied and maintained, fracture will result. All deformation up to this point is uniform throughout the narrow region of the tensile specimen. However, at this maximum stress, a small constriction or neck begins to form at some point, and all subsequent deformation is confined at this neck, as indicated by the schematic specimen insets in Figure 1.26. This phenomenon is termed "necking," and fracture ultimately occurs at the neck.

Ordinarily, when the strength of a material is cited for design

Introduction to Materials Science and Engineering　41

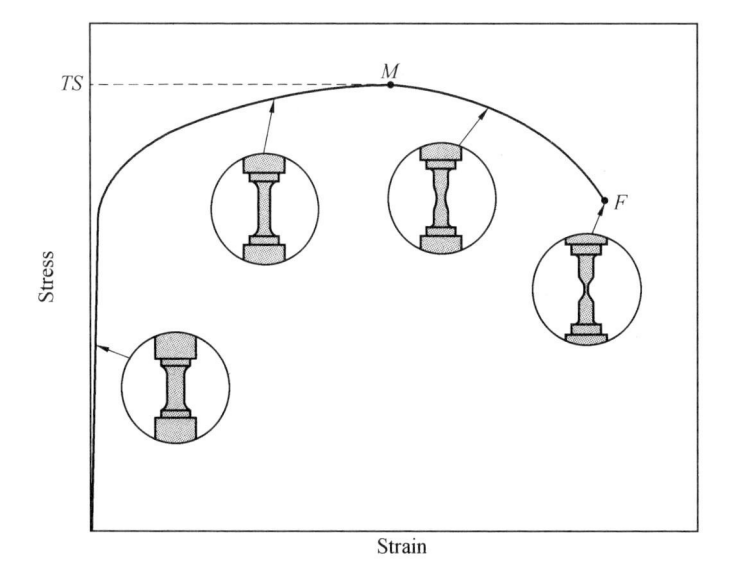

Figure 1.26 Typical engineering stress-strain behavior

purposes, the yield strength is used. This is because by the time a stress corresponding to the tensile strength has been applied, often a structure has experienced so much plastic deformation that it is useless.

1.4.1.3 *Ductility*

Ductility is another important mechanical property. It is a measure of the degree of plastic deformation that has been sustained at fracture. A material that experiences very little or no plastic deformation upon fracture is termed *brittle*.

Ductility may be expressed quantitatively as either *percent elongation* [*] or *percent reduction in area*. [*] The percent elongation δ is the percentage of plastic strain at fracture, or

$$\delta = (\frac{l_f - l_0}{l_0}) \times 100\% \tag{1.4}$$

where l_f is the fracture length and l_0 is the original gauge length [*]. Inasmuch as a significant proportion of the plastic deformation at fracture is confined to the neck region, the magnitude of δ will depend on specimen gauge length. The shorter l_0, the greater is the fraction of total elongation from the neck and the high the value of δ. Therefore, l_0 should be specified when percent elongation values are cited.

Percent reduction in area ψ is defined as

$$\psi = (\frac{A_0 - A_f}{A_0}) \times 100\% \qquad (1.5)$$

where A_0 is the original cross-sectional area and A_f is the cross-sectional area at the point of fracture. Percent reduction in area values are independent of both l_0 and A_0. Furthermore, for a given material the magnitudes of δ and ψ will, in general, be different.

A knowledge of the ductility of materials is important for at least two reasons. First, it indicates to a designer the degree to which a structure will deform plastically before fracture. Second, it specifies the degree of allowable deformation during fabrication operations.

1.4.1.4 *Hardness*

Another mechanical property that may be important to consider is hardness, which is a measure of the resistance to penetration of the surface of a material by a hard object. A variety of hardness tests have been devised, but the most commonly used are the Rockwell and the Brinell test.

In the *Brinell hardness* [*] *test* a hard steel sphere, usually 10 mm in diameter, is forced into the surface of the material. The diameter of the impression left on the surface is measured and the Brinell hardness number (HB) is calculated from the following equation.

$$HB = \frac{2P}{\pi D(D - \sqrt{D^2 - d^2})} \qquad (1.6)$$

where P is the applied load in kilograms, D is the diameter of the indentor [*] in millimeters, and d is the diameter of the impression in millimeters.

The *Rockwell harness* [*] *test* uses either a small diameter steel ball for soft materials or a diamond cone for harder materials. The depth of penetration of the indentor is automatically measured by the testing machine and converted to a Rockwell harness number. Several variations of the Rockwell test are used.

The Vickers and Knoop tests are microhardness tests; they form such small indentation that a microscope is required to obtain the measurement.

1.4.1.5 Modulus of Elasticity *

The *modulus of elasticity*, *or Young's modulus* *, is the slope of the stress-strain curve in the elastic region. This relationship is *Hooke's law*.

$$E = \frac{\sigma}{\varepsilon} \qquad (1.7)$$

The modulus is closely related to the forces bonding the atoms in the material. A steep slope in the force-interatomic spacing graph at the equilibrium spacing indicates that high forces are required to separate the atoms and cause the metal to stretch elastically. Thus, the metal has a high modulus of elasticity. Binding forces, and consequently the modulus of elasticity, are higher for high melting point metals.

The modulus is a measure of the *stiffness* of the material. A stiff material, with a high modulus of elasticity, maintains its size and shape even under an elastic load. If we are designing a shaft * and bearing *, we may need very close tolerances *. But if the shaft deforms elastically, those close tolerances may cause excessive rubbing, wear, or seizing.

Key words:
yield strength [屈服强度]   proportional limit [比例极限]
tensile strength [抗拉强度]   percent elongation [延伸率]
gauge length [标距]   Brinell hardness [布氏硬度]
indentor [压头]   Rockwell hardness [洛氏硬度]
modulus of elasticity [弹性模量]   Young's modulus [杨氏模量]
shaft [轴]   bearing [轴承]
tolerance [公差]
percent reduction in area [断面收缩率]

44　*English in Materials Science and Engineering*

Notes:

[1] 在这种情况下,必须知道材料的特性,并对其组成元素进行设计,使得外力造成的变形不会过大,也不会出现断裂。

[2] 对逐渐发生这种弹性-塑性转变的金属来说,屈服点可以通过应力－应变曲线开始偏离线性关系来确定。

Questions:

1) How is the yield strength of metal defined?

2) What is the importance of ductility?

1.4.2 Electrical Properties

In many applications, the electrical behavior of the material is more critical than the mechanical behavior. Metal wire used to transfer current over long distances must have a high electrical conductivity so that little power is lost by heating of the wire. Ceramic insulators must prevent arcing between conductors. To select and use materials for electrical and electronic applications, we must understand how properties such as electrical conductivity are produced and controlled. We must also realize that electrical behavior is influenced by the structure of the material, the processing of the material, and the environment to which the material is exposed. To accomplish these goals, we must examine the electronic structure of groups of atoms.

1.4.2.1 *Band Theory* *

The electrons in a single atom occupy discrete energy levels. The Pauli exclusion principle * permits each energy level to contain only two electrons. For example, the $2s$ level of a single atom contains one energy level and two electrons. The $2p$ level contains three energy levels and a total of six electrons.

When N atoms come together to produce a solid, the Pauli principle still requires that only two electrons in the entire solid have the same energy.[1] Each energy level broadens into a band (Figure 1.27). Consequently, the $2s$ band in a solid contains N discrete energy levels and $2N$ electrons. Since the three $2p$ bans actually

Introduction to Materials Science and Engineering 45

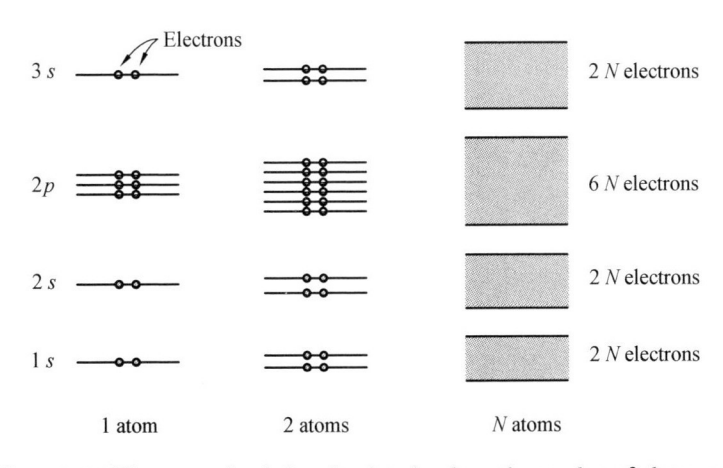

Figure 1.27 The energy levels broaden into bands as the number of electrons grouped together increases

overlap, we could alternately describe a single broad $2p$ band containing $3N$ energy levels and $6N$ electrons. Furthermore, bands will contain the electrons that resided in the corresponding levels of the isolated atoms. Of course, there will be empty bands and, possibly, bands that are only partially filled.

The electrical properties of a solid material are a consequence of its electron band structure, that is, the arrangement of the outermost electron bands and the way in which they are filled with electrons. Four different types of band structures are possible at 0 K, as shown in Figure 1.28.

In the first (Figure 1.28a), one outermost band is only partially filled with electrons. The energy corresponding to the highest filled state at 0 K is called the **Fermi energy** [*] E_F. This energy band structure is typified by some metals, in particular those that have a single s valence electron (e.g., copper). Each copper atom has one $4s$ electron. For a solid comprised of N atoms, the $4s$ band is capable of accommodating $2N$ electrons. Thus only half the available electron positions within this $4s$ band are filled. For the second band structure, also found in metals (Figure 1.28b), there is an overlap of an empty band and a filled band. Magnesium has this band structure. Each

46   *English in Materials Science and Engineering*

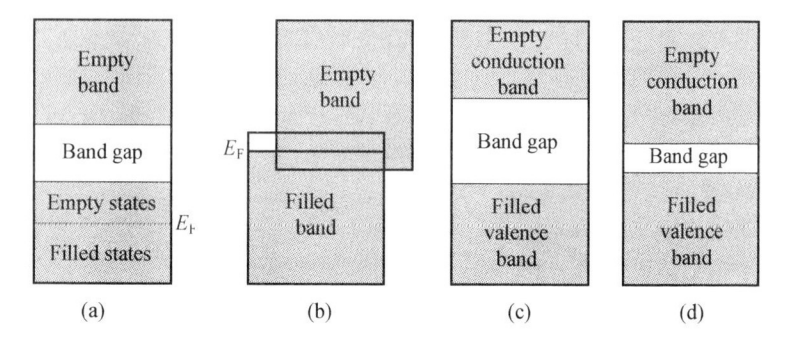

Figure 1.28 The various possible electron band structures in solids at 0 K

isolated Mg atom has two $3s$ electrons. However, when a solid is formed, the $3s$ and $3p$ bands overlap. In this instance and at 0 K, the Fermi energy is taken as that energy below which, for N atoms, N states are filled, two electrons per state. The Final two band structures are similar; one band (the **valence band** *) that is completely filled with electrons is separated from an empty **conduction band** *; and an **energy band gap** lies between them.[2] The difference between the two band structures lies in the magnitude of the energy gap. For materials that are insulators, the band gap is relatively wide (Figure 1.28c), whereas for semiconductors it is narrow (Figure 1.28d). The Fermi energy for these two band structures lies within the band gap—near its center.

1.4.2.2 *Conduction in Terms of Band and Atomic Bonding Models*

Only electrons with energies greater than the Fermi energy may be acted on and accelerated in the presence of an electric field. These are the electrons that participate in the conduction process, which are termed free electrons. Another charged electronic entity called a **hole** * is found in semiconductors and insulators. Holes have energies less than E_F and also participate in electronic conduction. The electrical conductivity * is a direct function of the numbers of free electrons and holes. In addition, the distinction between conductors and nonconductors lies in the number of these free electron and hole charge

Introduction to Materials Science and Engineering 47

carriers.

For an electron to become free, it must be excited or promoted into one of the empty and available energy states above E_F. For metals having either of the band structures shown in Figures 1.28(a) and 1.28(b), there are vacant energy states adjacent to the highest filled state at E_F. Thus very little energy is required to promote electrons into the low-lying empty states, as shown in Figure 1.29. Generally, the energy provided by an electric field is sufficient to excite large numbers of electrons into these conducting states.

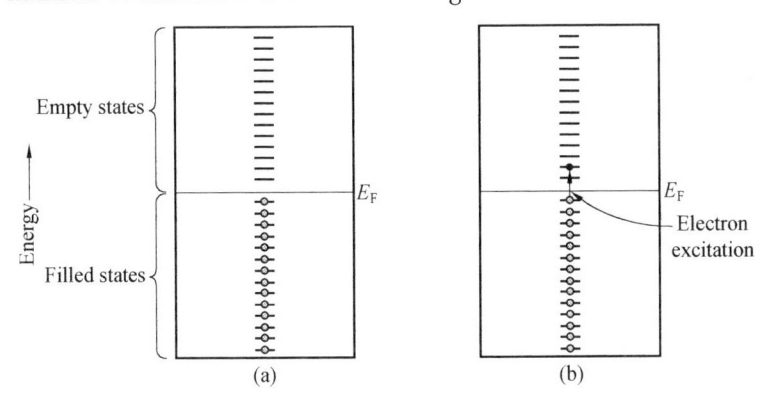

Figure 1.29 For a metal, occupancy of electron states

For insulators and semiconductors, empty states adjacent to the top of the filled valence band are not available. To become free, therefore, electrons must be promoted across the energy band gap and into empty states at the bottom of the conduction band. This is possible only by supplying to an electron the difference in energy between these two states, which is approximately equal to the band gap energy E_g. This excitation process is demonstrated in Figure 1.30. For many materials this band gap is several electron volts wide. Most often the excitation energy is from a nonelectrical source such as heat or light, usually the former. The number of electrons excited thermally into the conduction band depends on the energy band gap width as well as temperature. At a given temperature, the larger the E_g, the lower

48　*English in Materials Science and Engineering*

the probability that a valance electron will be promoted into an energy state within the conduction band. Thus, the distinction between semiconductors and insulators lies in the width of the band gap.

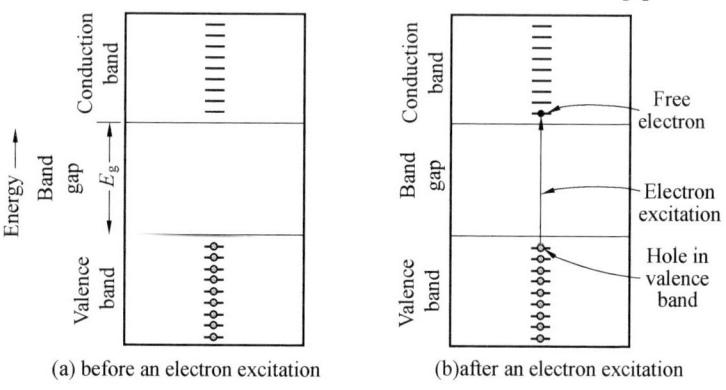

(a) before an electron excitation　　　(b)after an electron excitation

Figure 1.30 For an insulator or semiconductor, occupancy of electron states

1.4.2.3 *Electrical Conductivity*

When an electric field is applied, a force is brought to bear on the charge carriers. **Ohm's law** relates the current I—or time rate of charge passage—to the applied voltage V as follows:

$$V = IR \qquad (1.8)$$

where V is the voltage (volts, V), I is the current (amps, A), and R is the resistance (ohms, Ω) to the current flow. The resistance R is a characteristic of the materials that compose the circuit.

$$R = \rho \frac{l}{A} = \frac{l}{\sigma A} \qquad (1.9)$$

where l is the length (m) of the conductor, A is the cross-sectional area (m^2) of the conductor, ρ is the electrical resistivity ($\Omega \cdot m$), and σ which is the reciprocal of ρ, is the electrical conductivity ($\Omega^{-1} \cdot m^{-1}$).

A second form of Ohm's law can be expressed as

$$J = \sigma \xi \qquad (1.10)$$

where J is the current density, and ξ is the electric field intensity. We can also determine that the current density J is

$$J = nqv_d \tag{1.11}$$

where n is the number of charge carriers, q is the charge on each carrier, and v_d is the average drift velocity at which the charge carriers move. Define the **mobility** μ as

$$\mu = \frac{v_d}{\xi} \tag{1.12}$$

Then,

$$\sigma = nq\mu \tag{1.13}$$

So, we can control the electrical conductivity of a material by controlling the number of charge carriers in the material or by controlling the mobility, or ease of movement, of the charge carriers.

Electrons are the charge carriers in conductors, semiconductors, and insulators whereas ions carry the charge in most ionic compounds. The mobility depends on atomic bonding, lattice imperfections, microstructure, and, in ionic compounds, diffusion rates.

1.4.2.4 *Controlling the Conductivity of Metals*

The conductivity of a pure, defect-free metal is determined by the electronic structure of the atoms. But we can significantly affect the conductivity by influencing the mobility μ of the carriers. The mobility is proportional to the drift velocity, which is low if the electrons collide with imperfections in the lattice. The mean free path* is the average distance between collisions. A long mean free path permits high mobilities and high conductivities. If the metal contains no lattice defects and performs at absolute zero degrees, the mean free path is infinite and the electrical resistivity is zero. However, no metals are perfect nor do they operate at absolute zero.

Temperature Effect

When the temperature of a metal increases, thermal energy causes the atoms to vibrate. At any instant the atom may not be in its equilibrium position and therefore interacts with and scatters electrons. The mean free path decreases, the mobility of electrons is reduced, and the resistivity increases. The change in resistivity with temperature

50 *English in Materials Science and Engineering*

can be estimated from the equation

$$\rho_t = \rho_0 + a \Delta T \qquad (1.14)$$

where ρ_0 is the resistivity at room temperature, ΔT is the temperature difference between the temperature of interest and room temperature, and a is the *temperature resistivity coefficient*. The relationship between resistivity and temperature is linear over a wide temperature range.

Effect of Lattice Defects

Lattice imperfections scatter electrons and thus reduce the mobility and conductivity of the metal. Greater numbers of defects reduce the mean free path and have pronounced effect on the conductivity. For example, the increase in the resistivity due to solid solution[*] atoms is

$$\rho_d = b(1 - x)x \qquad (1.15)$$

where ρ_d is the increase in resistivity due to the defects, x is the atomic fraction of the impurity or solid solution atoms present, and b is the *defect resistivity coefficient*. In a similar manner, vacancies, dislocations, and surface defects, such as grain boundaries, also reduce the conductivity of the metal. The effect of the defects is independent of temperature.

Effect of Processing And Strengthening

Strengthening mechanisms and metal processing techniques affect the electrical properties of a metal in different ways. Solid solution strengthening is a poor way to obtain high strength in metals intended to have high conductivities. The mean free paths are very short due to the random distribution of the interstitial[*] or sustitutional atoms[*]. Age hardening[*] and dispersion strengthening[*] reduce the conductivity less than solid solution strengthening. In the dispersion-strengthened two-phase alloys, the electrical resistivity can be estimated from the rule of mixtures. Strain hardening and grain size control have less effect on conductivity. Since dislocations and grain boundaries are further apart than solid solution atoms, there are large volumes of metal that have a long mean free path. Consequently, cold working is an effective way to increase the strength of a metallic conductor without seriously impairing the electrical properties of that material. In addition, the effects of cold working on conductivity can be eliminated by the low temperature recovery heat treatment, in which good conductivity is restored while the strength is retained.

Key words:

band theory [能带理论]   Pauli exclusion principle [泡利不相容原理]
Fermi energy [费密能级]   valence band [价带]
conduction band [导带]   hole [空穴]
electrical conductivity [电导率] dislocation [位错]
mean free path [平均自由程]   age hardening [时效硬化]
solid solution [固溶体]   interstitial [间隙的]
substitutional atom [置换原子]   dispersion strengthening [弥散强化]

Notes:

[1] 当 N 个原子聚集到一起形成固体时,泡利不相容原理仍然要求整个固体中只能有两个电子的能量相同。

[2] 后两种能带结构是相似的,一个全部填满电子的能带(价带)和一个全空的导带完全分开,中间隔着一个能隙。

Questions:

1) What is the band theory?

2) How can the conductivity of metals be controlled?

1.4.3 Dielectric* and Magnetic Properties

The response of a material to an electric field can be used to advantage even when no charge is transferred. These effects are described by the dielectric properties of the material. Dielectric materials possess a large energy gap between the valence and conduction bands; thus the materials have a high electrical resistivity. Two important applications for dielectric materials include electrical insulators and capacitors*.

The effects of a magnetic field on a material are equally profound. Some magnetic materials possess a permanent magnetization for applications ranging from toys to computer storage; other magnetic materials are used in electric motors and transformers.

Although the responses of a material to an electric or magnetic

52   *English in Materials Science and Engineering*

field are based on very different phenomena, a similar approach is used to describe the two effects.

1.4.3.1 *Dipoles*

In both electrical and magnetic materials, the application of a field causes the formation and movement of dipoles. *Dipoles* are atoms or group of atoms that have an unbalanced charge. In an imposed field, the dipoles become aligned in the material. Alignment of the dipoles causes *polarization* in and electric field and *magnetization* in a magnetic field.[1] The ease with which polarization and magnetization occur determines the behavior of the dielectric or magnetic material.

1.4.3.2 *Polarization in and Electric Field*

When an electric field is applied to a material, dipoles are induced within the atomic or molecular structure and become aligned with the direction of the field. In addition, any permanent dipoles already present in the material are aligned with the field. The material is polarized. The polarization P is

$$P = Zqd \qquad (1.16)$$

where Z is the number of charge centers that are displaced per cubic meter, q is the electronic charge, and d is the displacement between the positive and negative ends of the dipole. Four mechanisms cause polarization—electronic polarization, ionic polarization, molecular polarization, and space charges, as shown in Figure 1.31.

1.4.3.3 *Dielectric Properties and Capacitors*

A capacitor is an electrical device used to store charge received from a circuit. The capacitor may smooth out fluctuations in signal, accumulate charge to prevent damage to the rest of the circuit, store charge for later distribution, or even change the frequency of the electric signal. Capacitors are designed so that the charge is stored in a polarized material between tow conductors. The material between the conductors must easily polarize yet have a high electrical resistivity to prevent the charge from passing from one plate to the next.[2]

Dielectric materials satisfy both of these requirements.

Dielectric Constant [*]

The charge Q that can be stored by a capacitor is

$$Q = CV \qquad (1.17)$$

where V is the voltage across the plates of the capacitor and C is the *capacitance* [*]. The capacitance depends on both the material between the plates and the design of the device. For a simple parallel plate capacitor with only two plates

$$C = \varepsilon \frac{A}{d} \qquad (1.18)$$

where A is the area of each plate and d is the distance between the plates. The *permittivity* ε is the ability of the material to polarize and store a charge. The *relative permittivity* or *dielectric constant*$_\kappa$ is the ratio between the permittivity of the material and the permittivity of a vacuum, ε_0.

$$\kappa = \frac{\varepsilon}{\varepsilon_0} \qquad (1.19)$$

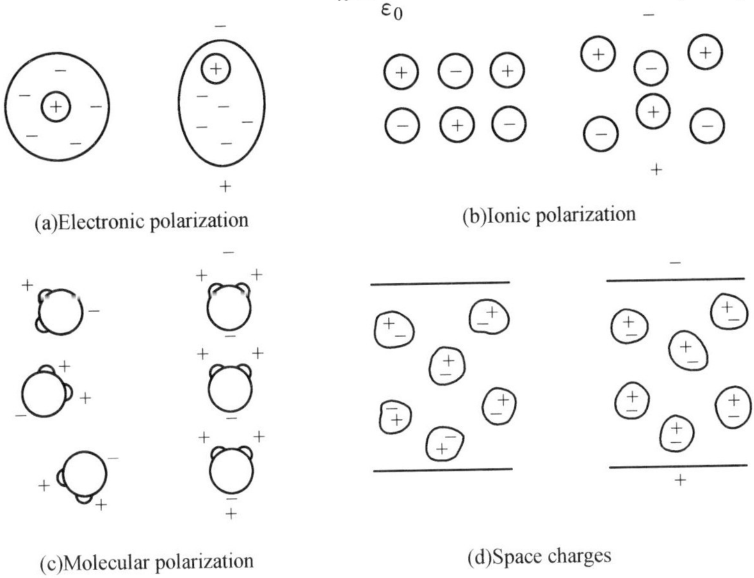

(a)Electronic polarization

(b)Ionic polarization

(c)Molecular polarization

(d)Space charges

Figure 1.31 Polarization mechanisms in materials

54   *English in Materials Science and Engineering*

The dielectric constant κ, which depends on the material, temperature, and frequency, is related to polarization.

$$P = (\kappa - 1)\varepsilon_0 \xi \qquad (1.20)$$

where ξ is the strength of the electric field.

Dielectric Strength *

Small separations and high voltages cause the capacitor to break down and discharge. The breakdown voltage, or dielectric strength, must be considered in addition to the dielectric constant. The dielectric strength is the maximum electric field ξ that can be maintained between the plates. The dielectric strength therefore places an upper limit on C and Q. In order to construct smaller capacitors capable of storing large charges in an intense field, we must select materials with a high dielectric strength and a high dielectric constant.

1.4.3.4 *Controlling Dielectric Properties*

Dielectrics for capacitors should exhibit a large degree of polarization over a wide range of temperatures and frequencies. Several important factors influence dielectric behavior.

Electrical Resistivity

All effective dielectrics have a high electrical resistivity to prevent leakage or discharge of the stored energy. Common dielectrics have resistivities of $10^{11}VA^{-1}m$ or greater.

Structure

Most of the dielectric materials for capacitors fall into one of three groups—liquids composed of polar molecules, polymers, and certain ceramics. All possess permanent dipoles that move easily in an electric field yet still produce high dielectric constants. Water, which has a high dielectric constant, is corrosive, relatively conductive, and difficult to use in constructing capacitor devices. Organic oils or waxes are more effective. These materials contain relatively long chainlike molecules that serve as dipoles yet are easily aligned. Often they are impregnated into paper, which itself is a dielectric. In amorphous polymers, segments of the chains possess sufficient mobility to cause polarization. Capacitors frequently use polyester*, polystyrene*, polycarbonate*, and cellulose* as dielectrics. Glass, an amorphous ceramic, behaves in much the same way. Glassy polymers and crystalline materials have lower dielectric constants and dielectric strengths than their amorphous counterparts. Polymers with asymmetrical chains have a higher dielectric constant, even though the chains may not easily align, because the strength of each molecular dipole is greater.[3] Thus, polyvinyl chloride* and polystyrene have dielectric strengths greater than polyethylene.

Frequency

Dielectric materials are often used in alternating-current circuits. The dipoles must therefore switch directions, often at a high frequency, in order for the electronic device to perform satisfactorily. Electronic polarization occurs easily even at frequencies as high as 10^{16} Hz, since no rearrangement of atoms is necessary. Ionic polarization also occurs readily up to 10^{13} Hz; only a simple elastic distortion of the bonds between the ions is required. However, materials that rely on molecular polarization are very sensitive to frequency, since entire atoms or groups of atoms must be rearranged. Consequently, the response of the dielectric material to an alternating field is reduced and complete polarization may not occur. The structure also influences the frequency effect. Gases and liquids polarize at higher frequencies than solids. Amorphous polymers and ceramics polarize at higher frequencies than their crystalline counterparts. Polymers with bulky asymmetrical groups attached to the chain polarize only at low frequencies.

Voltage

Increasing the voltage of the applied field forces permanent dipoles into alignment more easily and completely. Eventually, all of the dipoles are aligned, a saturation polarization is achieved, and further increases in voltage have little effect on polarization. However, high voltages may cause breakdown of the dielectric.

56   *English in Materials Science and Engineering*

Temperature

When the temperature increases, permanent dipoles have a greater mobility, polarize more easily, and give a higher dielectric constant. However, the higher temperatures again permit the dielectric to break down and may cause the crystal structure to change to a less polar condition, which greatly reduces the polarization.

1.4.3.5 *Magnetization and Permeability*

In dielectric materials, polarization occurs when induced or permanent electric dipoles arc oriented by an interaction between the material and the electrical field. In an analogous manner, *magnetization* occurs when induced or permanent magnetic dipoles are oriented by an interaction between the magnetic material and the magnetic field.[4] Magnetization enhances the influence of the magnetic field, permitting larger magnetic energies to be stored than if the material were absent. This energy can be stored permanently or temporarily and can be used to do work.

When a magnetic field is applied in a vacuum, lines of magnetic flux are produced. A greater number of lines of flux increases the work that the magnetic field can accomplish. The flux density, or inductance*, is related to the applied field by

$$B = \mu_0 H \qquad (1.21)$$

where B is the inductance, H is the magnetic field, and μ_0 is the *magnetic permeability** of a vacuum. The permeability in a vacuum is a constant.

When we place a material within the magnetic field, the magnetic inductance is determined by the manner in which induced and permanent magnetic dipoles interact with the field. The magnetic inductance now is

$$B = \mu H \qquad (1.22)$$

where μ is the magnetic permeability of the material in the field.

We can describe the influence of the magnetic material by the relative permeability μ_r, where

$$\mu_r = \frac{\mu}{\mu_0} \tag{1.23}$$

A large relative permeability means that the material has amplified the effect of the magnetic field. Thus the relative permeability has the same importance that the dielectric constant has in dielectrics.

The magnetization M represents the increase in the magnetic inductance due to the core material, so we can rewrite the equation for inductance as

$$B = \mu_0 H + \mu_0 M \tag{1.24}$$

Because the term $\mu_0 M$ is often much greater than $\mu_0 H$, we can frequently equate $B = \mu_0 M$. We sometimes interchangeably refer to either inductance or magnetization. Normally we are interested in producing a high inductance B or magnetization M. This is accomplished by selecting materials that have a high relative permeability.

1.4.3.6 Domain* Structure

When a magnetic field is applied to a collection of atoms, several types of behavior may be observed: diamagnetic* behavior, paramagnetism*, ferromagnetism*, antiferromagnetism*, and ferrimagnetism*.

Ferromagnetic materials have their powerful influence on magnetization because of the positive interaction between the dipoles of neighboring atoms. Within the grain structure of a ferromagnetic material, a substructure composed of magnetic domains is produced, even in the absence of an external field. *Domains* are regions in the material in which all of the dipoles are aligned. In a material that has never been exposed to a magnetic field, the individual domains have a random orientation. The net magnetization in the material as a whole is zero.

Boundaries, called *Bloch walls*, separate the individual domains, much like grain boundaries. The Bloch walls are narrow zones in which the direction of the magnetic moment gradually and continuously

58   *English in Materials Science and Engineering*

changes from that of one domain to that of the next.

When a magnetic field is imposed on the materials, domains that are already lined up with the field grow at the expense of unaligned domains. In order for the domains to grow, the Bloch walls must move. The imposed magnetic field provides the force required for the walls to migrate. As the strength of the field increases, favorably oriented domains continue to grow and a greater net magnetization occurs (Figure 1.32). The *saturation magnetization*, produced when all of the domains are properly oriented, is the greatest amount of magnetization that the material can obtain.

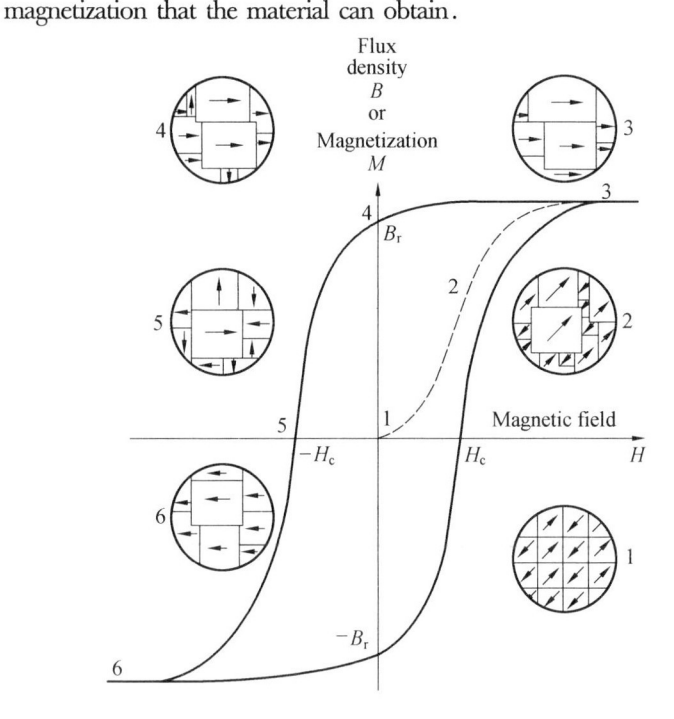

Figure 1.32 The ferromagnetic hysteresis loop

When the field is removed, the resistance offered by the domain walls prevents regrowth of the domains into random orientations. As a result, many of the domains remain oriented near the direction of the

Introduction to Materials Science and Engineering 59

original field and a residual magnetization, known as the *remanence** , is present in the material. The material acts as a permanent magnet.

If we now apply a field in the reverse direction, the domains grow with an alignment in the opposite direction. A *coercive** *field* H_c is required to force the domains to be randomly oriented and cancel one another's effect. Further increases in the strength of the field eventually align the domains to saturation in the opposite direction. As the field continually alternates, the magnetization versus field relationship traces out a *hysteresis** *loop*. The hysteresis loop describes the strength and direction of the magnetization in an alternating magnetic field.

1.4.3.7 *Application of the Magnetization-Field Curve*

The behavior of a material in a magnetic field is related to the size and shape of the hysteresis loop (Figure 1.33). Let's look at three applications for magnetic materials.

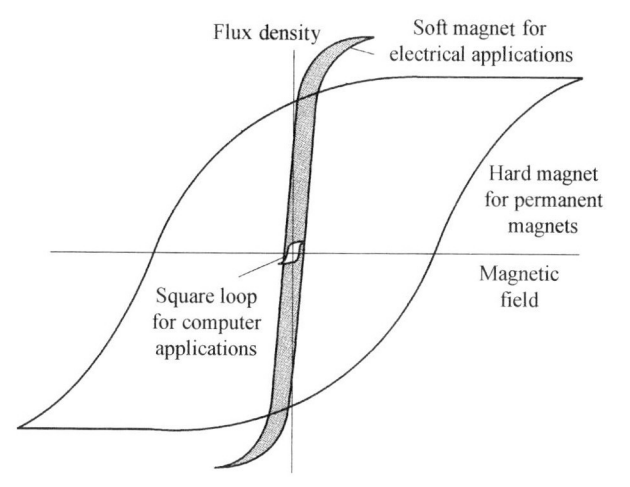

Figure 1.33 Comparison of the hysteresis loops for three applications of ferromagnetic materials

Magnetic Materials for Electrical Applications

Ferromagnetic materials are used to enhance the magnetic field produced when an electric current is passed through the material. The

60   *English in Materials Science and Engineering*

magnetic field is then expected to do work. Applications include cores for electromagnets, electric motors, transformers, generators, and other electrical equipment. These devices utilize an alternating field, so that the core material is continually cycled through the hysteresis loop. Electrical magnetic materials, often called soft magnets, should have the following characteristics.

(1) A high saturation magnetization permits the material to do the most work.

(2) The domains can be reoriented with the smallest imposed field if the coercive field is very small.

(3) A small hystersis loop gives small energy losses when a material is cycled through an alternating field.

(4) A small remanence is desired.

(5) The dipoles must be easily realigned at the frequency at which the material operates. If the frequency is so high that the domains cannot be realigned each cycle, then the device may heat due to dipole friction.

(6) If the electrical resistivity is too low, current may leak from the field as eddy currents and again may cause heating of the device.

Magnetic Materials for Computer Memories

Ferromagnetic materials are used to store bits of information in computers. Memory is stored by magnetizing the material in a certain direction. For this application, materials with a square hysteresis loop, a low remanence, a low satuation magnetization, and a low coercive field are preferable. The square loop assures that a bit of information placed in the material by a field remains stored; a steep and abrupt change in magnetization is required to remove the information from storage in the ferromagnet. Furthermore, the magnetization is produced by small external fields, so the coercive field, saturation magnetization, and remanence should be low.

Magnetic Materials for Permanent Magnets

Permanent magnets require high remanence, high permeability, high coercive fields, and high power. The power of the magnet is related to the size of the hysteresis loop, or the maximum product of B and H. The area of the largest rectangle that can be drawn in the second or fourth quadrants of the $B - H$ curve is related to the energy required to demagnetize the magnet. For the product to be large, both the remanence and the coercive field should be large.

Key words:
dielectric [介电的]   capacitor [电容]
dipole [偶极子]   capacitance [电容]
permittivity[介电常数]   dielectric strength [介电强度]
polyester [聚酯]   polystyrene [聚苯乙烯]
polycarbonate [聚碳酸酯]   cellulose [纤维素]
polyvinyl chloride [聚氯乙烯] inductance [感应]
diamagnetic [抗磁性的]   paramagnetism [顺磁性]
ferromagnetism [铁磁性]   ferrimagnetism [亚铁磁性]
domain [磁畴]   remanence [剩磁]
coercive [强制的]   hysteresis [磁滞]
dielectric constant [相对介电常数]
magnetic permeability [磁导率]
antiferromagnetism [反铁磁性]

Notes:
[1] 偶极子的定向排列在电场中引起极化效应,在磁场中引起磁化效应。
[2] 导体中间的这种材料必须很容易极化,而又有很高的电阻率,以防止电荷从一块板转移到另一块板上。
[3] 非对称链结构的聚合物,尽管分子链不容易定向排列,但由于每个分子偶极子的强度比较大,因此其介电常数较大。
[4] 与此相类似,磁性材料和磁场相互作用,会使感生的或永久的磁偶极子定向排列,产生磁化现象。

Questions:

1) What is a dipole?

2) What is the difference between the dielectric constant and the permittivity?

3) What is the ferromagnetic hysteresis loop?

1.4.4 Optical Properties

1.4.4.1 *Emission of Continuous and Characteristic Radiation*

Energy, or radiation in the form of waves or particles called *photons*[*], can be emitted from a material. The important characteristics of the photons—their energy E, wavelength λ, and the frequency ν—are related by the equation

$$E = h\nu = \frac{hc}{\lambda} \qquad (1.25)$$

where c is the speed of light and h is Planck's constant. This equation permits us to either consider the photon as a particle of energy E or as a wave with a characteristic wave length and frequency.

A stimulus such as an accelerated electron is decelerated when it strikes a material. As the electron decelerates, energy is given up and emitted as photons. Each time the electron strikes an atom, more of its energy is given up. Each interaction, however, may be more or less severe, so the electron gives up a different fraction of its energy each time, producing photons of different wavelengths. A *continuous spectrum*, or *white radiation*, is produced.

If the incoming stimulus has a sufficient energy, an electron from an inner energy level is excited into an outer energy level. To restore equilibrium, the empty inner level is filled by electrons from a higher level. There are discrete energy differences between any two energy levels. When an electron drops from one level to a second level, a photon having that particular energy and wavelength is emitted. Photons with this energy and wavelength comprise the *characteristic spectrum*[*] and are X rays.

1.4.4.2 *Interaction of Photons with a Material*

Photons, either characteristic or continuous, cause a number of optical phenomena when they interact with the electronic or crystal structure of a material.

Introduction to Materials Science and Engineering 63

Absorption

If the incoming photons interact with the material, they give up their energy and are absorbed. Most metals absorb photons with wavelengths shorter than infrared radiation, including visible light. Because the valence band is not filled in metals, almost any photon has a sufficient energy to excite an electron to a higher energy level in the conduction band (Figure 1.34a). Therefore metals, unless they are exceptionally thin, absorb visible light and are opaque*. Absorption is given by

$$\ln(\frac{I}{I_0}) = -\mu x \qquad (1.26)$$

where x is the path through which the photons move and μ is the *linear absorption coefficient* of the material for the photons. The absorption coefficient is related to the density of the material, the wavelength of the radiation, and the energy gap between the conduction and valence bands.

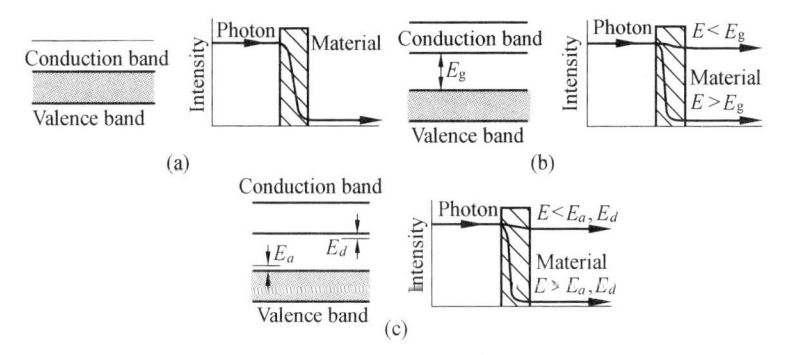

Figure 1.34 Relationship between absorption and the energy gap

Transmission

If the photons do not possess enough energy to excite an electron to a higher energy level, the photons may be transmitted rather than absorbed and the material is transparent (Figure 1.34b). Whether a photon is absorbed or transmitted depends on the relationship between the energy of the photon and the energy gap between the conduction and valence bands. In metals, there is no gap and almost all photons are absorbed unless the metal is exceptionally thin. In simple, high-purity ceramics and polymers, the energy gap is large and the material is transparent to even high-energy photons, including visible light. In semiconductors, however, electrons can be excited into the acceptor levels or out of the donor levels. The photons are absorbed unless their energies are smaller than the donor or acceptor energy gaps (Figure 1.34c). Semiconductors are therefore opaque to short wavelength radiation but transparent to very long wavelength photons. The degree of transmission is also related to the overall atomic arrangement. Amorphous materials, such as glass and simple polymers, may be transparent. However, when the material crystallizes, photons can interact with the crystal structure and are at least partially absorbed.

Refraction[*]

Even when photons are transmitted by the material, the photon loses some of its energy and therefore has a slightly longer wavelength. The photon then behaves as though the speed of light in the material has been reduced and the beam of photons changes directions (Figure 1.35). If α and β are respectively the angles that the incident and refracted beams make with the normal to the surface of the material, then

$$n = \frac{c}{v} = \frac{\lambda_{\text{vacuum}}}{\lambda} = \frac{\sin\alpha}{\sin\beta} \qquad (1.27)$$

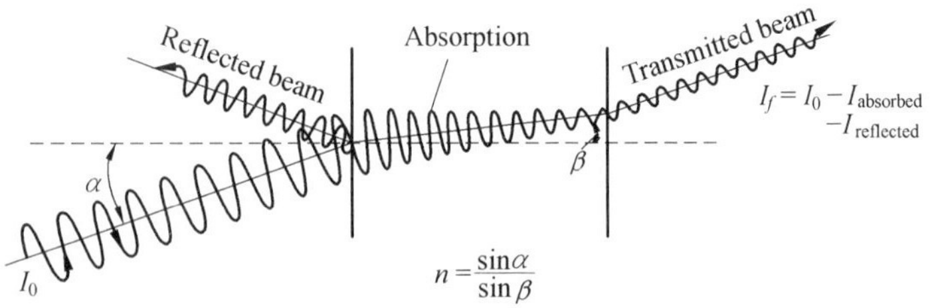

Figure 1.35 A beam of photons changes direction as a result of interactions as it passes through a material

Introduction to Materials Science and Engineering   65

The ratio n is the *index of refraction*, c is the speed of light in a vacuum and v is the speed of light in the material.

Reflection

If the surface of the material is smooth and if the incoming photons have a low energy, a portion of the incoming photons are reflected from the material's surface. The *reflectivity* R is related to the index of refraction. In a vacuum,

$$R = (\frac{n-1}{n+1})^2 \times 100\% \qquad (1.28)$$

Materials with a high index of refraction have a higher reflectivity than materials with a low index—light is transmitted rather than reflected in these materials

Diffraction[*]

In X-ray diffraction, the wavelike nature of X rays is used to determine information about the crystal structure and atom location within the material. The wavelike X-ray radiation interacts with the electronic dipoles and is scattered in all directions. The radiation scattered from one atom interacts destructively with radiation from other atoms except in certain directions (Figure 1.36). In these directions, the scattered radiation is reinforced rather than destroyed. The radiation, which is of the identical wavelength as the original X-ray beam, is reinforced in the angles given by Bragg's law.

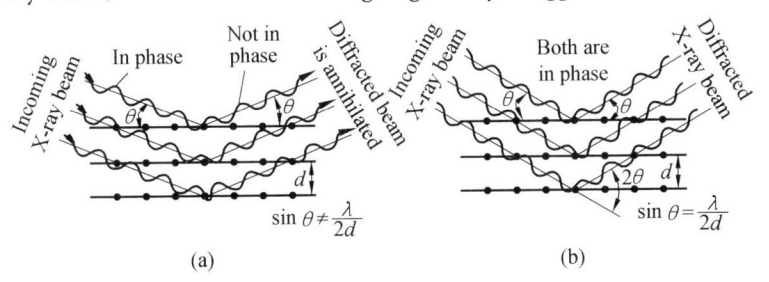

Figure 1.36 Destructive and reinforcing interactions between X rays and the crystal structure of a material

66 *English in Materials Science and Engineering*

$$\sin\theta = \frac{\lambda}{2\,d_{hkl}} \qquad (1.29)$$

where the angle θ is half of the angle between the diffracted beam and the original beam direction, λ is the wavelength, and d_{hkl} is the interplanar spacing that causes constructive reinforcement of the beam. Analysis of the angle θ permits us to identify d_{hkl} and eventually the identity, lattice parameter, and other information concerning the crystal.

Key words:
photon [光子]   characteristic spectrum [特征谱]
opaque [不透明的]   refraction [折射]
diffraction [衍射]

Questions:

1) Why are metals opaque?
2) What is the difference between refraction and diffraction?

1.4.5 Thermal Properties

Thermal properties, including heat capacity, thermal conductivity, and thermal expansion, are influenced by atomic vibration and in the case of thermal conductivity, transfer of energy by electrons. The vibration may be expressed as an energy or the wavelike nature of the energy can be utilized.

1.4.5.1 *Heat Capacity*[*]

At absolute zero, the atoms gain thermal energy and vibrate at a particular amplitude and frequency. This vibration produces an elastic wave called a *phonon*[*]. The energy of the phonon can be expressed in terms of wavelength or frequency. The material gains or loses heat by gaining or losing phonons.

The heat capacity is the energy required to raise the temperature of one mole of a material one degree. The heat capacity can be expressed either at constant pressure, C_p, or at a constant volume, C_v.

Introduction to Materials Science and Engineering   67

The *specific heat** is the energy required to raise the temperature of a particular weight or mass of a material one degree. The relationship between specific heat and heat capacity is

$$\text{specifi cheat} = \frac{\text{heat capacity}}{\text{atomic weight}} \qquad (1.30)$$

In most engineering calculations, the specific heat is more conveniently used.

1.4.5.2 *Thermal Expansion*

An atom that gains thermal energy and begins to vibrate behaves as though it has a larger atomic radius. The average distance between the atoms and the overall dimensions of the material increase. The change in the dimensions of the material Δl per unit length is given by the *linear coefficient of thermal expansion* α.

$$\alpha = \frac{\Delta l}{l\Delta T} \qquad (1.31)$$

where ΔT is the increase in temperature and l is the initial length.

The linear coefficient of thermal expansion is related to the strength of the atomic bonds. In order for the atoms to move from their equilibrium separation, energy must be introduced to the material. If a very deep energy trough caused by strong atomic bonding is characteristic of the material, the atoms separate to a lesser degree and have a low linear coefficient of thermal expansion. This relationship also indicates that materials having a high melting temperature, also due to strong atomic attractions, have low linear coefficients of thermal expansion.

1.4.5.3 *Thermal Conductivity*

The *thermal conductivity* K is a measure of the rate at which heat is transferred through a material. The conductivity relates the heat Q transferred across a given plane of area A per second when a temperature gradient $\Delta T / \Delta x$ exists.

$$\frac{Q}{A} = K \frac{\Delta T}{\Delta x} \qquad (1.32)$$

68   *English in Materials Science and Engineering*

The thermal conductivity K plays the same role in heat transfer that the diffusion coefficient D does in mass transfer.

If valence electrons are easily excited into the conduction band, thermal energy can be transferred by the electrons. The amount of energy transferred depends on the number of excited electrons and their mobility; thus we expect a relationship between thermal and electrical conductivity.

$$\frac{K}{\sigma T} = L = 2.3 \times 10^{-8} \text{W} \cdot \Omega \cdot \text{K}^{-2} \qquad (1.33)$$

where L is the Lorentz constant.

Key words:
heat capacity [热容]   phonon [声子]
specific heat [比热容]

2

Materials

2.1 Ferrous Alloys

More than 90% by weight of the metallic materials used by human beings are ferrous alloys. This represents an immense family of engineering materials with a wide range of microstructures and related properties. The majority of engineering designs that require structural load support or power transmission involve ferrous alloys. As a practical matter, these alloys fall into two broad categories based on the carbon in the alloy composition. Steel generally contains between $w_C = 0.05\%$ and $w_C = 2.0\%$. The cast irons generally contain between $w_C = 2.0\%$ and $w_C = 4.5\%$. Within the steel category, we shall distinguish whether or not a significant amount of alloying elements other than carbon is used. A composition of 5% total noncarbon additions will serve as an arbitrary boundary between low alloy and high alloy steels. These alloy additions are chosen carefully because they invariably bring with them sharply increased material costs. [1] They are justified only by essential improvements in properties such as higher strength or improved corrosion resistance.

70   *English in Materials Science and Engineering*

Note:

[1] 由于加入这些合金元素会急剧提高材料成本,故要慎重选用。

Questions:

1) How do you distinguish steel from cast iron?

2) How do you distinguish low alloy steel from high alloy steel?

2.1.1 Iron and Steel

The earth contains a large number of metals which are useful to man. One of the most important of these is iron. Modern industry needs considerable quantities of this metal, either in the form of iron or in the form of steel. A certain number of non-ferrous metals, including aluminum and zinc, are also important, but even today the majority of our engineering products are of iron or steel. Moreover, iron possesses magnetic properties, which have made the development of electrical power possible.

The iron ore* which we find on earth is not pure. It contains some impurities that must be removed by smelting. The process of smelting consists of heating the ore in a blast furnace* with coke* and limestone*, and reducing it to metal.[1] Blasts of hot air enter the furnace from the bottom and provide the oxygen that is necessary for the reduction of the ore. The ore becomes molten, and its oxides combine with carbon from the coke. The non-metallic constituents of the ore combine with the limestone to form a liquid slag*. This floats on top of the molten iron, and passes out of the furnace through a tap*. The metal which remains is pig iron*.

We can melt this down again in another furnace—a cupola*—with more coke and limestone, and tap it out into a ladle* or directly into molds. This is cast iron. Cast iron does not have the strength of steel. It is brittle and may fracture under tension. But it possesses certain properties that make it very useful in the manufacture of machinery. In the molten state it is very fluid, therefore, it is easy to cast it into intricate shapes. Also it is easy to machine it. Cast iron contains small proportions of other substances. These non-metallic constituents of cast iron include carbon, silicon and sulphur, and the presence of these substances affects the behavior of the metal. Iron which contains a negligible quantity of carbon, for example, wrought* iron behaves differently from iron which contains a lot of carbon. [2]

The carbon in cast iron is present partly as free graphite and partly as a chemical combination of iron and carbon which is called cementite. *[3] This is a very hard substance, and it makes the iron hard too. However, iron can only hold about 1.5% of cementite. Any carbon content above that percentage is present of the form of a flaky* graphite. Steel contains no free graphite, and its carbon content ranges from almost nothing to 1.5%. We make wire and tubing from mild steel with a very low carbon content, and drills and cutting tools from high carbon steel.

Key words:

ore[矿]	blast furnace[高炉]	coke[焦炭]
limestone[石灰石]	slag[熔渣]	tap[口]
pig iron[生铁]	cupola[冲天炉]	ladle[钢(铁)水包]
wrought[可锻的]	cementite[渗碳体]	flaky[片状的]

Notes:

[1] 冶炼过程是在有焦炭和石灰石存在的高炉中加热矿石,从而把它提炼成金属。

[2] 含有极少量碳的铁如精炼铁,其特性与含大量碳的铁不同。

[3] 在铸铁中的碳部分作为自由的石墨存在,部分以被称为渗碳体的铁和碳的化学混合物存在。

Questions:

1) How is the steel made?

2) If you want to have a high strength iron based material, what should you do?

3) What is the function of the coke when producing pig iron?

4) What is the difference between the pig iron and the cast iron?

2.1.2 Carbon and Alloy Steel

◆ Carbon Steel

A plain carbon steel is one in which carbon is the only alloying element. The amount of carbon in the steel controls its hardness, strength, and ductility. The higher the carbon content, the harder the steel.

Carbon steels are classified according to the percentage of carbon they contain. They are referred to as low, medium, high, and very-high-carbon steels.

Low-carbon Steels

Steels with a carbon range of 0.05 to 0.30 percent are called low-carbon steels. Steels in this class are tough, ductile, and easily machined, formed, and welded. Most of them do not respond to any heat treating process except case hardening. *

Medium-carbon Steels

These steels have a carbon range from 0.30 to 0.45 percent. They are strong and hard but cannot be worked or welded as easily as low-carbon steels. Because of their higher carbon content, they can be heat treated. Successful welding of these steels often requires special electrodes, but even then greater care must be taken to prevent formation of cracks around the weld area. [1]

High and Very-high-carbon Steels

Steels with a carbon range of 0.45 to 0.75 percent are classified as high-carbon and those with 0.75 to 1.7 percent carbon as very-high-carbon steels. Both of these steels respond well to heat treatment. As a rule, steels up to 0.65 percent carbon can be welded with special electrodes, although preheating and stress relieving techniques must often be used after the welding is completed. [2] Usually it is not practical to weld steels in the very-high-carbon range.

Carbon is the principal element controlling the structure and properties that might be expected from any carbon steel. The influence that carbon has in strengthening and hardening steel is dependent upon

Materials 73

the amount of carbon present and upon its microstructure. Slowly cooled carbon steels have a relatively soft iron pearlitic* microstructure; whereas rapidly quenched carbon steels have a strong, hard, brittle, martensitic microstructure. *

In carbon steel, at normal room temperature, the atoms are arranged in a body-centered lattice* . This is known as alpha iron. Each grain of the structure is made up of layers of pure iron (ferrite) and a combination of iron and carbon. The compound of iron and carbon, or iron carbide* , is called cementite* . The cementite is very hard and has practically no ductility.

In a steel with 0. 8 percent carbon, the grains are pearlitic, meaning that all the carbon is combined with iron to form iron carbide. This is known as a eutectoid* mixture of carbon and iron. See Figure 2.1.

If there is less than 0. 8 percent carbon, the mixture of pearlite and ferrite is referred to as hypoeutectoid. An examination of such a mixture would show grains of pure iron and grains of pearlite as shown in Figure 2.2.

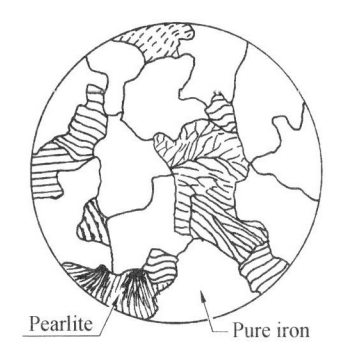

Pearlite ⎯   ⎯ Pure iron

Figure 2.1 Pearlite grains   Figure 2.2 Hypoeutectoid*

When the metal contains more than 0. 8 percent carbon, the mixture consists of pearlite and iron carbide and is called hypereutectoid. Notice in Figure 2. 3 how the grains of pearlite are surrounded by iron carbide. In general, the greatest percentage of steel

74　*English in Materials Science and Engineering*

used is of the hypoeutectoid type, that which has less than 0.8 percent carbon.

◆ Alloy Steel

An alloy steel is a steel to which one or more of such elements as nickel, chromium*, manganese, molybdenum*, titanium*, cobalt*, tungsten*, or vanadium* have been added. The addition of these elements gives steel greater

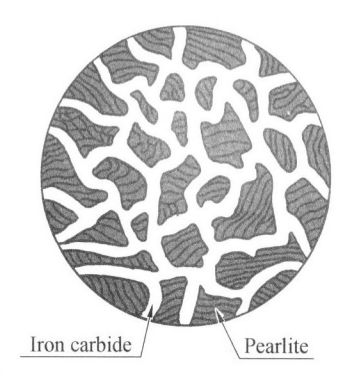

Iron carbide　Pearlite

Figure 2.3 Hypereutectoid*

toughness, strength, resistance to wear, and resistance to corrosion. Alloy steels are called by the predominating element which has been added. Most of them can be welded, provided special electrodes are used.

The common elements added to steel and their effects are explained as the following.

Manganese

The addition of manganese to steel produces a fine grain structure which has greater toughness and ductility. Manganese always presents in a steel to some extent because it is used as a deoxidiser.

Silicon

Always present to some extent, because it is used with manganese as a deoxidiser.*

Chromium

When quantities of chromium are added to steel the resulting product is a metal having extreme hardness and resistance to wear without making it brittle.[3] Chromium also tends to refine the grain structure of steel, thereby increasing its toughness. It is used either alone in carbon steel or in combination with other elements such as nickel, vanadium, molybdenum, or tungsten.

Nickel

The addition of nickel increases the ductility of steel while allowing it to maintain its strength. When large quantities of nickel are added (25 to 35 percent), the steels not only become tough but also develop high resistance to corrosion and shock.

Tungsten

Tungsten is used mostly in steels designed for metal cutting tools. Tungsten steels are tough, hard, and very resistant to wear.

Molybdenum

Molybdenum produces the greatest hardening effect of any element except carbon and at the same time it reduces the enlargement of the grain structure. The result is a strong, tough steel. Although molybdenum is used alone in some alloys, often it is supplemented by other elements, particularly nickel or chromium or both.

Vanadium

Vanadium is a strong carbide forming element. Addition of this element to steel promotes fine grain structure when the steel is heated above its critical range for heat treatment. It also imparts toughness and strength to the metal. It can cause reheat cracking.

Titanium

Titanium is a strong carbide forming element. It is not used on its own, but added as a carbide stabiliser to some austenitic stainless steels.

Key words:
case hardening [表面(渗碳)硬化]
pearlitic microstructure [珠光体组织]
martensitic microstructure [马氏体组织]
body-centered lattice [体心晶格]

quench [淬火]	ferrite [铁素体]
carbide [碳化物]	cementite [渗碳体]
eutectoid [共析的,共析]	hypoeutectoid [亚共析]
hypereutectoid [过共析]	nickel [镍]
chromium [铬]	manganese [锰]
molybdenum [钼]	titanium [钛]
cobalt [钴]	tungsten [钨]
vanadium [钒]	deoxidiser [脱氧剂]

76　*English in Materials Science and Engineering*

Notes:

[1] 通常需要采用特殊焊条才能成功地焊接这类钢材,即使这样,也要非常小心,避免在焊接区周围形成裂纹。

[2] 通常来说,碳的质量分数在 0.65% 以下的钢都可以采用特殊的焊条进行焊接,尽管通常需要采用预热以及焊后消除应力处理。

[3] 钢中加入大量的铬以后,硬度变得非常高,非常耐磨而又不脆。

Questions:

1) It is very difficult to weld steel with 1.0 percent carbon. (T/F)

2) All elements added to steel make it hard. (T/F)

3) Vanadium and titanium are all strong carbide forming elements. (T/F)

2.1.3 Cast Irons

As stated earlier, we define cast irons as the ferrous alloys with greater than 2% (w) carbon. They also generally contain up to 3% (w) silicon for control of carbide formation kinetics. Cast irons have relatively low melting temperatures and liquid phase viscosities*, do not form undesirable surface films when poured, and undergo moderate shrinkage* during solidification and cooling.[1] The cast irons must balance good formability of complex shapes against inferior mechanical properties compared to wrought alloys.

A cast iron is formed into a final shape by pouring molten metal into a mold. The shape of the mold is retained by the solidified metal. Inferior mechanical properties result from a less uniform microstructure, including some porosity*. Wrought alloys are initially cast but are rolled or forged into final, relatively simple shapes (in fact, "wrought" simply means "worked").

There are four general types of cast irons. White iron has a characteristic white, crystalline fracture surface. Large amounts of Fe_3C are formed during casting, giving a hard, brittle material. Gray iron has a gray fracture surface with a finely faceted structure. A significant silicon content ($w_{Si} = 2\% \sim 3\%$) promotes graphite (C) precipitation rather than cementite (Fe_3C). The sharp, pointed graphite flakes contribute to characteristic brittleness in gray iron. By adding a small amount($w = 0.05\%$) of magnesium* to the molten metal of the gray iron composition, spheroidal graphite precipitates rather than flakes are produced.[2] This resulting ductile iron derives its name from the improved mechanical properties. Ductility is increased by a factor of 20, and strength is doubled. A more traditional form of cast iron with reasonable ductility is malleable* iron, which is first cast as white iron and then heat treated to produce nodular* graphite precipitates.[3]

Key words:
viscosity[粘性]   shrinkage[收缩]   porosity[多孔]
magnesium[镁]   malleable[可锻的]   nodular[球状的]

Notes:

[1] 铸铁具有比较低的熔点和液相粘性。浇注时不形成不需要的表面膜，并且在固化和冷却过程中收缩适度。

[2] 通过将少量的 Mg ($w = 0.05\%$)添加到灰铁成分的熔融金属中,就形成球状石墨沉淀而不是片状石墨。

[3]具有适当韧性的更传统形式的铸铁是可锻铸铁。它首先被铸成白口铁,然后热处理形成小球状石墨沉淀。

Questions:

1) The name "cast iron" derives from the fact that there is only iron in cast irons. (T/F)

2) How is malleable cast iron obtained?

3) What is the function of the element of magnesium when it is added into the cast iron?

2.2 Non-ferrous Alloys

Although ferrous alloys are used in the majority of metallic applications in current engineering designs, non-ferrous alloys play a large and indispensable role in our technology. As for ferrous alloys, the list of non-ferrous alloys is, of course, long and complex. We shall briefly list the major families of non-ferrous alloys and their key attributes. Aluminum alloys are best known for low density and corrosion resistance. Electrical conductivity, ease of fabrication, and appearance are also attractive features. Because of these, the world production of aluminum roughly doubled in one recent 10 year period. Ore reserves* for aluminum are large(representing 8% of the earth's crust*)and aluminum can be easily recycled.

Magnesium alloys have even lower density than aluminum and, as a result, appear in numerous structural applications such as aerospace designs. Aluminum is a fcc material and therefore has numerous(12) slip systems, leading to good ductility. By contrast, magnesium is hcp* with only three slip systems and characteristic brittleness.

Titanium* alloys have become widely used since World War II. Before that time, a practical method of separating titanium metal from reactive oxides and nitrides* was not available. Once formed, titanium's reactivity works to its advantage.[1] A thin, tenacious* oxide coating forms on its surface, giving excellent resistance to corrosion. This "passivation" will be discussed in detail later. Titanium alloys, like Al and Mg, are of lower density than iron. Although more dense than Al or Mg, titanium alloys have a distinct advantage of retaining strength at moderate service temperatures, leading to numerous aerospace design applications. Titanium shares the hcp structure with magnesium leading to characteristically low ductility. However, a high temperature bcc structure can be stabilized at room temperature by certain alloy additions such as vanadium*.

Copper alloys possess a number of superior properties. Their excellent electrical conductivity makes copper alloys the leading material for electrical wiring. Their excellent thermal conductivity leads to applications for radiators and heat exchangers. Superior corrosion resistance is exhibited in marine and other corrosive environments. The fcc structure contributes to their generally high ductility and formability. Their coloration is frequently used for architectural appearance. Widespread uses of copper alloy through history has led to a somewhat confusing collection of descriptive terms. The mechanical properties of these alloys rival the steels in their variability. High purity copper is an exceptionally soft material. The addition of 2 w beryllium followed by a heat treatment to produce CuBe precipitates is sufficient to push the tensile strength beyond 1 000 MPa.

Nickel alloys have much in common with copper alloys. We have already used the Cu-Ni system as the classic example of complete solid solubility. Monel* is the name given to commercial alloys with Ni-Cu ratios of roughly 2:1 by weight. These are good examples of solution hardening. Nickel is harder than copper, but Monel is harder than nickel. Nickel exhibits excellent corrosion resistance and high temperature strength. Zinc alloys are ideally suited for die castings due to their low melting point and lack of corrosive reaction with steel crucibles and dies. Automobile parts and hardware are typical structural applications. Zinc coatings on ferrous alloys are important means of corrosion protection. This method is termed as galvanization*.

Lead* alloys are durable and versatile materials. The lead pipes installed by the Romans at the public baths in Bath, England, nearly 2 000 years ago are still in use. Lead's high density and deformability combined with a low melting point adds to its versatility. Lead alloys find use in battery grids (alloyed with calcium* or antimony*), solders (alloyed with tin*), radiation shielding, and sound control structures. The toxicity of lead restricts design applications and the handling of its alloys.[2]

The refractory* metals include molybdenum*, niobium*, tantalum, and tungsten. They are, even more than the superalloys, especially resistant to high temperatures. However, their general reactivity with oxygen requires the high temperature service to be in a controlled atmosphere or with protective coatings.

The precious metals include gold, iridium*, osmium*, palladium*, platinum*, rhodium*, ruthenium*, and silver. Excellent corrosion resistance combined with various inherent properties justify the many costly applications of these metals and alloys. Gold

80   *English in Materials Science and Engineering*

circuitry in the electronics industry, various dental alloys, and platinum coatings for catalytic* converters are a few of the better-known examples.

Key words:

reserve[蕴藏]	crust[壳层]	hcp[密堆六方]
titanium[钛]	nitride [氮化物]	tenacious[坚韧的]
vanadium[钒]	monel[蒙耐合金]	galvanization[镀锌]
lead[铅]	calcium[钙]	antimony[锑]
tin[锡]	refractory[耐火的]	molybdenum[钼]
niobium[铌]	iridium[铱]	osmium[锇]
palladium[钯]	platinum[铂]	rhodium[铑]
ruthenium[钌]	catalytic[接触反应的]	

Notes:

[1] 钛一旦形成,它就显示出优越的反应活性。

[2] 铅合金广泛应用于电池栅电极、焊料、辐射屏蔽和隔音结构。然而铅的毒性限制了它的应用及其合金的加工。

Questions:

1) There are a lot of alloys in which there is no iron. (T/F)

2) Tungsten can bear the temperature of 2 000℃ in air. (T/F)

3) List the applications that the copper alloy may have.

2.3 Advanced Structural Ceramics

Advanced structural ceramics are ceramic materials that demonstrate enhanced mechanical properties under demanding conditions. Because they serve as structural members, often being subjected to mechanical loading, they are given the name structural ceramics.[1] Ordinarily, for structural applications ceramics tend to be expensive replacements for other materials, such as metals, polymers, and composites. For especially erosive, corrosive, or high temperature environments, however, they may be the material of choice. This is because the strong chemical bonding in ceramics. Chemical bonds makes them exceptionally robust* in demanding situations. For example, some advanced ceramics display superior wear resistance, making them ideal for tribological (wear) applications such as mineral processing equipment. Others are chemically inert and therefore are used as bone replacements in the highly corrosive environment of the human body. High bond strengths also make ceramics thermochemically inert; this property shows promising areas of application in engines for automobiles, aerospace vehicles, and power generators.[2]

A number of technological barriers have to be surmounted* in order to make advanced structural ceramics an everyday reality. The most significant challenges are the inherent flaw sensitivity, or brittleness, of ceramics and the variability of their mechanical properties.

Key words:
robust[强健的]   surmount[战胜]

Notes:

[1] 因为它们是作为结构件使用的,经常承受机械载荷,所以被称为结构陶瓷。

[2]高的键强度也使得陶瓷具有热化学惰性,这一性能在发动机方面有广泛的应用前景, 如汽车、航天器和能源装置的发动机。

Questions:

1) Ceramics can be substituted by steel in some case according to the passage. (T/F)

2) The ceramics can work in those environments such as...

3) The ceramics can be used as bone replacement since the ceramics is _____ .

4) What is the main problem that prevents the extensive application of the ceramics?

Among the strategies for achieving ceramics with improved mechanical properties, especially toughness, some involve the engineering of microstructures that either resist the propagation of cracks or absorb energy during the crack propagation process. Both

82 *English in Materials Science and Engineering*

goals can be achieved simultaneously in microstructures with fibrous or interlocked grains. In ceramics produced with such microstructures, cracks are deflected* from a straight path, leading to a dramatic increase in crack length; at the same time particles behind the advancing crack tip bridge the crack, tending to hold it closed. Crack deflection and crack bridging also occur in whisker reinforced and fibre reinforced ceramic composites. The result is increased fracture surface area and much greater energy absorption.

Another mechanism that can lead to increased fracture toughness in ceramics is microcracking, which occurs in single phase polycrystalline ceramics whose grains are anisotropic (that is, whose mechanical properties vary with direction) or in intentionally biphasic polycrystalline microstructures.[1] In these materials tiny microcracks open up to either side of the main crack path ahead of the advancing crack tip. This phenomenon has two effects. First, the energy that goes into the opening of the subsidiary* cracks increases the energy needed for propagation of the main crack. Second, as the main crack propagates, microcracks opening up in the wake or process zone adjacent to the main crack but behind the crack front result in an increase in volume, which tends to close the main crack. The resistance to propagation thus increases the farther the crack propagates.

Key words:
deflect[使偏斜]   subsidiary[二次的]
Note:
[1] 提高陶瓷断裂韧性的另一种机制是微裂纹,它存在于各向异性的单相多晶体中,或者双相多晶体组织中。

Questions:

1) There are two ways to improve the toughness of the ceramic material, what are they?

2) What are the functions of the particles and whiskers?

3) If a lot of cracks are generated, the toughness is improved.

(T/F)

4) How will be the property if many microcracks are generated?

The most promising toughening mechanism for ceramic materials involves a phase transformation; the method is referred to as transformation toughening. Although other materials such as alumina can be transformation toughened, zirconia (zirconium dioxide, ZrO_2) is the prototype* material for this process. Pure zirconia, upon cooling below 1 150℃, undergoes a dramatic three percent volume expansion as it transforms from a tetragonal form to a monoclinic* form.[1] This expansion can be used to advantage by dispersing extremely fine tetragonal particles in a matrix of cubic zirconia or alumina. The small size of the particles (less than 1 micrometer) and their intimate contact with the matrix induce the tetragonal structure to remain stable at room temperature. Ahead of an advancing crack, however, a stress field triggers the transformation of the embedded tetragonal particles to the monoclinic form. Behind the advancing crack, a process zone forms in which all the tetragonal particles have transformed to the monoclinic form. The cumulative increase in volume exerts* a closing force on the advancing crack, as well as a corresponding resistance to crack propagation that increases with crack length.[2] Ceramics such as transformation toughened zirconia (TTZ) are often referred to as ceramic steel because the strain, or change in dimension, in response to stress behaviour resembles that of steel instead of a brittle ceramic. Also, the underlying phase transformation is called martensitic, after a similar transformation in rapidly quenched steel to a phase known as martensite.

Key words:
prototype[原型]　　　　monoclinic[单斜]　　　　exert[发挥]
Notes:
　[1] 当冷却到1 150℃以下时,纯氧化锆从四角晶系转变成单斜晶系的同时,还伴随着3%的体积膨胀。
　[2] 体积的逐渐增加会对扩展裂纹的尖端施加一个闭合力,以及随着裂

84　*English in Materials Science and Engineering*

纹长度而增加的裂纹传播阻力。

Questions:

1) The ceramic material can be toughened by phase transformation. (T/F)

2) Why the transformation toughened zirconia (TTZ) is often referred to ceramic steel?

3) The transformation in ceramics is triggered by _____ at room temperature.

Although toughened ceramics are far less tough than metals, they represent a vast improvement over conventional ceramics and glass. Fracture toughness is defined as the stress intensity factor at a critical point where crack propagation becomes rapid. It is given the symbol Kic and is measured in units of megapascals times the square root of the distance measured in metres (with glass, an extremely brittle material, having a Kic value of 1, all other materials can be assigned values relative to that of glass). Metals thus have relative Kic in the 30 ~ 45 range (aluminum alloys) or the 40 ~ 65 range (steels). In comparison, conventional ceramics have relative fracture toughness in the 3 ~ 4 range and are there fore brittle like glass. Ceramics with fibrous or interlocked microstructures and particle reinforced composites fall in the 4 ~ 6 range. Whisker reinforced and fibre reinforced composites have toughnesses in the 8 ~ 10 and 10 ~ 25 range, respectively. Transformation toughened ceramics fall in the 6 ~ 15 range. At such toughness large TTZ ball bearings can be repeatedly bounced on concrete floors without noticeable surface damage.

Despite their superior properties, toughened ceramics have not achieved wide spread use. One reason for this is that they are costly to produce. Therefore, they will not displace their metallic counterparts[*] unless they display such cost saving performance features as increased operating temperature or dramatically increased lifetime. Toughened ceramics also can lose their properties at elevated temperatures. As temperature rises, the driving force for the phase transformation in

TTZ decreases and then disappears altogether. As a result, the material loses its toughness. Whiskers and fibres in ceramic matrix composites are often susceptible* to high temperature oxidation.[1] This virtually eliminates them as toughening agents, so that the ceramic matrix reverts* to brittle behaviour. One of the challenges facing ceramic engineers is the engineering of tough ceramic microstructures that are stable at elevated temperatures.

Key words:
counterpart[副本]   susceptible[敏感的]   revert[恢复]
Note:
[1] 陶瓷基复合材料中的晶须和纤维通常对高温氧化敏感。

Questions:

1) The toughened ceramics are tougher than steels. (T/F)

2) The stress intensity factor can't be used to measure the toughness of the ceramics. (T/F)

3) The toughened ceramics are not expensive. (T/F)

4) The whisker can not only increase the toughness of the ceramics, but also increase its heat resistance behavior. (T/F)

2.4 Functional Ceramics

Capacitors are devices that store electric energy in the form of an electric field generated in the space between two separated, oppositely charged electrodes. Their capacity to store energy makes them essential components in many electric circuits, and that capacity can be greatly increased by inserting a solid dielectric material into the space separating the electrodes. Dielectrics are materials that are poor conductors of electricity. The non-conducting properties of ceramics are well known, and some ceramics are made into extremely effective dielectrics. Indeed, more than 90 percent of all capacitors are produced with ceramic materials serving as the dielectric.

Piezoelectrics are materials that generate a voltage when they are subjected to mechanical pressure; conversely, when subjected to an electromagnetic field, they exhibit a change in dimension.[1] Many piezoelectric devices are made of the same ceramic materials as capacitor dielectrics.

It can be explained that low electric conductivity is a factor of the chemical bonds that form a material. In dielectrics, unlike in conductive materials such as metals, the strong ionic and covalent bonds holding the atoms together do not leave electrons free to travel through the material under the influence of an electric field. Instead, the material becomes electrically polarized, its internal positive and negative charges separating somewhat and aligning parallel to the axis of the electric field.[2] When employed in a capacitor, this polarization acts to reduce the strength of the electric field maintained between the electrodes, which in turn raises the amount of charge that can be stored.

Notes:

[1] 压电材料是当受到机械压力作用时会产生电压,反之当受到电磁场作用时就会变形的材料。

[2] 而是材料受到电极化,其内部的正负电荷分离且与电场方向平行排列。

Questions:

1) The ceramic is dielectric material by using which the capacity can be greatly increased. (T/F)

2) In order to have a good dielectric property, the ceramics should be conductor. (T/F)

3) An electric field can make the electrons in the ceramics move. (T/F)

4) What kind of bond is it between the moleculars of ceramics?

Most ceramic capacitor dielectrics are made of barium titanate* (BaTiO$_3$) and related compounds. In the case of BaTiO$_3$, at high temperatures (above approximately 120℃), the crystal structure consists of a tetravalent* titanium ion (Ti^{4+}) sitting at the centre of a cube with the oxygen ions (O^{2-}) on the faces and the divalent* barium ions (Ba^{2+}) at the corners.[1] Below 120℃, however, a transition occurs. the Ba^{2+} and O^{2-} ions shift from their cubic positions, and the Ti^{4+} ion shifts away from the cube centre. A permanent dipole* results, and the symmetry of the atomic structure is no longer cubic (all axes identical) but rather tetragonal (the vertical axis different from the two horizontal axes). There is a permanent concentration of positive and negative charges toward opposite poles of the vertical axis. This spontaneous polarization is known as ferroelectricity* ; the temperature below which the polarity is exhibited is called the Curie* point. Ferroelectricity is the key to the utility of $BaTiO_3$ as a dielectric material.

Within local regions of a crystal or grain that is made up of these polarized structures, all the dipoles line up in what is referred to as a domain, but, with the crystalline material consisting of a multitude of randomly oriented domains, there is overall cancellation of the polarization. However, with the application of an electric field, as in a capacitor, the boundaries between adjacent domains can move, so that domains aligned with the field grow at the expense of out of alignment domains, thus producing large net polarizations. The susceptibility of these materials to electric polarization is directly related to their capacitance, or capacity to store electric charge.[2] The capacitance of a specific dielectric material is given a measure known as the dielectric constant, which is essentially the ratio between the capacitance of that material and the capacitance of a vacuum. In the case of the perovskite ceramics, dielectric constants can be enormous—in the range of 1 000 ~ 5 000 for pure $BaTiO_3$ and up to 50 000 if the Ti^{4+} ion is replaced by zirconium (Zr^{4+}).

Key words:
titanate[钛酸钡]   tetravalent[四价的]   divalent[二价的]
dipole[偶极子]   ferroelectricity[铁电性]   Curie[居里]
Notes:
[1] 对于钛酸钡,高温时的晶体结构由位于立方体中心的正四价钛离

88 *English in Materials Science and Engineering*

子,位于面上的负二价的氧离子和位于顶角的正二价的钡离子组成。

[2] 这些材料的电极化系数直接与材料的电容或者说贮存电荷的能力相关。

Questions:

1) Why the barium titanate* is most frequently used for making capacitors?

2) The barium titanate is a polarized material. (T/F)

3) Different ceramics have different dielectric constant. (T/F)

Chemical substitutions in the $BaTiO_3$ structure can alter a number of ferro electric properties. For example, $BaTiO_3$ exhibits a large peak in dielectric constant near the Curie point—a property that is undesirable for stable capacitor applications. This problem may be addressed by the substitution of lead (Pb^{2+}) for Ba^{2+}, which increases the Curie point; by the substitution of strontium (Sr^{2+}), which lowers the Curie point; or by substituting Ba^{2+} with calcium (Ca^{2+}), which broadens the temperature range at which the peak occurs.

Barium titanate can be produced by mixing and firing barium carbonate and titanium dioxide, but liquid-mix techniques are increasingly used in order to achieve better mixing, precise control of the barium titanium ratio, high purity, and submicrometre particle size.[1] Processing of the resulting powder varies according to whether the capacitor is to be of the disk or multilayer type. Disks are dry pressed or punched from tape and then fired at temperatures between 1 250 and 1 350℃. Silver-paste screen printed electrodes are bonded to the surfaces at 750℃. Leads are soldered to the electrodes, and the disks are epoxy coated or wax impregnated for encapsulation.

The capacitance of ceramic disk capacitors can be increased by using thinner capacitors; unfortunately, fragility* results. Multilayer capacitors (MLCs) overcome this problem by interleaving* dielectric and electrode layers. The electrode layers are usually palladium or a palladium-silver alloy. These metals have a melting point that is higher than the sintering temperature of the ceramic, allowing the two materials to be cofired. By connecting alternate layers in parallel, large capacitances can be realized with the MLC. The dielectric layers are processed by tape casting or doctor blading and then drying. Layer thickness as small as 5 micrometres have been achieved. Finished "builds" of dielectric and electrode layers are then diced into cubes and cofired. MLCs have the advantages of small size, low cost, and good performance at high frequencies, and they are suitable for surface mounting on circuit boards. They are increasingly used in place of disk capacitors in most electronic circuitry. Where monolithic* units are still employed, tubular capacitors are often used in place of disks, because the axial wire lead configuration of tubular capacitors is preferred over the radial configuration of disk capacitors for automatic circuit board insertion machines. [2]

Key words:
fragility[脆弱]   interleave[插入]   monolithic[完整的]
Notes:
[1] 钛酸钡可以利用混合和烧结碳酸钡和氧化钛的方法制得,但是越来越多地利用液体混合技术可以使混合得更充分,而且可以精确控制碳酸钡的比例,保证碳酸钡的纯度和粒子的亚微米尺寸。
[2] 在使用单块集成电路的地方,管状电容器通常代替片状电容器,这是由于对于自动控制插入器件而言,管状电容器的轴向引线结构比片状电容器的径向引线结构优越。

Questions:

1) How do you alter the Curie point of the ceramic material?

2) How many types of capacitors are there and what are they?

3) What kind of capacitor is most frequently used on circuit boards?

As is noted above, barium titanate based MLCs usually require firing temperatures in excess of 1 250℃. To facilitate cofiring with electrode alloys of lower melting temperatures, the sintering temperature of the ceramic can be reduced to the neighbourhood of 1 100℃ by adding low melting glasses or fluxing* agents. [1] In order to reduce the costs associated with precious metal electrodes such as palladium and silver, ceramic compositions have been developed that can be cofired with less expensive nickel or copper at lower temperatures.

Two other strategies to produce ceramic materials with high dielectric constants involve surface barrier layers or grain boundary barrier layers; these are referred to as barrier layer (BL) capacitors. In each case conductive films or grain cores are formed by donor* doping* or reduction firing of the ceramic. The surface or grain boundaries are then oxidized to produce thin resistive layers. In surface BL capacitors oxidation is accomplished by adding oxidizing agents such as manganese oxide or copper oxide to the silver electrode paste prior to firing. In grain boundary BL capacitors slow cooling in air or oxygen allows oxygen to diffuse into the grain boundaries and reoxidize thin layers adjacent to the boundaries. Oxidizing agents such as bismuth and copper oxides can also be incorporated into the electrode paste to diffuse along grain boundaries during firing.[2] In either case very high apparent dielectric constants, 50 000 to 100 000, can be obtained. Care must be taken in using BL capacitors, however, as they have very low dielectric breakdown strengths. Dielectric breakdown involves sudden failure of and catastrophic* discharge through the dielectric material, with usually irreversible* damage to the ceramic. In BL capacitors the barriers are so thin that local fields can be quite intense.

Key words:
flux［熔剂］   donor［施主］   dope［掺杂］
catastrophic［灾难的］   irreversible［不可逆转的］

 Notes:

［1］为了与低熔点电极合金一起烧结,加入低熔点的玻璃或溶剂可以使陶瓷烧结温度降低到 1 100℃左右。

［2］氧化剂如氧化铋和氧化铜也可被溶入到电极上从而可在烧结时沿晶界扩散。

Questions:

1) Why the sintering temperature of the ceramics needs to be lowered?

2) In order to have a high dielectric constants, the ceramic materials should be treated so that to have a surface barrier layer. (T/F)

3) The BL capacitors are very easy to be destroyed. (T/F)

An extremely important application of thin film ferroelectrics is in random access memories (RAMs) for computers. Because of their larger dielectric constants, titanate based ferroelectrics can achieve higher bit densities than silica based semiconductors when used as thin film capacitors in dynamic random access memories (DRAMs). They also can be used as ferroelectric random access memories (FERAMs), where the opposing directions of polarization can represent the two states of binary logic. [1] Unlike conventional semiconductor RAM, the information stored in FERAMs is non-volatile; i. e., it is retained when the power is turned off.

Many of the ferroelectric perovskite materials described above are also piezoelectric; that is, they generate a voltage when stressed or, conversely, develop a strain when under an applied electromagnetic field. These effects result from relative displacements of the ions, rotations of the dipoles, and redistributions of electrons within the unit cell. Only certain crystal structures are piezoelectric. They are those which, like $BaTiO_3$, lack what is known as an inversion center, or center of symmetry—that is, a center point from which the structure is virtually identical in any two opposite directions. In the case of $BaTiO_3$, the center of symmetry is lost owing to the transition from a cubic to a tetragonal structure, which shifts the Ti^{4+} ion away from the central position that it occupies in the cube. [2] Quartz is a naturally occurring crystal that lacks a center of symmetry and whose piezoelectric properties are well-known. Among the polycrystalline

92   *English in Materials Science and Engineering*

ceramics that display piezoelectricity, the most important are PZT(lead zirconate titanate, Pb [Zr, Ti] O_2) and PMN (lead magnesium niobate, Pb [$Mg_{1/3} Nb_{2/3}$] O_3). These materials are processed in a similar manner to capacitor dielectrics except that they are subjected to poling, a technique of cooling the fired ceramic piece through the Curie point under the influence of an applied electric field in order to align the magnetic dipoles along a desired axis.

Notes:

[1] 它们也可用作铁电随机存贮器,其中两个不同的极化方向可代表二进制逻辑的两个状态。

[2] 以碳酸钡为例,由于从立方晶体转变为正方晶体的过程中,正四价的钛偏离立方体的中心,所以对称中心就不再存在。

Questions:

1) Some ceramics are used in the random access memory circuits. (T/F)

2) The ferroelectric materials can change its shape when a voltage is applied on. (T/F)

3) Some of the ceramics are piezoelectric materials. (T/F)

4) How do you let the dipoles line up along a desired axis?

There are numerous uses of piezoelectrics. For instance, plates cut from a single crystal can exhibit a specific natural resonance* frequency (i. e., the frequency of an electromagnetic wave that causes it to vibrate mechanically at the same frequency); these can be used as a frequency standard in highly stable crystal controlled clocks and in fixed frequency communications devices. Other resonant applications include selective wave filters and transducers for sound generation, as in sonar*. Broadband resonant devices (e. g., for ultrasonic cleaning and drilling) and non-resonant devices (e. g., accelerometers, pressure gauges, microphone pickups) are dominated by ceramic piezoelectrics. Precision positioners made from piezoelectric ceramics are utilized in the manufacture of integrated circuits and also in scanning tunneling* microscopes, which obtain atomic scale resolution images of materials surfaces.[1]

Domestic uses of piezoelectrics include buzzers* and manually operated gas igniters*.

Key words:
resonance[共振]   sonar[声纳]   tunnel[隧道]
buzzer[蜂鸣器]   igniter[点火器]

Note:

[1] 由压电陶瓷制成的精密定位器被用来制造集成电路以及扫描隧道显微镜,这种显微镜可以获得材料表面原子尺度的图像。

Questions:

1) There are piezoelectric materials in the electric clock. (T/F)

2) Those piezoelectric materials used in the clock are single crystal. (T/F)

3) There are a lot of situations where the piezoelectric material is useful. (T/F)

2.5 Polymer

Polymers are chemical compounds that consist of long, chainlike molecules made up of multiple repeating units. The term polymer was coined in 1832 by the Swedish chemist Jins Jacob Berzelius from the Greek polys, or "many" and meros, or "parts." Polymers are also referred to as macromolecules, or "giant molecules"—a term introduced by the German chemist Hermann Staudinger in 1922. Some giant molecules occur naturally. Proteins, for example, are natural polymers of amino acids that make up much of the structural material of animals; and the polymers deoxyribonucleic acid (DNA) and ribonucleic acid (RNA) are linear strands of nucleotides* that define the genetic* makeup of living organisms.[1] Other examples of natural polymers are silk, wool, natural rubber, cellulose, and shellac*. These materials have been known and exploited since ancient times. Indeed, people in what is now Switzerland cultivated* flax*, a source

94   *English in Materials Science and Engineering*

of polymeric cellulose fibres, during the Neolithic* Period, or New Stone Age, some 10 000 years ago, while other ancients collected proteinaceous wool fibres from sheep and silk fibres from silkworms. About five millennia ago, tanners* produced leather through the cross linking of proteins by gallic acid forming the basis of the oldest industry in continuous production. Even embalming*, the art for which ancient Egypt is famous, is based on the condensation and cross linking of proteins with form aldehyde*.

Key words:
nucleotide[核苷酸]   genetic[遗传的]   shellac[虫漆]
cultivate[种植]   flax[亚麻]   neolithic[新石器时代]
tanner[制革工]   embalm[防腐]   formaldehyde[甲醛]

Note:

[1] 例如,蛋白质是氨基酸的天然聚合物,是构成大多数动物的结构材料。脱氧核糖核酸和核糖核酸聚合物是核苷酸的线性连接结构,该核苷酸定义着生物机体的遗传结构。

Questions:

1) The molecules of the polymers is very long. (T/F)

2) What are the terms that can be used to substitute the name "polymer"?

3) Are there any polymer materials natural? And what are they?

Early developments in polymer technology, taking place in the 19th century, involved the conversion of natural polymers to more useful products—for example, the conversion of cellulose, obtained from cotton or wood, into celluloid*, one of the first plastics. Before the 1930s only a small number of synthetically produced polymers were available commercially, but after that period and especially after World War Ⅱ, synthetic compounds came to dominance.[1] Derived principally from the refining of petroleum and natural gas, synthetic polymers are made into the plastics, rubbers, man-made fibres, adhesives*, and surface coatings that have become so ubiquitous in modern life.

Key words:

celluloid[赛璐珞]   adhesive[粘接剂]

Note:

[1] 1930 年以前只有很少量商业现成的合成聚合物,但自那以后,尤其是在第二次世界大战以后,合成复合材料开始占据主导地位。

Questions:

1) The plastics are also a kind of polymers.(T/F)

2) When were the polymer techniques invented?

3) What are the most polymer materials made from?

As an important materials, the polymers are available in a wide variety of commercial forms: fibers, thin films and sheets, foams and in bulk *. A common synonym * for polymers is "plastics," a name derived from the deformability associated with the fabrication of most polymeric products. To some critics, "plastic" is a synonym for modern culture. Accurate or not, it represents the impact that this complex family of engineering materials has had on our society.

Polymers are distinguished from our previous types of materials by chemistry. Metals, ceramics, and glasses are inorganic * materials. The polymers discussed here are organic *. The student should not be concerned about a lack of background in organic chemistry. This passage is intended to provide any of the fundamentals of organic chemistry needed to appreciate the unique nature of polymeric materials. We begin our discussion of polymers by investigating polymerization, the process by which long chain or network molecules are made from relatively small organic molecules.[1] The structural features of the resulting polymers are rather unique compared to the inorganic materials. In general, the melting point and rigidity of polymers increase with the extent of polymerization and with the complexity of the molecular structure.

We shall find that polymers fall into one of two main categories. Thermoplastic * polymers are materials that become less rigid upon heating, and thermosetting* polymers become more rigid upon heating. For both categories, it is important to appreciate the roles played by additives*, which provide important features such as color and resistance to combustion. As with ceramics and glasses, we shall discuss important mechanical and optical properties of polymers. Mechanically, polymers exhibit behavior associated with their long chain molecular structure. Examples include viscoelastic and elastomeric deformation. Optical properties such as transparency and color, so important in ceramic technology, are also significant in the selection of polymers.

Key words:
bulk[块]   synonym[同义词]   inorganic[无机的]
organic[有机的]   thermoplastic[热塑]   thermoset[热固]
additive[添加剂]

Note:
[1] 我们通过研究聚合反应来对聚合物展开讨论,聚合反应指的是相对较小的有机分子结成长链状或网状大分子的过程。

Questions:

1) How can we distinguish the polymer from other kind of material?

2) What happens during the polymerization?

3) The behavior of the polymer is associated with _____ .

2.5.1 Polymerization*

The term polymer simply means "many mers" where mer is the building block of the long chain or network molecule. There are two distinct ways in which a poly merization reaction can take place. Chain growth(also known as addition polymerization)involves a rapid "chain reaction" of chemically activated monomers. Step growth(also known as condensation polymerization)involves individual chemical reactions between pairs of reactive monomers and is a much slower process. In either case, the critical feature of a monomer, which permits it to join with similar molecules and form a polymer, is the presence of reactive sites, that is double bonds(chain growth) or reactive functional groups (step growth).[1] Each covalent bond is a pair of electrons shared between adjacent atoms. The double bond is two such pairs. The chain growth reaction converts the double bond in the monomer to a single bond in the mer. The remaining two electrons become parts of the single bonds joining adjacent mers.

Key words:
polymerization[聚合]
Note:
[1] 无论在哪种情况下,可以与相似的分子相连接形成聚合物的单节分子的主要特征就是存在活性区域,即双键(链状生长),或活性功能团(台阶状生长)。

Questions:

1) How are the monomers polymerizated?

2) Chain reaction is faster than individual chemical reactions between pairs of reactive monomers. (T/F)

2.5.2 Thermal Plastic Polymers

Thermoplastic polymers become soft and deformable upon heating. This is characteristic of linear polymeric molecules. The high temperature plasticity is due to the ability of the molecules to slide past one another. This is another example of a thermally activated, or Arrhenius process. In this sense, thermoplastic materials are similar to metals that gain ductility at high temperatures. The key distinction between thermoplastics and metals is what we mean by "high" temperatures. The secondary bonding, which must be overcome to deform thermoplastics, may allow substantial deformation around 100℃, whereas metallic bonding generally restricts creep deformation to temperature closer to 1 000℃ in typical alloys. It should be noted that, as with metals, the ductility of thermoplastic polymers is lost upon cooling.

98   *English in Materials Science and Engineering*

Question:

What kind of polymer has the property of thermoplasticity?

2.5.3 Thermal Setting Polymers

Thermosetting polymers are the opposite of the thermoplastics. They become hard and rigid upon heating. Unlike thermoplastic polymers, this phenomenon is not lost upon cooling. This is characteristic of network molecular structures formed by the step growth mechanism. The chemical reaction "steps" are enhanced by higher temperatures and are irreversible, that is, the polymerization remains upon cooling. In fabricating thermosetting products, they can be removed from the mold at the fabrication temperature (typically 200℃ to 300℃). By contrast, thermoplastics must be cooled in the mold to prevent distortion. It might also be noted that network copolymers can be formed similar to the block and graft copolymers. The network copolymer will result from polymerization of a combination of more than one species of polyfunctional monomers.

Question:

What is the difference between the thermoplastic and thermosetting polymers?

2.5.4 Additives

Copolymers and blends were discussed above as analogs of metallic alloys. There are several other alloylike additives that traditionally have been used in polymer technology to provide specific characteristics to the polymers. A plasticizer* is added to soften a polymer. This addition is essentially blending* with a low molecular weight(approximately 300 amu) polymer.

A filler*, on the other hand, is added to strengthen a polymer primarily by restricting chain mobility. it also provides dimensional stability and reduced cost. Relatively inert* materials are used. Examples include shortchanger cellulose (and organic filler) and asbestos* (and inorganic filler). Roughly one third of the typical automobile tire is a filler (i. e. , carbon black). Reinforcements such as glass fibers are also categorized as additives but produce such fundamentally different materials (e. g. , fiberglass) that they are properly discussed later on composites.

Stabilizers* are additives used to reduce polymer degradation*. They represent a complex set of materials because of the large variety of degradation mechanisms(oxidation, thermal, and ultraviolet*). As an example, polyisoprene can absorb up to 15% oxygen at room temperature with its elastic properties being destroyed by the first 1%. Natural rubber latex* contains complex phenol* groups that retard the room temperature oxidation reactions. However, these naturally occurring antioxidants are not effective at elevated temperatures. Therefore, additional stabilizers (e. g. , other phenols, amines*, sulphur compounds, etc.) are added to rubber intended for tire applications.

Flame retardant are added to reduce the inherent combustibility of certain polymers such as polyethylene. Combustion is simply the reaction of a hydrocarbon with oxygen accompanied by substantial heat evolution. Many polymeric hydrocarbons exhibit combustibility. Others, such as polyvinyl chloride (PVC), do not. The resistance of PVC to combustion appears to come from the evolution of the chlorine atoms from the polymeric chain. These halogens* hinder* the process of combustion by terminating free radical chain reactions. Additives that provide this function for halogen free polymers include chlorine*, bromine, and phosphorus containing reactants*.

Colorant* are additions to provide color to a polymer where appearance is a factor in materials selection. Two types of colorants are used, pigments* and dyes*. A pigment is an insoluble, colored material added in powered form. Typical examples are crystalline ceramics such as titanium oxide and aluminum silicate, although

100　*English in Materials Science and Engineering*

organic pigments are also available. Dyes are soluble, organic colorants that can provide transparent colors.

Key words:

plasticizer[增塑剂]	blending[混合]	filler[填充剂]
inert[惰性的]	asbestos[石棉]	stabilizer[稳定剂]
degradation[退化]	ultraviolet[紫外的]	latex[乳液]
phenol[石炭酸]	amine[胺类]	halogen[卤素]
hinder[妨碍]	chlorine[氯]	reactant[反应物]
colorant[着色剂]	pigment[色素]	dye[染料]

Questions:

1) Why the additives should be added into the polymers?

2) List types of the additives.

2.5.5 Viscoelastic Deformation

At relatively low temperature, polymers are rigid solids and deform elastically. At relatively high temperatures, they are liquidlike and deform viscously. The boundary between elastic and viscous behavior is again known as the glass transition temperature, T_g. However, the variation in polymer deformation with temperature is not demonstrated in the same way. For glasses, the variation in viscosity was plotted against temperature. For polymers, the modulus of elasticity is plotted instead of viscosity. There is a drastic and complicated drop in modulus with temperature for a typical, commercial thermoplastic with approximately 50% crystallinity. The magnitude of the drop is illustrated by the use of a logarithmic scale for modulus. At "low" temperatures (well below T_g), a rigid modulus occurs corresponding to mechanical behavior reminiscent of metals and ceramics. However, the substantial component of secondary bonding in the polymers causes the modulus for these materials to be substantially lower than the ones found for metals and ceramics, which were fully bonded by primary chemical bonds (metallic, ionic, and covalent*). In the glass transition temperature (T_g) range, the modulus drops precipitously and the mechanical behavior is leathery. The polymer can be extensively deformed and slowly returns to its original shape upon stress removal. Just above T_g, a rubbery plateau is observed. In this region, extensive deformation is possible with rapid spring back to the original shape when stress is removed. These last two regions(leathery and rubbery) extend our understanding of elastic deformation. Sometimes the elastic deformation meant a relatively small strain directly proportional to applied stress. For polymers, extensive, non-linear deformation can be fully recovered and is, by definition, elastic. This concept will be explored shortly when we discuss elastomers, those polymers with predominant rubbery region.

Key words:
modulus[模量]   viscoelastic[粘滞弹性的]
reminiscent[回忆的]   covalent[共价的]

Questions:

1) What is the glass transition temperature?

2) Talk something about the properties of the polymer as temperature changes.

2.5.6 Elastomers

Typical linear polymers exhibits a rubbery deformation region. For certain polymers known as elastomers, the rubbery plateau is pronounced* and establishes the normal room temperature behavior of these materials.(For these materials, the glass transition temperature is below room temperature.) This subgroup of thermoplastic polymers includes the natural and synthetic rubbers (such as polyisoprene). These materials provide a dramatic example of the uncoiling of a linear polymer. As a practical matter, the complete uncoiling of the molecule is not achieved, but huge elastic strains* do occur. The stress-strain curve for the elastic deformation of an elastomer shows dramatic contrast to the stress-strain curve for a common metal. In that case, the elastic modulus was constant throughout the elastic region (stress

102 *English in Materials Science and Engineering*

was directly proportional to strain). While the elastic modulus(slope of the stress-strain curve) increases with increasing strain. For low strains, the modulus is low corresponding to the small forces needed to overcome secondary bonding and to uncoil the molecules. For high strains, the modulus rises sharply, indicating the greater force needed to stretch* the primary bonds along the molecular "backbone".[1] In both regions, however, there is a significant component of secondary bonding involved in the deformation mechanism, and the moduli are much lower than those for common metals and ceramics. Tabulated values of moduli for elastomers are generally for the low strain region in which the materials are primarily used. Finally, it is important to emphasize that we are talking about elastic or temporary deformation. The uncoiled polymer molecules of an elastomer recoil to their original lengths upon removal of stress.

Key words:
pronounced[显著的]   strain[应变]   stretch[伸展]
Note:
[1] 在高应变区,弹性模量急剧增加,这意味着沿分子的主干方向拉伸需要更大的力。

Questions:

1) The stress-strain curve of the elastomer is just like that of the plain steel. (T/F)

2) The elastic modulus does not change during its deformation. (T/F)

2.5.7 Stress Relaxation

For metals and ceramics, we found creep* deformation to be an important phenomenon at high temperatures(greater than one half the absolute melting point). A similar phenomenon, termed stress relaxation, occurs in polymers. This is perhaps more significant to polymers. Because of their low melting points, stress relaxation can occur at room temperature. A familiar example is the rubber band, understress for a long period of time, which does not snap back to its original size upon stress removal.

Creep deformation involves increasing strain with time for metals and ceramics under constant stresses. By contrast, stress relaxation involves decreasing stress with time for polymers under constant strains. The mechanism of stress relaxation in viscous flow, is that, molecules gradually sliding pass each other over an extended period of time.[1] Stress relaxation is characterized by a relaxation time, defined as the time necessary for the stress to fall to 0.37 of the initial stress. In general, stress relaxation is an Arrhenius phenomenon, as was creep for metals and ceramics.

Key words:
creep[蠕变]
Note:
[1] 粘滞流体的应力松弛机理就是在长时间内分子相互间的慢慢滑动。

Questions:

1) What is the difference between creep and relaxation?
2) What is the mechanism of the relaxation?

2.6 Semiconductor

Following the discussion of intrinsic*, elemental semiconductors we note that the Fermi function indicates that the number of charge carriers increases exponentially with temperature. This effect so dominates the conductivity of semiconductors that conductivity also follows an exponential increase with temperature(an example of an Arrhenius equation). This increase is in sharp contrast to the behavior of metals.

We consider the effect of impurities in extrinsic, elemental semiconductors. Doping* a group Ⅳ A material(such as Si) with a group Ⅴ A impurity(such as P) produces an n-type semiconductor in which negative charge carriers(conduction electrons) dominate. The "extra" electron from the group Ⅴ A addition produces a donor level in the energy band structure of the semiconductor. As with intrinsic semiconductors, extrinsic semiconduction exhibits Arrhenius behavior. In n-type material, the temperature span between the regions of extrinsic and intrinsic behavior is called the exhaustion[*] range. A p-type semiconductor is produced by doping a group IV A material with a group III A impurity (such as Al). The group III A element has a "missing" electron producing an acceptor level in the band structure and leading to formation of positive charge carriers (electron holes). The region between extrinsic and intrinsic behavior for p-type semiconductors is called the saturation range. Hall effect measurements can distinguish between n-type and p-type conduction.

Compound semiconductors usually have an MX composition with an average of four valence electrons per atom. The III - V and II - VI compounds are the common examples. Amorphous semiconductors are the non-crystalline materials with semiconducting behavior. Elemental and compound materials are both found in this category. To appreciate the applications of semiconductors, we review a few of the simple devices that have been developed in the past few decades. The solid state rectifier[*] (or diode[*]) contains a single p-n junction. Current flows readily when this junction is forward biased[*] but is almost completely choked[*] off when reverse biased. The transistor is a device consisting of a pair of nearby pn junctions. The net result is a solid state amplifier. Replacing vacuum tubes with solid state elements such as these produced substantial miniaturization[*] of electrical circuits. Further miniaturization has resulted by the production of microcircuits consisting of precise patterns of n-type and p-type regions on a single crystal chip.

The major electrical properties needed to specify an intrinsic semiconductor are band gap, electron mobility, hole mobility, and conduction electron density (= electron hole density) at room temperature. For extrinsic semiconductors, one needs to specify either the donor level (for n-type material) or the acceptor level (for p-type material).

Key words:

intrinsic[本质的]   dope[掺杂]   exhaustion[耗尽]
rectifier[整流器]   diode[二极管]   bias[偏置]
choke[阻塞]   miniaturization[小型化]

Questions:

1) The size of transistor is larger than that of vacuum tube. (T/F)

2) The higher the temperature is, the higher the resistance of the semiconductor. (T/F)

3) The current in p-type semiconductor is in fact the motions of electrons in micro scale. (T/F)

2.7 Composites

One category of structural engineering materials is that of composites. These materials involve some combination of two or more components from the "fundamental" material types. A key philosophy* in selecting composite materials is that they provide the "best of both worlds," that is, attractive properties from each component.[1] A classic example is fiberglass. The strength of small diameter glass fibers is combined with the ductility of the polymeric* matrix. The combination of these two components provides a product superior to either component alone. Many composites, such as fiberglass, involve combinations that cross over the boundaries of different kinds of materials. Others, such as concrete, involve different component from within a single material type.[2] In general, we shall use a fairly narrow definition of composites. We shall consider only those materials that combine different components on the microscopic (rather than macroscopic) scale. We shall not include multiphase alloys and ceramics, which are the result of routine processing. Similarly, the microcircuits be discussed later are not included because each component retains its distinctive character in these material systems. In spite of these restrictions, we shall find this category to include a tremendously diverse collection of materials, from the common to some of the most sophisticated.

We shall consider three categories* of composite materials. Conveniently, these categories are demonstrated by three of our most common structural materials, fiberglass, wood, and concrete. Fiberglass(or glass fiber reinforced polymer) is an excellent example of a human made fiber reinforced* composite. The glass-polymer system is just one of many important examples. The fiber reinforcement is generally found in one of three primary configurations: aligned in a single direction, randomly chopped, or woven in a fabric that is laminated* with the matrix. Wood is a structural analog of fiberglass, that is, a natural fiber reinforced composite. The fibers of wood are elongated, biological cells. The matrix corresponds to lignin* and hemicellulose deposits. Concrete is our best example of an aggregate* composite, in which particles rather than fibers reinforce a matrix. Common concrete is rock and sand in a calcium aluminosilicate (cement*) matrix. While concrete has been a construction material for centuries, there are numerous composites developed in recent decades that use a similar particulate reinforcement concept.

The concept of property averaging is central to understanding the utility of composite materials. An important example is the elastic modulus of a composite. The modulus is a sensitive function of the geometry of the reinforcing component. Similarly important is the strength of the interface between the reinforcing component and the matrix. We shall concentrate on these mechanical properties of composites in regard for their wide use as structural materials. So called "advanced" composites have provided some unusually attractive features, such as high strength to weight ratios. Some care is required in citing these properties, as they can be highly directional in nature.

Key words:
philosophy[原理]   polymeric[聚合物的]   category[种类]
reinforce[增强]   laminated[成层的]   lignin[木质素]
aggregate[聚集态的]   cement[水泥]

Notes:

[1] 选择复合材料的关键是它提供了'两个世界中最好的',即来自于每一个组元的最优异的性能。

[3] 其他的材料,如水泥,含有属于同一材料类型中的不同组元。

Questions:

1) Three kinds of composite materials are considered in this passage, what are they?

2) Why is the composite material so popular?

2.7.1 Human-made Fiber Reinforced Composite

Let us begin by concentrating on fiberglass, or glass fiber reinforced polymer. This is a classic example of a modern composite system. A typical fracture surface of a composite shows fibers embedded* in the polymeric matrix, such fibers may have different composition since each is the result of substantial development that has led to optimal suitability for specific applications. For example, the most generally used glass fiber composition is E glass, in which E stands for "electrical type." The low sodium content of E glass is responsible for its especially low electrical conductivity and its attractiveness as a dielectric*. Its popularity in structural composites is related to the chemical durability of the borosilicate composition. We should note that optimal strength is achieved by the aligned, continuous fiber reinforcement. Caution is necessary, however, in citing this strength because it is maximal only in the direction parallel to the fiber axes.[1] In other words, the strength is highly anisotropic*.

The fiber reinforced composites include some of the most sophisticated materials developed by man for some of the most demanding engineering applications. Important examples include boron* reinforced aluminum, graphite epoxy*, and Al_2O_3 reinforced aluminum. Metal fibers are frequently small diameter wires. Especially high strength reinforcement come from "whiskers," which are small, single crystal fibers that can be grown with a nearly perfect crystalline structure. Unfortunately, whiskers cannot be grown as continuous

108 *English in Materials Science and Engineering*

filaments * in the manner of glass fibers or metal wires.

Key words:
embed [嵌入]   dielectric[介电的]   anisotropic[各向异性的]
boron[硼]   epoxy[环氧树脂]   filament [细丝]
Note:
[1] 在谈及该强度时必须注意的是该强度只有在平行于纤维方向上才是最大的。

Questions:

1) Since it is very good material, the composite has a uniformly distributed properties. (T/F)

2) What can the "whiskers" be used for?

2.7.2 Wood, Natural Fiber Reinforced Composite

Like so many accomplishments of human beings, those fiber reinforced composites imitate nature. Common wood is such a composite, which serves as an excellent structural material. In fact, the weight of wood used each year in the United States exceeds the combined total for steel and concrete. We find two categories, softwoods and hardwoods. These are relative terms, although softwoods generally have lower strengths. The fundamental difference between the categories is their seasonal nature. Softwoods are "evergreens" with needlelike leaves and exposed seeds. Hardwoods are deciduous(i.e., lose their leaves annually) with covered seeds(i.e., nuts).

The microstructure of wood illustrates its commonality with the human-made composites. The dominant feature of the microstructure is the large number of tubelike cells oriented vertically. These longitudinal cells are aligned with the vertical axis of the tree. There are some radial cells perpendicular to the longitudinal ones. As the name implies, the radial cells extend from the center of the tree trunk out radically toward the surface. The longitudinal cells carry sap and other fluids critical to the growth process. Early season cells are of larger diameter than later season cells. This growth pattern leads to the characteristic "ring structure," which indicates the tree's age. The radial cells store food for the growing tree. The cell walls are composed of cellulose. These tubular *cells serve the reinforcing role played by glass fibers in "fiberglass" composites.[1] The strength of the cells in the longitudinal direction is a function of fiber alignment in that direction. The cells are held together by a matrix of lignin and hemicellulose. Lignin is a phenol * propane * network polymer, and hemicellulose is polymeric cellulose with a relatively low degree of polymerization.

The complex chemistry and microstructure of wood are manifest * as a highly anisotropic macrostructure.[2] Related to this, the dimensions as well as the proper ties of wood vary significantly with atmospheric moisture levels. Care will be required in specifying the atmospheric conditions for which mechanical property data apply.

Key words:
tubular[管状的]   phenol[石炭酸]
propane[丙烷]   manifest[明白]

Notes:

[1]这些管状细胞提供了一种类似于玻璃纤维在纤维玻璃复合材料中所起的增强作用。

[2]木材这种复杂的化学和微观结构表明它在宏观上是高度各向异性。

Questions:

1) The property of the wood does not change when the environmental condition changes.(T/F)

2) Man-made composites do not imitate natural ones.(T/F)

2.7.3 Aggregate Composite

Fiberglass was a convenient and familiar example of fiber reinforced composites. Similarly, concrete is an excellent example of an aggregate composite. As with wood, this common construction material is used in staggering * quantities. The weight of concrete used

110 *English in Materials Science and Engineering*

annually exceeds that of all metals combined.

For concrete, the term "aggregate" refers to a combination of sand(fine aggregate) and gravel* (coarse aggregate). This component of concrete is a "natural" material in the same sense as wood. Ordinarily, these materials are chosen for their relatively high density and strength. A table of aggregate compositions would be complex and largely meaningless. In general, aggregate materials are geological* silicates* chosen from locally available deposits. As such, these materials are complex and relatively impure examples of the crystalline silicates. Igneous* rocks are common examples. "Igneous" means solidified from a molten state. For quickly cooled igneous rocks, some fraction of the resulting material may be non-crystalline, corresponding to the glassy silicates. The relative particle sizes of sand and gravel are measured(and controlled) by passing these materials through standard screens(or sieves*). The reason for a combination of fine and coarse aggregate in a given concrete mix is that the space is more efficiently filled by a range of particle sizes. The combination of fine and coarse aggregate accounts for 60 to 75 percent of the total volume of the final concrete.

The matrix that encloses the aggregate is cement, which, as the name implies, bonds the aggregate particles into a rigid solid.[1] Modern concrete uses portland cement, which is a calcium aluminosilicate. There are five common types of portland cement. They vary in the relative concentrations of four calcium containing minerals. The matrix is formed by the addition of water to the appropriate cement powder. The particle sizes for the cement powders are relatively small compared to the finest of the aggregates. Variation in cement particle size can strongly affect the rate at which the cement hydrates. It is this hydration reaction which hardens the cement and produces the chemical bonding of the matrix to the aggregate particles.[2] As one might expect from inspecting the complex compositions of portland cement, the chemistry of the hydration process is equally complex.

Materials 111

In polymer technology, we noted several "additives," which provided certain desirable features to the end product. In cement technology, there are a number of admixtures, which are additions providing certain features. Any component of concrete other than aggregate, cement, or water is, by definition, an admixture. One of the admixtures is an "air entrainer," which reminds us that air can be thought of as a fourth component of concrete. Virtually all structural concrete contains some entrapped air. The air entrainer admixture increases the concentration of entrapped air bubbles, usually for the purpose of workability(during forming) and increased resistance to freeze thaw* cycles.

While concrete is an important engineering material, a large number of other composite systems are based on particle reinforcement. Particulate composites refer specifically to systems with relatively large size dispersed particles(at least several micrometers in diameter), and the particles are in relatively high concentration(greater than 25 φ and frequently between 60 φ and 90 φ) of small diameter oxide particles. The oxide particles strengthen the metal by serving as obstacles to dislocation motion.

Key words:
staggering[惊人的]   gravel[碎石]
geological[地质学的]   silicate[硅酸盐]
igneous[火成的]   sieve[筛子]
thaw[融化]

 Notes:
[1] 包围颗粒的基体是水泥,顾名思义,它将颗粒粘结成刚性固体。
[2] 正是该水和反应使水泥硬化并产生基体与颗粒间的化学键。

Questions:

1) Why aggregates with different size were used in the concrete?
2) Why different cement needs different time for solidification?
3) Why it is necessary for the air to be added into the concrete?

112 *English in Materials Science and Engineering*

2.7.4 Property Averaging

It is obvious that the properties of composites must, in some way, represent an average of the properties of their individual components.[1] However, the precise nature of the "average" is a sensitive function of microstructural geometry. Because of the wide variety of such geometry in modern composites, we must be cautious of generalities. But we will identify a few of the important examples.

Take the three idealized geometries: (1) a direction parallel to continuous fibers in a matrix; (2) a direction perpendicular to the direction of the continuous fibers; and (3) a direction relative to a uniformly dispersed aggregate composite. The first two cases represent extremes in the highly anisotropic nature of fibrous composites such as fiberglass and wood. The third case represents an idealized model of the relatively isotropic nature of concrete. We shall now consider these cases individually. Each time, we will use the modulus of elasticity to illustrate how a property is averaged. This is consistent with our emphasis on the structural applications of composites.

Note:

[1] 很显然,在某些方面,复合材料的性能一定是各个组元性能的平均值。

Questions:

1) How to decide the properties of the composite?

2) What are the three geometries of the composite mentioned in this passage?

2.7.5 Loading Parallel to Reinforcing Fibers——Isostrain *

In this case, if the matrix is intimately bonded to the reinforcing fibers, the strain of both the matrix and the fibers must be the same. This isostrain condition is true even though the elastic moduli of each component will tend to be quite different.[1] It is apparent that the load carried by the composite is the simple sum of loads carried by each component. For the fiberglass example under discussion, nearly the entire uniaxial* load is carried by the high modulus fibers. This geometry is an ideal application of a composite. The high modulus and strength of the fibers are effectively transmitted to the composite as a whole. At the same time, the ductility of the matrix is available to produce a substantially less brittle material than glass by itself.

2.7.6 Loading Perpendicular to Reinforcing Fibers—Isostress*

A substantially different result is obtained for the case of perpendicular loading of the reinforcing fibers. In this case, the total elongation of the composite in the direction of stress application is the sum of the elongation of matrix and fiber components, but most elongation come form the matrix since the fiberglass has a much higher modulus value.

2.7.7 Interfacial Strength

The averaging of properties in a useful composite material can be represented by the typical examples just discussed. We must note an important consideration so far taken for granted*. That is the interface between the matrix and discontinuous phase must be strong enough to transmit the stress or strain due to a mechanical load from one phase to the other. Without this strength, the dispersed phase can fail to "communicate" with the matrix.[2] Rather than have the "best of both worlds" as implied in the introduction, we may obtain the worst behavior of each component. Reinforcing fibers slipping out of a matrix would be an example. Substantial effort has been devoted to providing interfacial strength. Surface treatment, chemistry, and temperature are a few considerations in the "art and science" of interfacial bonding.

Key words:
isostrain[等应变]   uniaxial[单轴的]
isostress[等应力]   grant[认可]

114   *English in Materials Science and Engineering*

Notes:

[1] 即使各种组元的弹性模量差别很大时,这种等应变条件也是正确的。

[2] 如果没有界面强度,分散相就不能同基体发生(应力或应变)传递。

Questions:

1) When loading parallel to reinforcing fibers, how is the strain distributed and how is the load distributed?

2) When loading perpendicular to reinforcing fibers, how is the strain distributed and how is the load distributed?

3) The interfacial strength is not important for a composite material. (T/F)

3

Welding

3.1 Introduction to Welding Processes

3.1.1 Definition and Classification of Welding Processes

Welding is essential for the manufacture of a range of engineering components, which may vary from very large structures such as ships and bridges to miniature components for microelectronic applications.[1]

Several alternative definitions are used to describe a weld, for example:

> A union between two pieces of metal rendered* plastic or liquid by heat or pressure or both. A filler metal* with a melting temperature of the same order of that of the parent metal* may or may not be used.

or alternatively:

116 *English in Materials Science and Engineering*

> A localized coalescence* of metals or nonmetals produced either by heating the materials to the welding temperature, with or without the application of pressure, or by the application of pressure alone, with or without the use of a filler metal.

Based on these definitions welding processes may be classified into those which rely on the application of pressure and those which used elevated temperatures to achieve the bond. The most important processes are shown in Figure 3.1.

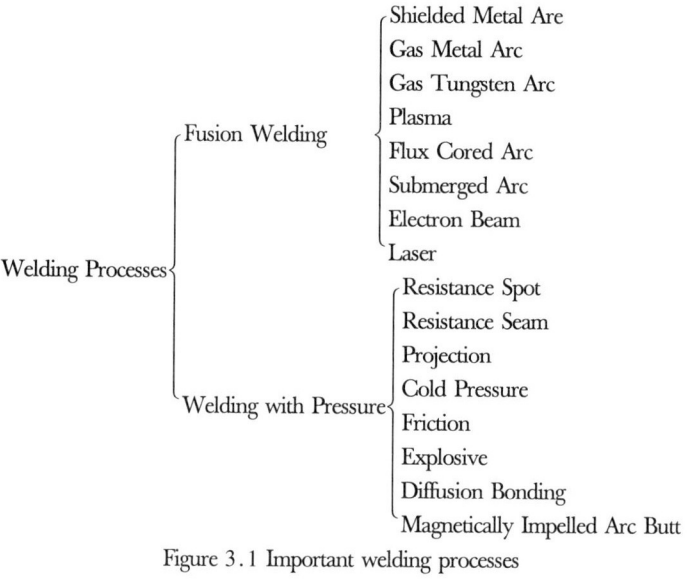

Figure 3.1 Important welding processes

Key words:
render [给予,提供]   filler metal [填充金属]
parent metal [母材]   coalescence [结合]
Note:
[1] 焊接在很多工程零部件的生产中都是必需的,大到船舶、桥梁,小到微电子应用的微小零件。

Questions:

1) A filler metal must be used in a welding process. (T/F)

2) Welding processes can be classified into two groups according

to whether pressure is applied. (T/F)

3.1.2 Fusion Welding

The most widely used welding processes rely on fusion of the components at the joint line. In fusion welding*, a heat source melts the metal to form a bridge between the components.

A widely used heat source is electric arc, as shown in Figure 3.2.

The molten metal must be protected from the atmosphere—absorption of oxygen and nitrogen leads to a poor quality weld. Air in the weld area can be replaced by a gas which does not contaminate the metal, or the weld can be covered with a flux*.

A large number of fusion welding* processes and techniques are available. No process is universally best. Each has its own

Figure 3.2 Welding arc

special attributes and must be matched to the application. Choosing the most suitable process requires consideration of a number of factors, including type of metal, type of joint, material thickness, production constraints, equipment availability, labour availability, labour costs, costs of consumables, health, safety and the environment consideration.

Key words:
fusion welding [熔化焊]   flux [焊剂]

3.1.2.1 *Shielded Metal Arc Welding* (SMAW)*

Shielded metal arc welding process, shown in Figure 3.3, is also known as manual metal arc welding (MMA) in Europe.

It has for many years been one of the most common techniques applied to the fabrication of steels. The process uses an arc as the heat source and shielding is provided by gases generated by the decomposition of the electrode* coating material and by the slag* produced by the melting of mineral constituents of the coating.[1] In addition to heating and melting the parent material the arc also melts the core of the electrode and thereby provides filler material for the joint*. The electrode coating may also be used as a source of alloying

Figure 3.3 Shielded metal arc welding

elements and additional filler material. The flux and electrode chemistry may be formulated to deposit wear- and corrosion-resistant layers for surface protection.

Significant features of the process are:

(1) equipment requirements are simple;

(2) a large range of consumables are available;

(3) the process is extremely portable;

(4) the operating efficiency is low;

(5) it is labour intensive.

For these reasons the process has been traditionally used in structural steel fabrication, shipbuilding and heavy engineering as well as for small batch production and maintenance.

Key words:

shielded metal arc welding (SMAW) [手工电弧焊]

electrode [焊条,电极]   slag [熔渣]   joint [接头]

Note:

[1] 该工艺采用电弧作为热源,由焊条药皮分解产生的气体和药皮中的矿物质成分熔化形成的熔渣提供保护。

Questions:

1) What are the features of the SMAW process?

Welding   119

2) How is the shielding realized in the SMAW process?

3.1.2.2 *Gas Metal Arc Welding (GMAW)* [*]

Gas metal arc welding, shown in Figure 3.4 and Figure 3.5, is also known as metal inert gas (MIG) [*] or metal active gas (MAG) [*] welding in Europe.

Gas metal arc welding uses the heat generated by an electric arc to fuse the joint area. The arc is formed between the tip of a consumable [*], continuously fed filler wire and the workpiece and the entire arc area is shielded by an inert MIG/MAG

Figure 3.4 Gas Metal Arc Welding

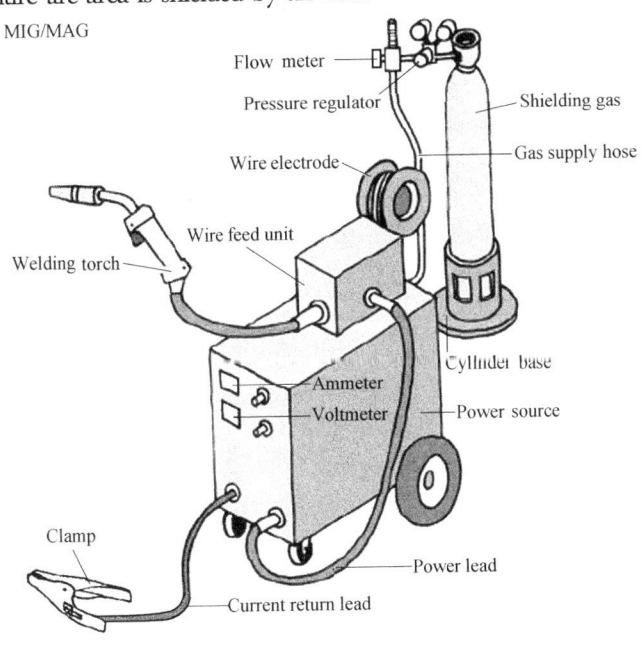

Figure 3.5 GMAW system

120   *English in Materials Science and Engineering*

gas. The principle of operation is illustrated in Figure 3.6.

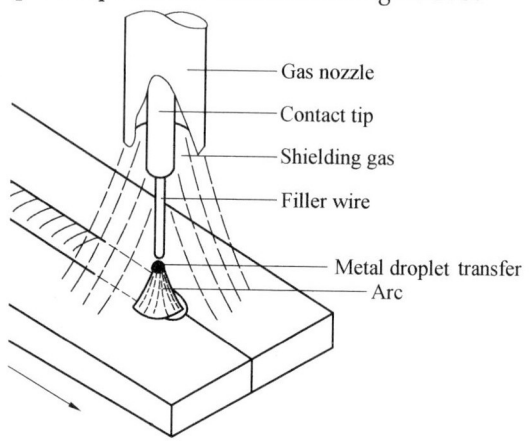

Figure 3.6 The operating principle of gas metal arc welding

Some of the more important features of the process are summarized below:

(1) low heat input (compared with SMAW and SAW);

(2) continuous operation;

(3) high deposition rate;

(4) no heavy slag—reduced post-weld cleaning;

(5) low hydrogen—reduces risk of cold cracking.

Depending on the operating mode of the process it may be used at low currents for thin sheet or positional welding.

The process is used for joining plain carbon steel sheet from 0.5 to 2 mm thick in the following applications: automobile bodies, exhaust systems, storage tanks, tubular steel furniture, heating and ventilating ducts. The process is applied to positional welding* of thick plain carbon and low alloy steels in the following areas: oil pipelines, marine structures and earth-moving equipment. At higher currents high deposition rates may be obtained and the process is used for downhand and horizontal-vertical welds in a wide range of materials—include earth-moving equipment, structural steelwork, weld surfacing with nickel or chromium alloys, aluminum alloy cryogenic vessels and

Welding 121

military vehicles.

Key words：
gas metal arc welding（GMAW）［熔化极气体保护焊］
metal inert gas（MIG）welding［熔化极惰性气体保护焊］
metal active gas（MAG）welding［熔化极活性气体保护焊］
consumable［焊丝］
positional welding［全位置焊］

3.1.2.3 *Gas Tungsten Arc Welding*（GTAW）*

Gas tungsten arc welding, shown in Figure 3.7, is also known as tungsten inert gas（TIG）* welding in most of Europe.

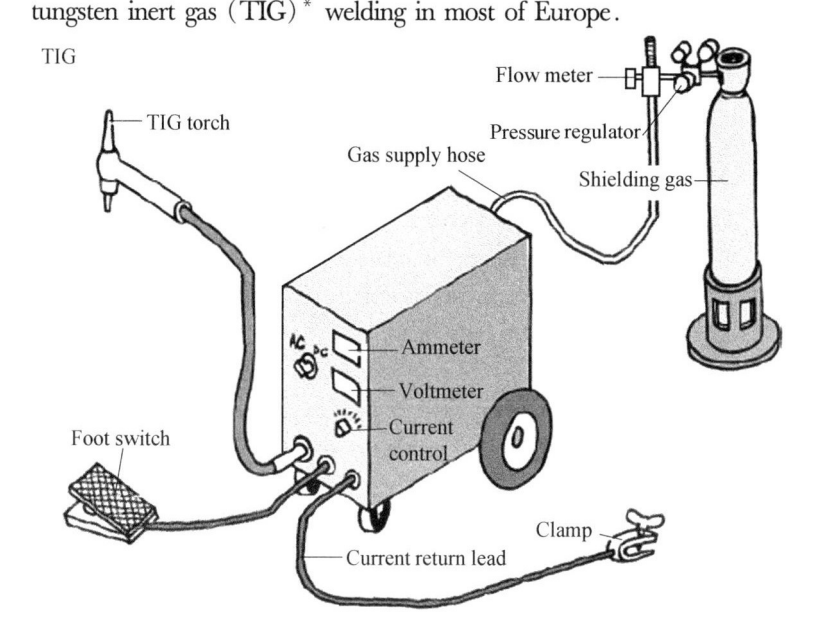

Figure 3.7 GTAW system

In the gas tungsten arc welding process the heat generated by an arc which is maintained between the workpiece and a non-consumable tungsten electrode is used to fuse the joint area. The arc is sustained in an inert gas which serves to protect the weld pool and the electrode from atmospheric contamination. The principle of operation is

122　*English in Materials Science and Engineering*

illustrated in Figure 3.8.

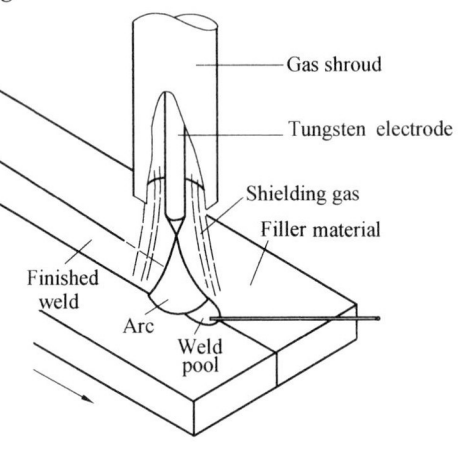

Figure 3.8 The operating principle of gas tungsten arc welding

The process has the following features:

(1) it is conducted in a chemically inert atmosphere;

(2) the arc energy density is relatively high;

(3) the process is very controllable;

(4) joint quality is usually high;

(5) deposition rates and joint completion rates are low.

The process may be applied to the joining of a wide range of engineering materials including stainless steel, aluminum alloys and reactive metals such as titanium. These features of the process lead to its widespread application in the aerospace, nuclear reprocessing and power generation industries as well as in the fabrication of chemical process plant, food processing and brewing equipment.

Key words:

gas tungsten arc welding (GTAW) [钨极惰性气体保护焊(钨极氩弧焊)]

tungsten inert gas (TIG) welding [钨极惰性气体保护焊(钨极氩弧焊)]

Questions:

1) What is the difference between GMAW process and GTAW process?

2) The GTAW process can be used to join titanium. (T/F)

3.1.2.4 *Plasma Welding**

The arc used in TIG welding can be converted to a high energy jet by forcing it through a small hole in a nozzle. This constricts the arc and forms the plasma jet. Plasma welding uses the heat generated by the constricted arc to fuse the joint area, and the arc is formed between the tip of a non-consumable electrode and either the workpiece or the constricting nozzle, as shown in Figure 3.9. A wide range of shielding gases are used depending on the mode of operation and the application.

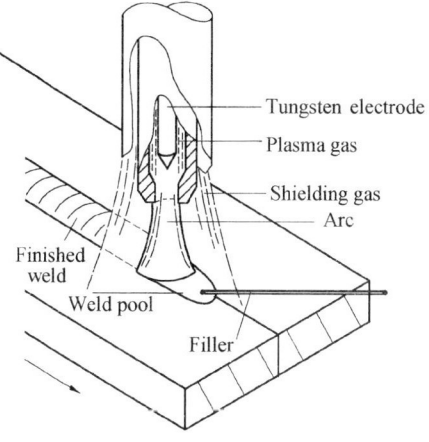

Figure 3.9 Plasma welding

In the normal transferred arc mode the arc is maintained between the electrode and the workpiece; the electrode is usually the cathode and the workpiece is connected to the positive side of the power supply. In this mode a high energy density is achieved and the process may be used effectively for welding.

Plasma welding relies on a special technique known as keyholing. First a hole is pierced through the joint by the plasma arc. As the torch is moved along the joint, metal melts at the front of the hole, swirls to the back and solidifies.

The features of the process depend on the operating mode and the

124   *English in Materials Science and Engineering*

current, but in summary the plasma process has the following characteristics:

(1) good low-current arc stability;

(2) improved directionality compared with TIG;

(3) improved melting efficiency compared with TIG;

(4) possibility of keyhole* welding.

These features of the process make it suitable for a range of applications including the joining of very thin materials, the encapsulation of electronic components and sensors, and high-speed longitudinal welds on strip and pipe.

Key words:
plasma welding [等离子焊]   keyhole [匙孔, 小孔]

Questions:

1) What are the relationship and differences between plasma welding and TIG welding?

2) A consumable electrode is used in plasma welding. (T/F)

3.1.2.5 *Flux-cored Wire Welding* (FCAW)

Flux-cored* wires consist of a metal outer sheath filled with a combination of mineral flux and metal powders, as shown in Figure 3.10. The FCAW process is operated in a similar manner to GMAW welding and the principle is illustrated in Figure 3.11. The most common production

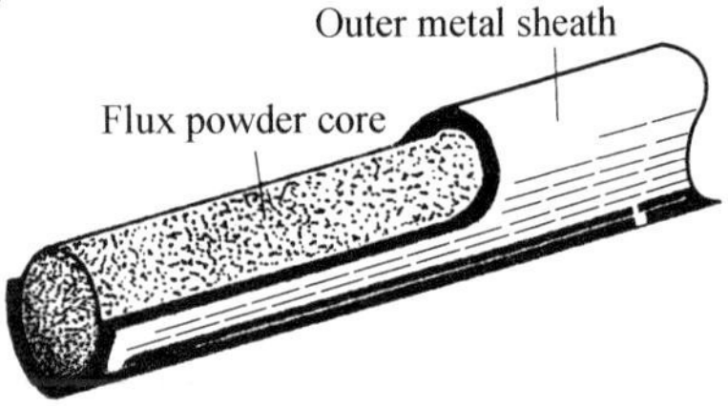

Figure 3.10 Construction of a flux-cored wire

technique used to produce the wire involves folding a thin metal strip into a U shape, filling it with the flux constituents, closing the U to form a circular section and reducing the diameter of the tube by drawing or rolling.[1] Alternative configurations, shown in Figure 3.12, may be produced by lapping or folding the strip or the

Welding 125

consumable may be made by filling a tube with flux followed by a drawing operation to reduce the diameter. Typical finished wire diameters range from 3.2 to 0.8 mm.

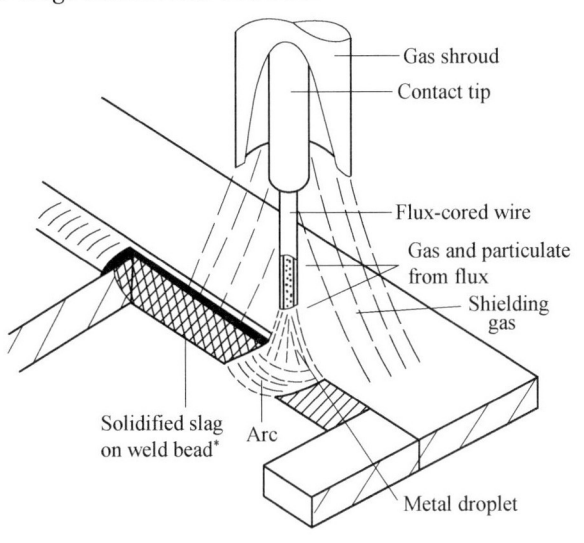

Figure 3.11 Principle of operation of FCAW

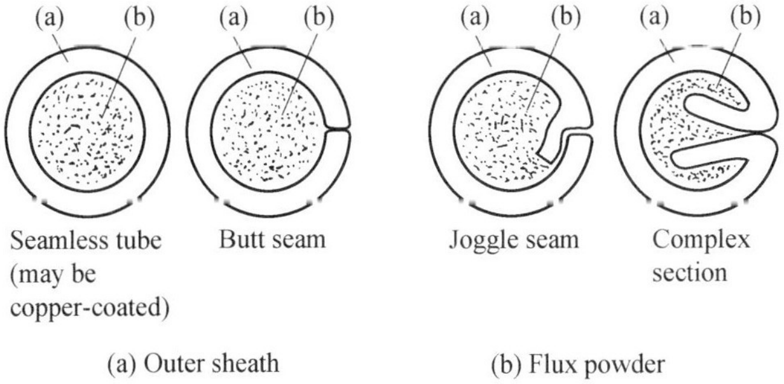

Figure 3.12 Alternative configurations of flux-cored wires

Flux-cored wires offer the following advantages:
(1) high deposition rates;
(2) alloying addition from the flux core;
(3) slag shielding and support;

126　*English in Materials Science and Engineering*

（4）improved arc stabilization and shielding.

Key words:
flux-cored wire ［药芯焊丝］　　　　weld bead ［焊缝］
Note:
［1］制造药芯丝的一般过程为:将薄钢带折成 U 型,在其中添加焊剂,将
U 型槽封口获得圆形截面的焊丝,最后通过拉拔或轧制使焊丝达到所需尺
寸。

3.1.2.6 *Submerged Arc Welding*（SAW）

　　Submerged arc welding, shown in Figure 3.13, is a consumable
electrode arc welding process in which the arc is shielded by a molten
slag and the arc atmosphere is generated by decomposition of certain
slag constituents. The filler material is a continuously fed wire and very
high melting and deposition rates are achieved by using high current
（e.g. 1 000 A）with relatively small-diameter wires（e.g. 4 mm）.

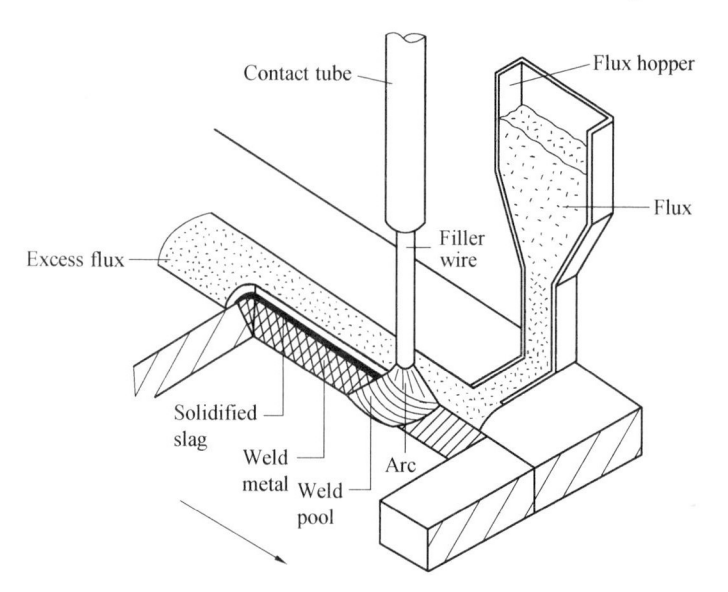

Figure 3.13 Submerged arc welding

The significant features of the process are:

(1) high deposition rates;

(2) automatic operation;

(3) no visible arc radiation;

(4) flexible range of flux/wire combinations;

(5) difficult to use positionally;

(6) best for thicknesses above 6mm.

The main applications of submerged arc welding are on thick-section plain carbon and low-alloy steels and it has been used on power generation plant, nuclear containment, heavy structural steelwork, offshore structures and shipbuilding. The process is also used for high-speed welding of simple geometric seams in thinner sections, for example in the fabrication of pressure containers for liquefied petroleum gas. Like shielded metal arc welding, with suitable wire/flux combinations the process may also be used for surfacing.

Key words:
Submerged arc welding (SAW) [埋弧焊]   weld pool [熔池]

Questions:

1) What are the differences between SAW and GMAW?

2) SAW is suitable for joining thin sheets. (T/F)

3.1.2.7 *Electron Beam Welding* (EBW)

A beam of electrons may be accelerated by a high voltage to provide a high-energy heat source for welding, as shown in Figure 3.14. The power density of electron beams is high (10^{10} to 10^{12} W/m^2) and keyhole welding is the normal operating mode. The problem of power dissipation when the electrons collide with atmospheric gas molecules is usually overcome by carrying out the welding operation in a vacuum.

Features of the process include:

(1) very high energy density;

(2) confined heat source;

(3) high depth to width ratio of welds;

(4) normally requires a vacuum;

128　*English in Materials Science and Engineering*

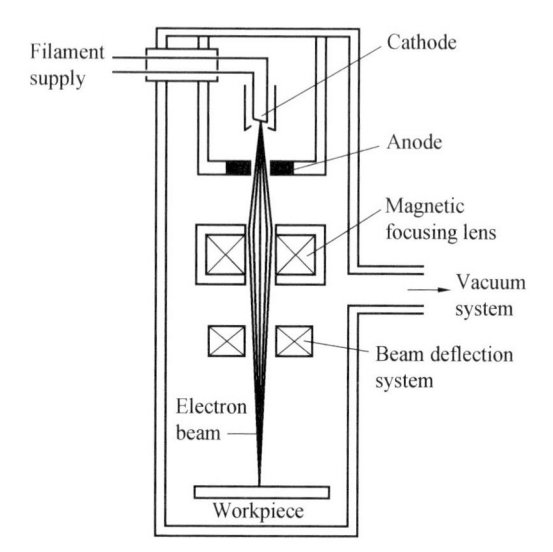

Figure 3.14 Principle of electron beam welding

(5) high equipment cost.

Applications of electron beam welding have traditionally included welding of aerospace engine components and instrumentation, but it may be used on a wide range of materials when high-precision and very deep penetration* welds* are required.

Key words:
penetration [熔深]　　　　weld [焊缝]

3.1.2.8 *Laser Welding*

The laser may be used as an alternative heat source for fusion welding. The focused power density of the laser can reach 10^{10} to 10^{12} W/m^2 and welding is often carried out using the "keyhole" technique. Significant features of laser welding are:

(1) very confined heat source at low power;

(2) deep penetration at high power;

(3) reduced distortion and thermal damage;

(4) out-of-vacuum technique;

(5) high equipment cost.

These features have led to the application of lasers for microjoining of electronic components, but the process is also being applied to the fabrication of automotive components and precision machine tool parts in heavy section steel.

Question:

What are the similarities and differences of electron beam welding and laser welding?

3.1.3 Welding with Pressure

3.1.3.1 *Resistance Spot Welding**

Spot welding, as shown in Figure 3.15, is one of a group of resistance welding processes that involve the joining of two or more metal parts together in a localized area by the application of heat and pressure. The heat is generated within the material being joined by the resistance to the passage of a high current through the metal parts. Resistance heating at the contact surfaces causes local melting and fusion. High currents (typically 10 000 A) are applied for short durations and pressure is applied to the electrodes prior to the application of current and for a short time after the current has ceased to flow.

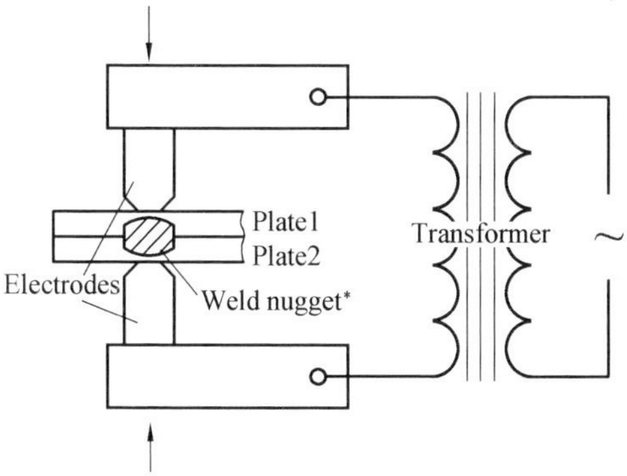

Figure 3.15 Resistance welding system

130　*English in Materials Science and Engineering*

The process is used for joining sheet materials and uses shaped copper alloy electrodes to apply pressure and convey the electrical current through the workpieces. Heat is developed mainly at the interface between two sheets, eventually causing the material being welded to melt, forming a molten pool, the weld nugget. The molten pool is contained by the pressure applied by the electrode tip and the surrounding solid metal.

Accurate control of current amplitude, pressure and weld cycle time are required to ensure that consistent weld quality is achieved but some variation may occur due to changes in the contact resistance of the material, electrode wear, magnetic losses or shunting of the current through previously formed spots.[1] These "unpredictable" variations in process performance have led to the practice of increasing the number of welds from the design requirement to give some measure of protection against poor individual weld quality. To improve this situation significant developments have been made in resistance monitoring and control, these allow more efficient use of the process.

Features of the basic resistance welding process include:

(1) the process requires relatively simple equipment;

(2) it is easily and normally automated;

(3) once the welding parameters are established it should be possible to produce repeatable welds for relatively long production runs.

The major applications of the process have been in the joining of sheet steel in the automotive and white-goods manufacturing industries.

Key words:
resistance spot welding [电阻点焊]　　　weld nugget [焊核]

Note:

[1] 要确保一致的焊接质量,就要精确控制电流幅值、压力和焊接循环时间,但有时材料接触电阻的变化、电极磨损、磁损以及已形成焊点的分流会造成焊接质量的变化。

3.1.3.2 *Resistance Seam Welding**

The seam welding process is an adaptation of resistance spot welding and involves making a series of overlapping spot welds by means of rotating copper alloy wheel electrodes to form a continuous leak tight* joint. The electrodes are not opened between spots. The electrode wheels apply a constant force to the workpieces and rotate at a controlled speed. The welding current is normally pulsed to give a series of discrete spots, but may be continuous for certain high speed applications where gaps could otherwise occur between individual spots. Seam welding equipment is normally fixed and the components being welded are manipulated between the wheels. The process may be automated; it is illustrated in Figure 3.16.

Figure 3.16 Resistance seam welding

Key words:
resistance seam welding [电阻缝焊]   leak tight [致密的]

3.1.3.3 *Resistance Projection Welding**

Projection welding is a development of resistance spot welding. In spot welding, the size and position of the welds are determined by the size of the electrode tip and the contact point on the workpieces, whereas in projection welding the size and position of the weld or welds are determined by the design of the component to be welded. The

132   *English in Materials Science and Engineering*

force and current are concentrated in a small contact area which occurs naturally, as in cross wire welding* or is deliberately introduced by machining or forming. An embossed dimple is used for sheet joining and a "V" projection or angle can be machined in a solid component to achieve an initial line contact with the component to which it is to be welded, see Figure 3.17.

In sheet joining using embossed* projection welds, a melted weld zone is produced, as in spot welding. However, when a solid formed or machined projection is used, a solid phase forge weld is produced without melting. The plastic deformation of the heated parts in contact produces a strong bond across the weld interface.

The process is well established and is applicable mainly to low carbon or microalloyed steels. The process is widely used on sheet metal assemblies in automotive and white goods industries for both sheet joining and attaching nuts and studs*.

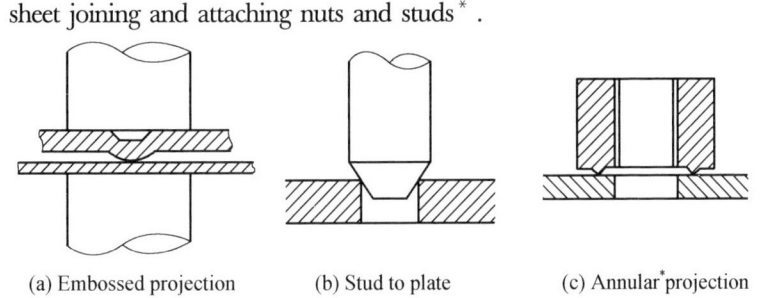

(a) Embossed projection   (b) Stud to plate   (c) Annular*projection

Figure 3.17 Example of projection welding configurations

Key words:
resistance projection welding [电阻凸焊]
cross wire welding [十字交叉线材焊接]
emboss [使凸起,压花]   stud [螺柱,销钉]   annular [环形的]

Questions:

1) What are the relationships and differences of spot welding, seam welding and projection welding?

2) Does a weld nugget always appear in the projection welding process?

3.1.3.4 Cold Pressure Welding

If sufficient pressure is applied to the cleaned mating surfaces to cause substantial plastic deformation the surface layers of the material are disrupted, metallic bonds form across the interface and a cold pressure weld is formed.[1]

The main characteristics of cold pressure welding are:

(1) the simplicity and low cost of the equipment;

(2) the avoidance of thermal damage to the material;

(3) most suitable for low-strength (soft) materials.

The pressure and deformation may be applied by rolling, indentation*, butt welding*, drawing or shear welding techniques. In general the more ductile materials are more easily welded.

This process has been used for electrical connections between small-diameter copper and aluminum conductors using butt and indentation techniques. Roll bonding is used to produce bimetallic sheets* such as Cu/Al for cooking utensils*, Al/Zn for printing plates and precious-metal contact springs for electrical applications.

Key words:
indentation [压痕]   butt weld [对焊]
bimetallic sheet [双金属板]   utensil [器具]

Note:

[1] 如果在清洁的配对表面上施加足够高的压力,造成显著的塑性变形,材料的表面层就会被破坏,在界面处形成金属键,从而形成冷压焊接头。

3.1.3.5 Friction Welding*

In friction welding, shown in Figure 3.18, a high temperature is developed at the joint by the relative motion of the contact surfaces. When the surfaces are softened a forging pressure is applied and the relative motion is stopped. Material is extruded from the joint to form an upset.

The process may be divided into several operating modes in terms of the means of supplying the energy:

134 *English in Materials Science and Engineering*

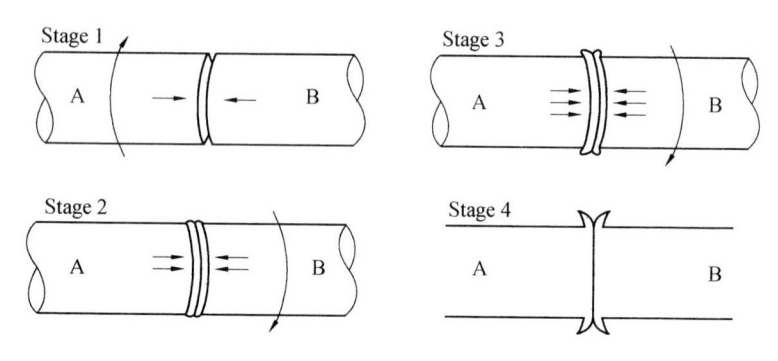

Figure 3.18 Friction welding

Stage 1: A fixed, B rotated and moved into contact with A.
Stage 2: A fixed, B rotated under pressure, interface heating.
Stage 3: A fixed, forge pressure applied.
Stage 4: Relative motion stopped, weld formed.

(1) Continuous drive: in which the relative motion is generated by direct coupling to the energy source. The drive maintains a constant speed during the heating phase.

(2) Stored energy: in which the relative motion is supplied by a flywheel which is disconnected from the drive during the heating phase.

The process may also be classified according to the type of motion as shown in Figure 3.19. Rotational motion is the most commonly used, mainly for round components where angular alignment of the two parts is not critical. If it is required to achieve a fixed relationship between the mating parts angular oscillation may be used and for non-circular components the linear and orbital techniques may be employed.

Features of the process include:

(1) one-shot process for butt welding sections;

(2) suitable for dissimilar metals;

(3) short cycle time;

(4) most suited to circular sections;

(5) robust and costly equipment may be required.

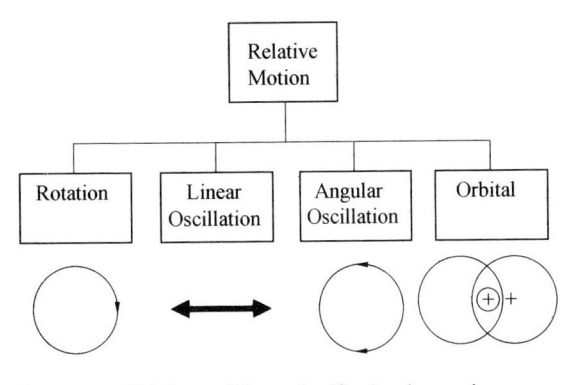

Figure 3.19 Friction welding: classification by motion type

The process is commonly applied to circular sections, particularly in steel, but it may also be applied to dissimilar metal joints such as aluminum to steel or even ceramic materials to metals. Early applications of the process included the welding of automotive stub axles* but the process has also been applied to the fabrication of high-quality aero-engine parts, duplex stainless steel pipe for offshore applications and nuclear components.

Key words:
friction welding [摩擦焊]   stub axle [(汽车的)转向节]

3.1.3.6 *Explosive Welding*

In explosive welding the force required to deform the interface is generated by an explosive charge*. In the most common application of the process two flat plates are joined to form a bimetallic structure, shown in Figure 3.20. An explosive charge is used to force the upper of "flyer*" plate on to the base plate in such a way that a wave of plastic material at the interface is extruded* forward as the plates join.[1] For large workpieces considerable force is involved and care is required to ensure the safe operation of the process.

Features of the process include:

(1) one-shot process—short welding time;

(2) suitable for joining large surface areas;

(3) suitable for dissimilar thickness and metals joining;

136　*English in Materials Science and Engineering*

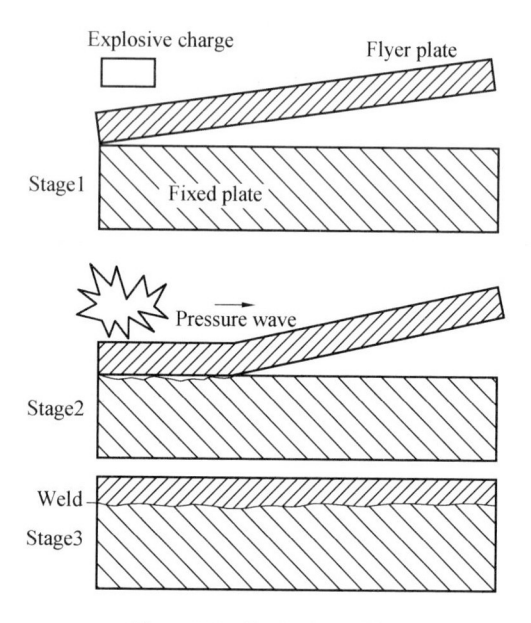

Figure 3.20 Explosive welding

(4) careful preparation required for large workpieces.

Key words:
explosive welding [爆炸焊]　　　explosive charge [炸药]
flyer [飞行物]　　　　　　　　　extrude [挤压]
　Note:
　[1]采用炸药爆炸把上面的动板压到基板上,在板的连接过程中,界面处的塑性材料被挤得呈波浪状向前推进。

3.1.3.7 *Diffusion Bonding*

In diffusion bonding the mating surfaces are cleaned and heated in an inert atmosphere. Pressure is applied to the joint and local plastic deformation is followed by diffusion during which the surface voids are gradually removed. The components to be joined need to be enclosed in a controlled atmosphere* and the process of diffusion is time and temperature dependent. In some cases an intermediate material is placed between the abutting* surfaces to form an interlayer.

Significant features of the process are:

Welding 137

(1) suitable for joining a wide range of materials;
(2) one-shot process;
(3) complex sections may be joined;
(4) vacuum or controlled atmosphere required;
(5) prolonged cycle time.

Key words:
diffusion bonding [扩散焊]   controlled atmosphere [受控气氛]
abut [邻接]

Question:

Do the mating surfaces melt in the diffusion bonding process?

3.1.3.8 *Magnetically Impelled Arc Butt Welding* (MIAB)*

Magnetically impelled arc butt (MIAB) welding is a one shot, forge welding process which is predominantly used in the European automotive industry for rapidly joining circular and non-circular thin wall (< 5 mm) steel tubes. This machine tool based process is attractive to the mass production industries because of the short cycle times and reproducible quality.

The first stage of a MIAB weld is to force the two tubulars* together whilst applying a DC welding current. They are then moved apart to a distance of 1 ~ 3 mm in order to strike an arc. This arc is rotated at high speed around the circumference of the weld interface using a static radial magnetic field which can be generated using permanent magnets or electromagnets.[1] Arc rotation is sustained for a few seconds until the joint faces are heated to a high temperature or are molten, as shown in Figure 3.21.

In the second stage of the process the tubulars are brought rapidly together under a pre-determined forging pressure and the arc is extinguished. The molten metal at the weld interface is expelled and a solid phase weld results from sustained forging pressure, which consolidates the joint. Typically weld cycle times range from 1-6 seconds depending on tube diameter.

Key words:
magnetically impelled arc butt (MIAB) welding [磁驱动电弧对焊]

Stage 1   Rotating arc heats end faces

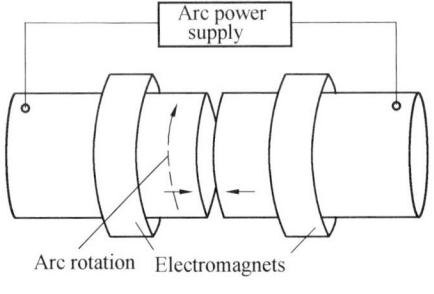

Stage 2   Forge pressure applied

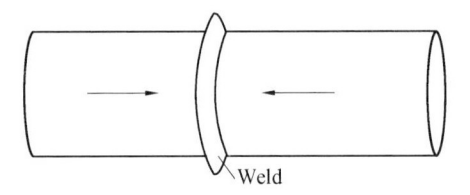

Figure 3.21 MIAB welding

tubular [管]

Note:

[1] 采用静态的径向磁场使电弧绕焊缝界面圆周高速旋转,磁场可以采用永久磁铁或电磁铁产生。

3.2 Welding Metallurgy

3.2.1 Introduction

3.2.1.1 *Welding Problems in Steels*

Carbon and alloy steels are more frequently welded than any other materials owing to their widespread applications and good weldability[*]. In general, carbon and alloy steels with higher strength levels are more difficult to weld, hydrogen cracking[*] and reheat cracking[*] being more likely to occur in these materials. Table 3.1 summarizes typical welding problems in carbon and alloy steels and their solutions.

Welding   139

Table 3.1 **Typical welding problems in carbon and alloy steels and their solutions**

Typical problems	Alloy types	Locations	Practical solutions
Porosity*	Carbon and low-alloy steels	Fusion zone*	Add deoxidizers (Al, Ti, Mn) in filler metal
Hydrogen cracking	Steels with high carbon equivalent*	Fusion zone and HAZ*	Use low-hydrogen or austenitic stainless-steel electrodes
Lamellar tearing*	Carbon and low-alloy steels	HAZ	Use joint designs that minimize transverse restraint.* Butter with a softer layer.
Reheat cracking		HAZ	Use low heat input to avoid grain growth. Minimize restraint and stress concentrations. Heat rapidly through critical temperature range, if possible.
Solidification cracking* and partially melted zone cracking	Carbon and low-alloy steels	Fusion zone and partially melted zone	Keep proper Mn/S ratio
Low HAZ toughness due to grain growth	Carbon and low-alloy steels	HAZ	Use carbide and nitride formers to suppress grain growth. Use low heat input.
Low fusion zone toughness due to coarse columnar grains	Carbon and low-alloy steels	Fusion zone	Grain refining.

140　*English in Materials Science and Engineering*

Key words:

weldability [焊接性]　　　　　hydrogen cracking [氢致裂纹]
reheat cracking [再热裂纹]
porosity [气孔]　　　　　　　fusion zone [熔合区]
carbon equivalent [碳当量]　　HAZ [热影响区]
lamellar tearing [层状撕裂]　 transverse restraint [横向拘束]
solidification cracking [凝固裂纹]

3.2.1.2 *Characteristics of Phase Transformations during the Welding of Steels*

The thermal processes during the welding and heat-treating of steels are different in a number of ways. First, the peak temperature of the HAZ during welding can be rather high. In fact, near the fusion boundary, where difficulties such as grain coarsening and underbead cracking often arise, the peak temperature can reach 1 400℃ or even higher. In the heat-treating of steels, on the other hand, the maximum temperature involved is usually only around 950℃. Second, the heating rate is very high, and the retention time at high temperatures is very brief during most welding processes. In the heat-treating of steels, the heating rate is much slower and the high-temperature retention time is much longer. Figure 3.22 shows the thermal processes during the welding and heat-treating of two steels.

As a result of the high heating rate during welding, diffusional transformations, such as ferrite + pearlite → austenite, become more difficult. Consequently, effective transformation temperatures, such as the lower critical temperature Ac_1 and the upper critical temperature Ac_3, tend to increase with increasing heating rate during welding (1, 2). For steels containing greater amounts of carbide-forming elements (such as V, W, Cr, Ti, and Mo), the effect of the heating rate becomes more pronounced. This is because the diffusion rate of such elements is orders of magnitude lower than that of carbon and also because those elements hinder the diffusion of carbon.[1] As a result, diffusional transformations are retarded to a greater extent.

The high the heating rate, together with the brief

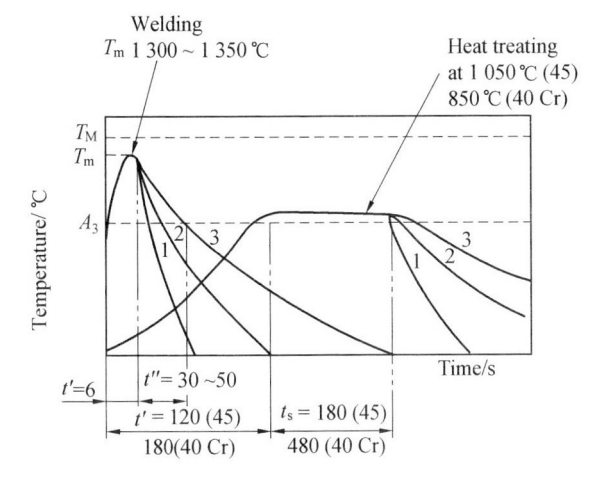

Figure 3.22 Temperature-time relationships for welding and heat treating of 45 steel and 40Cr steel

high-temperature retention time, can also result in the formation of nonhomogeneous austenite during welding. Such a nonhomogeneous austenite, upon subsequent rapid cooling, can cause the formation of localized high-carbon-martensite colonies. Consequently, the microhardness of the HAZ tends to scatter over a wide range.

As a result of high peak temperatures during welding, grain growth can take place near the fusion boundary. * Steels containing grain growth inhibitors (carbide and nitride formers such as Al, Ti, V, Nb, etc.) are more resistant to grain growth. The fine carbide or nitride particles tend to hinder the movement of grain boundaries, thus suppressing grain growth. In fact, the fine grain size in "microalloyed steels" is achieved by using such growth inhibitors.

Since the degree of grain growth increases with the high-temperature retention time, a higher heat-input welding process tends to produce more severe grain growth. Of course, under high heat inputs, carbide and nitride particles have a greater tendency to dissolve and coarsen, and their effectiveness as grain growth inhibitors diminishes. During the heat-treating of steels, the maximum temperature employed is only about 100 to 200°C above the upper critical temperature, and

142 *English in Materials Science and Engineering*

therefore no significant grain growth can occur.

Key words:
underbead cracking [焊道下裂纹]   fusion boundary [熔合线]
Note:
[1] 这是因为这些元素的扩散速度比碳的扩散速度低几个数量级,还因为这些元素妨碍了碳的扩散。

Questions:

1) What are the main characteristics of phase transformations during the welding of steels?

2) What are the results of high heating rate during welding?

3.2.2 The Fusion Zone

3.2.2.1 *Grain Structure of the Fusion Zone*

◆ Epitaxial Growth* at the Fusion Boundary

In autogenous welding*, the liquid metal of the weld pool is in intimate contact with a substrate of identical composition (the unmelted part of the base metal). Therefore, grain growth initiates from the substrate at the fusion boundary and proceeds toward the weld centerline.[1] Such a growth initiation process is called epitaxial growth (sometimes epitaxial nucleation). In this process, grain growth is initiated by arranging atoms from the liquid phase on the existing crystalline substrate, thereby extending it without altering the crystallographic orientation.[2]

◆ Competitive Growth in the Bulk Fusion Zone

In the bulk of the weld, the grain structure is governed by a different mechanism known as competitive growth.

During solidification, grains tend to grow in the direction perpendicular to the solid/liquid interface, since this is the direction of the maximum temperature gradient and thus the maximum driving force for solidification. However, grains also have their own preferred direction of growth called the easy growth direction—for example, ⟨100⟩ in face-centered-cubic and body-centered-cubic metals.

Welding   143

Therefore, during solidification, grains with their easy growth direction parallel to the direction of the maximum temperature gradient will grow more easily and crowd out* those other grains whose easy growth direction deviates significantly from the direction of the maximum temperature gradient.[3]

◆ Effect of Welding Parameters on Grain Structure

At high welding speeds the weld pool tends to be elongated, whereas at low welding speeds it tends to be elliptical. Since the boundary of the trailing portion of the tear-drop-shaped weld pool is essentially straight, the grains are also straight and growing essentially perpendicular to the pool boundary, as shown in Figure 3.23(a). On the other hand, since the boundary of the trailing portion of the elliptical weld pool is curved, the grains are also curved in order to grow perpendicular to the pool boundary, as shown in Figure 3.23 (b). Therefore, for weld metals free from heterogeneous nuclei, it can be expected that at high welding speeds columnar grains* will grow straight toward the weld center line and that at low welding speeds they will curve and grow in the direction of the maximum temperature gradient.

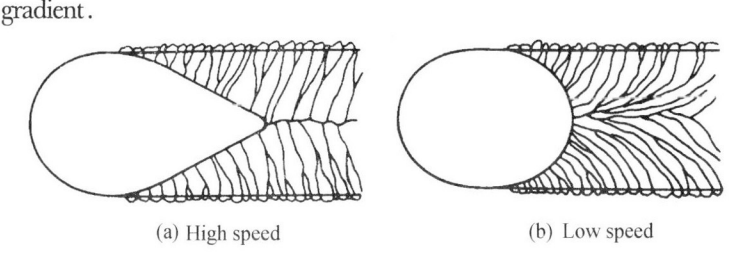

(a) High speed   (b) Low speed

Figure 3.23 Columnar-grain structure of welds made with tear-drop-shaped and elliptical weld pools

◆ Nucleation of New Grains in the Weld Metal

The growth of columnar grains can be interrupted by the formation of new grains, and if so, the development of grain structure in the fusion zone is no longer dominated by epitaxial and competitive growth of columnar grains. The formation of these new grains are

144   *English in Materials Science and Engineering*

often equiaxed * rather than columnar.

Figure 3.24(a) shows schematically the microstructure around the weld pool boundary of an alloy. Specifically, it shows dendrites in the mushy zone behind the trailing portion of the weld pool boundary and partially melted grains in the base metal adjacent to the leading portion of the weld pool boundary. Figure 3.24(a) illustrates three different mechanisms for the nucleation of new grains in the weld metal - dendrite fragmentation, grain detachment, and heterogeneous nucleation. * There is still another mechanism for the nucleation of new grains in the weld metal, surface nucleation, as illustrated in Figure 3.24(b).

Dendrite Fragmentation

Weld pool convection occurs during welding owing to various driving forces such as the electromagnetic force. Weld pool convection can in principle cause fragmentation of dendrite tips in the mushy zone, as illustrated in Figure 3.24(a). These dendrite fragments are carried into the bulk weld pool, where if able to survive the weld pool temperature, they can act as nuclei for new grains to form.

Grain Detachment

Where partially melted grains are loosely held together by the liquid films between them weld pool convection can also cause partially melted grains to detach themselves from the base metal immediately adjacent to the weld pool, as illustrated in Figure 3.24(a).[4] Like dendrite fragments, these partially melted grains, if they survive in the weld pool, can act as nuclei for the formation of new grains in the weld metal.

Heterogeneous Nucleation

According to the nucleation theory, atoms in a liquid metal have to overcome a critical energy barrier so that they can form solid nuclei that are larger than a critical size in order to be stable and able to grow into solid grains. Unfortunately, this critical energy barrier is usually high and difficult to overcome if these nuclei are to be formed solely by the atoms in the liquid themselves—the so-called homogeneous nuclei.

Welding 145

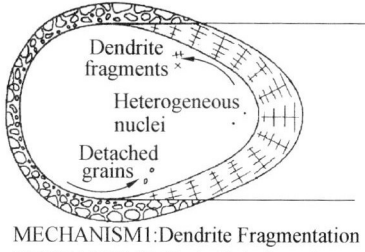

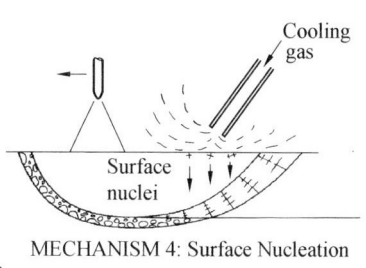

MECHANISM1:Dendrite Fragmentation
MECHANISM2: Grain Detachment
MECHANISM3: Heterogeneous Nucleation

MECHANISM 4: Surface Nucleation

(a) Top view

(b) Side view

Figure 3.24 Microstructure around the weld pool boundary of an alloy and nucleation mechanisms in weld metal

However, if the liquid metal already contains a significant number of foreign solid particles on which the atoms in the liquid metal can be arranged in a crystalline form, it is no longer necessary for the atoms in the liquid metal to form nuclei solely by themselves. These foreign particles are called heterogeneous nuclei.

Surface Nucleation

The weld pool surface can be undercooled thermally to induce surface nucleation by exposure to a stream of cooling gas or by instantaneous reduction or removal of the heat input. When this occurs, solid nuclci can foun at the weld surface, as illustrated in Figure 3.24(b). These solid nuclei then grow into new grains as they shower down from the weld pool surface, which they do because their density is higher than that of the surrounding liquid metal.

Key words:

epitaxial growth [外延生长]   autogenous welding [气焊]

crowd out [挤出,推开]   columnar grain [柱状晶]

equiaxed [等轴的]   heterogeneous nucleation [异质形核]

Notes:

[1] 于是,晶粒在熔合线处从母材开始长大,并向焊缝中心线生长。

[2] 在这一过程中,液相中的原子在已有晶体表面排列,晶粒开始长大,因此晶粒生长时不改变结晶方向。

[3] 因此,在结晶过程中,优先生长方向和最大温度梯度方向平行的晶

146 *English in Materials Science and Engineering*

粒更容易生长,优先生长方向和最大温度梯度方向偏离较大的晶粒则容易被挤掉。

[4] 如图 3.24(a)所示,半熔化的晶粒由处于这些晶粒之间的液态薄膜连在一起,熔池对流也能将这些半熔化的晶粒从紧邻熔池的母材上分离出来。

Questions:

1) What is the meaning of epitaxial growth?

2) How many mechanisms are there for nucleation of new grains in the weld pool? And what are they?

3.2.2.2 *Solidification Cracking of the Fusion Zone*

◆ Characteristics of Solidification Cracking

Solidification cracking, which is observed frequently in castings and ingots, can also occur in fusion welding. Such cracking is intergranular* —that is, along the grain boundaries of the weld metal. It occurs during the terminal stages of solidification, when the stresses developed across the adjacent grains exceed the strength of the almost completely solidified weld metal. [1] Such stresses can be induced either by the tendency of the workpiece to contract during cooling, by the tendency of the weld metal to contract during solidification, or both. The severity of such contraction stresses increases with both the degree of constraint and the thickness of the workpiece.

The various theories of solidification cracking are effectively identical and embody the concept of the formation of a coherent interlocking solid network separated by essentially continuous thin liquid films which are ruptured by the contraction stresses. [2] If a sufficient amount of liquid metal is present near the cracks, it can "backfill" and "heal" the incipient* cracks. Otherwise, the cracks appear as open tears. The tear fracture surface often reveals the dendritic morphology of the terminal stage of solidification.

Many different methods have been recommended for testing the solidification cracking susceptibility of weld metals. One is the "Houldcroft test*", which is often used for evaluating the solidification cracking susceptibility of sheet gage materials. The Design of the test specimen is shown in Figure 3.25. The specimen is free from constraints, and a progression of slots of varying depth allows the dissipation of stresses within it. In such a test, solidification cracking initiates from the starting edge of the test specimen and propagates along its centerline. As the heat source moves inward from the starting edge of the test specimen, solidification begins there immediately. The solidifying structure is torn apart, for the starting edge of the test specimen continues to expand as a result of continued heat input to the specimen. Because of the presence of the slots, the weld bead is subjected to a decreasing amount of stress along its length. The crack length from the starting edge of the test specimen is an index of solidification cracking sensitivity.

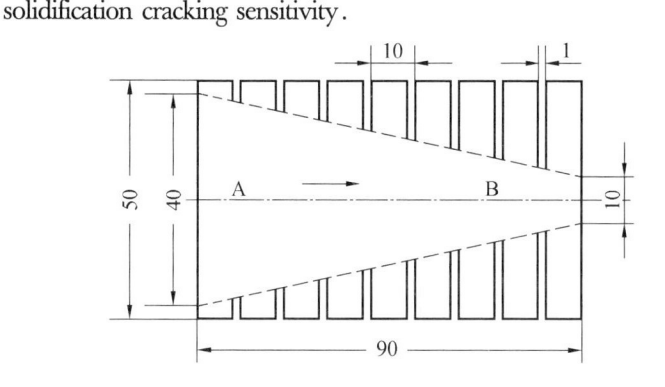

Figure 3.25 Houldcroft test

Key words:

intergranular [晶间的]   incipient [初期的]

Houldcroft test [鱼骨状裂纹试验]

 Notes:

[1] 它在结晶的后期,当邻近晶粒间的应力超过即将完全凝固的焊缝的强度时出现。

[2] 各种关于凝固裂纹的理论实际上都是一致的,都包含了这样的概念,即形成相互联结的固相物网络,而这些固相物被基本连续的液态薄膜隔开,在收缩应力的作用下,液态薄膜被破坏。

148　*English in Materials Science and Engineering*

Questions:

1) When does the solidification cracking occur?

2) How can solidification cracking sensitivity of a material be indicated by Houldcrost test?

◆ Metallurgical Factors of Solidification Cracking

Several metallurgical factors have been known to affect the solidification cracking susceptibility of weld metals.

Freezing Temperature Range And Amount of Low-melting-point Segregates

Generally speaking, the wider the freezing range, the larger the mushy zone *, and thus the larger the area that is weak and susceptible to weld solidification cracking. The freezing range of an alloy can be increased as a result either the intentional addition of alloying elements or the presence of undesirable impurities. The addition of Cu, Mg, or Zn in aluminum alloys is an example of the former case, and the presence of S and P in steels or nickel-base alloys is an example of the latter.

The effect of composition on the solidification cracking sensitivity of several aluminum alloys is shown in Figure 3.26.

As shown, the maximum cracking sensitivity occurs somewhere between pure aluminum and aluminum alloys with substantially high alloying contents. Pure aluminum is, of course, not susceptible to solidification cracking, since there is no low-melting-point eutectic * present at the grain boundary to cause solidification cracking. In high-alloy aluminums, on the other hand, the eutectic liquid is so abundant that it backfills and "heals" incipient cracks, resulting in low cracking sensitivity. Somewhere in between these two composition levels, however, the amount of eutectic liquid may be just large enough to form a continuous film at the grain boundary and render the materials rather susceptible to solidification cracking.

Sulfur * and phosphorus * tend to widen the freezing range of steels tremendously. Unlike the eutectic liquid in high-alloy

Welding 149

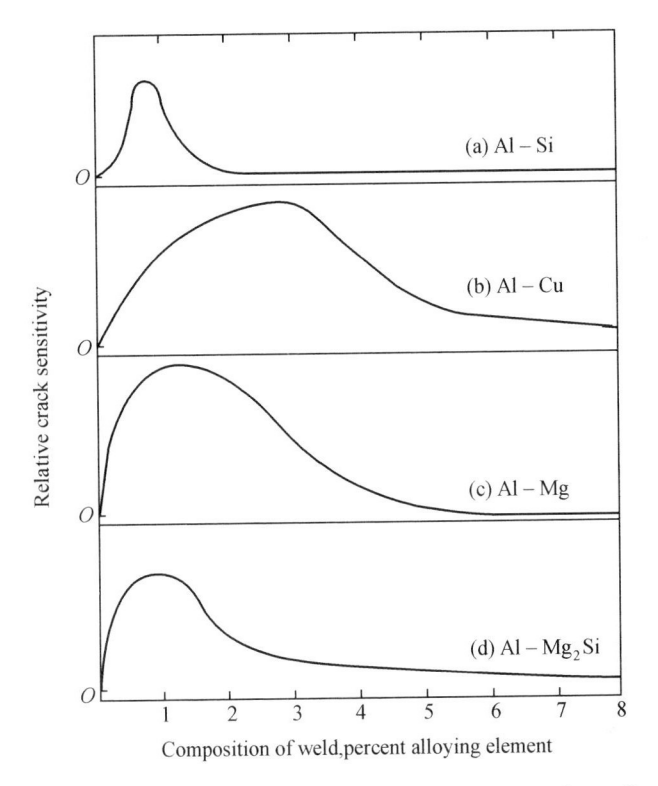

Figure 3.26 Solidification cracking sensitivity of some aluminum alloys

aluminums, the amount of low-melting-point segregates due to sulfur and /or phosphorus is too small to heal any incipient cracks. Since they have a rather strong tendency to segregate at grain boundary and form low-melting-point compounds (FeS in the case of S), they can cause severe solidification cracking even at relatively low concentrations. Sulfur and phosphorus can also cause severe solidification cracking in nickel-base alloys and ferritic stainless steels. In the case of austenitic stainless steels, their detrimental effect on solidification cracking can be significantly affected by the primary solidification phase.

Primary Solidification Phase

Figure 3. 27 shows the effect of δ-ferrite on the solidification

150   *English in Materials Science and Engineering*

cracking susceptibility of Cr (w_{Cr} = 17. 5%) stainless steels during casting. According to the Fe-Cr-Ni ternary phase diagram, the primary solidification phase changes from austenite (γ) to δ-ferrite when the nickel content falls below 12%. It is evident from Figure 3. 27 that, when austenite is the primary solidification phase, the ferrite content is practically zero, and the cracking susceptibility is high. When the primary solidification phase switches to δ-ferrite, the ferrite content increases, and the cracking susceptibility decreases.

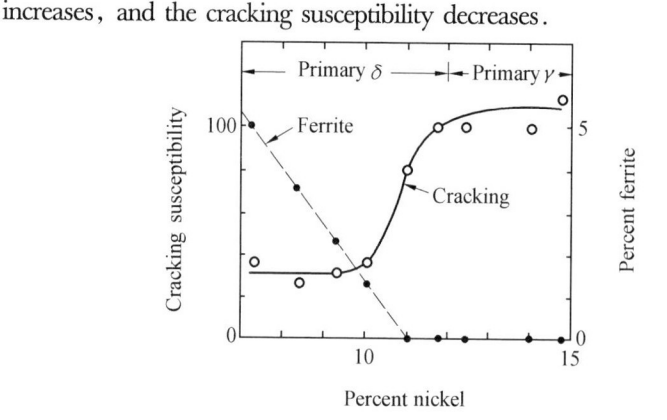

Figure 3.27 Solidification cracking susceptibility of Cr(w = 17.5%)stainless steels

Surface Tension of Grain Boundary Liquid

The effect of the amount of the grain boundary liquid on the solidification cracking of weld metals has been mentioned. However, not only the amount but also the distribution of the grain boundary liquid can significantly affect the solidification cracking tendency of weld metals. Figure 3. 28 shows the relationship between the surface tension, the dihedral* angle, and the distribution of the grain boundary liquid.

If the surface tension between the solid grains and the grain boundary liquid is very low, a liquid film will form between the grains, and the solidification cracking susceptibility will be high. On the other hand, if the surface tension is high, the liquid phase will be globular and will not wet the grain boundaries. Such discontinuous liquid globules do not significantly reduce the strength of the solid network and therefore are not as harmful. For example, FeS forms films at the grain boundaries of steels whereas MnS forms globules. Because of its globular morphology and higher melting point, MnS has been known to be far less harmful than FeS.

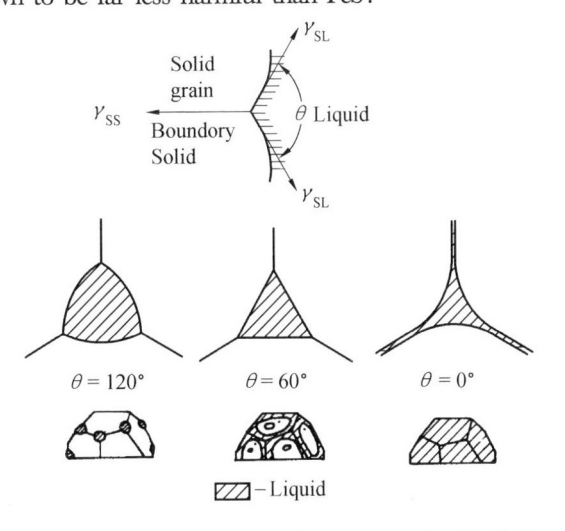

Figure 3.28 Relationship between the surface tension, the dihedral angle, and the distribution of the grain boundary liquid

Grain Structure of Fusion Zone

Coarse columnar grains are often more susceptible to solidification cracking than fine equiaxed grains. This can be because fine equiaxed grains can deform to accommodate contraction strains more easily. Liquid feeding and the healing of incipient cracks can also be more effective in fine-grained material. In addition, the grain boundary area is much greater in fine-grained material, and harmful low-melting-point segregates are therefore less concentrated at the grain boundary.

It is interesting to note that, owing to the steep angle of abutment between columnar grains growing from opposite sides of the weld pool, welds made with a tear-drop-shaped weld pool have been reported to be more susceptible to weld centerline solidification cracking than welds

152　*English in Materials Science and Engineering*

made with an elliptical weld pool.[1] A steep angle seems to favor the head-on impingement of columnar grains growing from opposite sides of the weld pool and the formation of the continuous liquid film of low-melting-point segregates at the weld centerline. As a result, centerline solidification cracking occurs under the influence of transverse contraction stresses.

Key words:
mushy zone [脆性温度区间]　　　eutectic [共晶,共晶的]
sulfur [硫]　　　phosphorus [磷]　　　dihedral [两面角]
Note:
[1] 有趣的是,由于从熔池两侧生长的柱状晶之间的夹角很小,由泪滴状熔池形成的焊缝对焊缝中心线凝固裂纹的敏感性比椭圆形熔池形成的焊缝更大。

Questions:

1) Why MnS is less harmful than FeS in weld of steels?

2) How many metallurgical factors of solidification cracking are there? And what are they?

◆ Mechanical factors of solidification cracking
Contraction Stresses

So far, the metallurgical factors of weld solidification cracking have been described. But without the presence of stresses acting on adjacent grains during solidification, no cracking can occur. Such stresses can be due to thermal contraction or solidification shrinkage or both. Austenitic stainless steels have relatively high thermal expansion coefficients * (compared to mild steels *) and are therefore often prone to solidification cracking. Aluminum alloys have both high thermal expansion coefficients and high solidification shrinkage. As a result, solidification cracking can be rather serious in some aluminum alloys, especially those with wide freezing ranges.

Degrees of Restraint

The degree of restraint of the workpiece is another mechanical factor of the solidification cracking. For the same joint design and material, the greater the restraint of the workpiece, the more likely solidification cracking will occur.

Key words:
thermal expansion coefficient [热膨胀系数]   mild steel [低碳钢]

3.2.3 Heat Affected Zone (HAZ)

3.2.3.1 HAZ *of Low-carbon Steels*

Essentially, the weld HAZ of low-carbon steels can be divided into three major regions: the partial grain-refining, grain-refining, and grain-coarsening regions. The partial grain-refining region was subjected to a peak temperature between the effective lower and upper critical temperatures, Ac_1 and Ac_3. The prior pearlite colonies in this region transformed to austenite (γ) and expanded slightly into the prior ferrite(α) colonies upon heating to above the Ac_1 temperature and then decomposed into very fine grains of pearlite and ferrite during cooling, as illustrated schematically in Figure 3.29. The prior ferrite colonies were essentially unaffected. The grain-refining region was subjected to a peak temperature just above the effective upper critical temperatures, Ac_3, thus allowing austenite grains to nucleate. Such austenite grains decomposed into small pearlite and ferrite grains during subsequent cooling. The distribution of pearlite and ferrite is not exactly uniform This is because insufficient time was allowed for the diffusion of carbon atoms owing to the rapid heating rate during welding, and the austenite phase formed was therefore not uniform in composition. Finally, the grain-coarsening region was subjected to a peak temperature well above the Ac_3 temperature, thus promoting the coarsening of austenite grains. Because of the relatively high cooling rate and the large grain size in this region, acicular, rather than blocky, ferrite formed at grain boundaries. Such a structure is often called the Widmanstatten[*] structure.

Although the HAZ contains both fine and coarse grains, its average grain size is much smaller than the coarse columnar grains of

154   *English in Materials Science and Engineering*

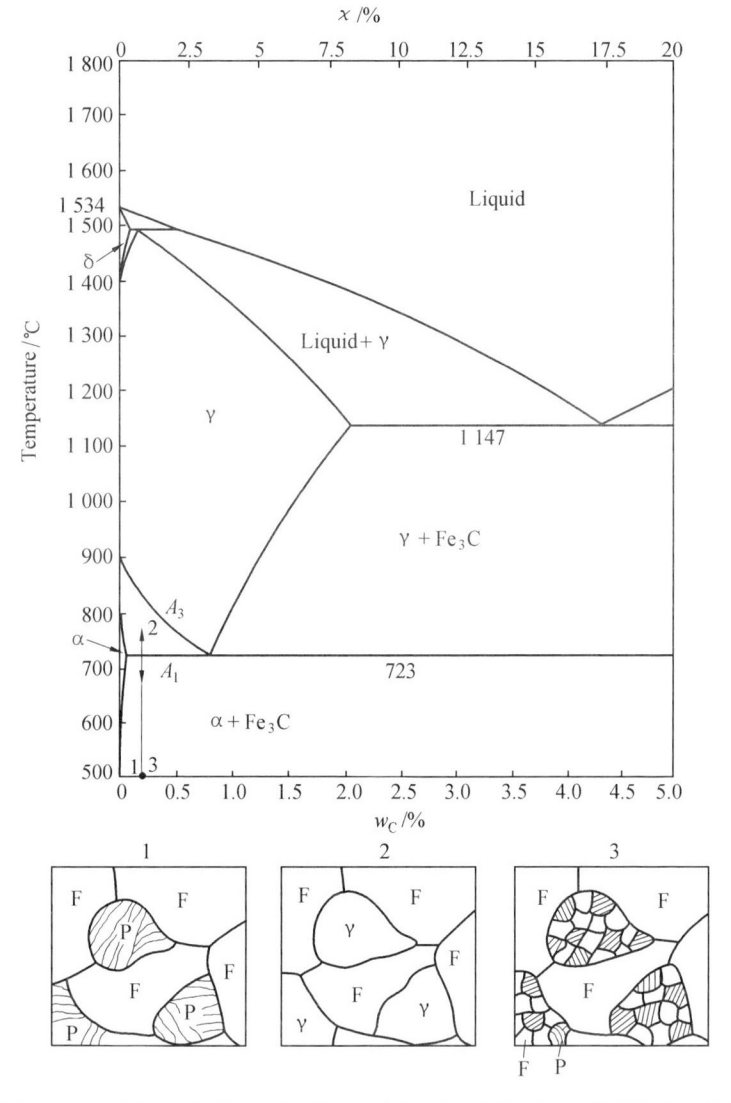

Figure 3.29 Schematic illustration for partial grain refining in the HAZ of a mild steel

the fusion zone. Therefore, if the fusion zone of a weld pass is replaced by the HAZs of its subsequent passes, the fusion zone of this weld pass is "grain-refined". Such grain refining is often desired in the multipass welding of carbon and alloy steels.

The HAZ microstructure mentioned above is expected when normal welding conditions are involved. However, when both the heating and the cooling rates are extremely high, as in the case of laser or electron beam welding, martensite can form in the HAZ of mild steels. The prior-pearlite colonies in the region subjected to a peak temperature just above Ac_1 did not have sufficient time to interact with their neighboring ferrite, and their carbon content consequently remained essentially unchanged. The austenite that formed in these prior-pearlite colonies during heating transformed into martensite during subsequent rapid cooling. The martensite formed is very hard and brittle because of the high carbon content. Further up into the HAZ, both the peak temperature and the diffusion time increased. As a result, the prior-pearlite colonies expanded while being austenized[*] and formed martensite colonies of lower carbon contents during subsequent cooling.

Key words:
Widmanstatten structure [魏氏组织]   austenize [奥氏体化]

Questions:

1) How many regions can the weld HAZ of low-carbon steels be divided into? And what are they?

2) Is Widmanstatten structure harmful? Why?

3.2.3.2 HAZ *of Medium- and High-carbon Steels*

The welding of medium- and high-carbon steels is more difficult than that of mild steels. This is because with higher carbon contents the tendency to form hard, brittle martensite in the weld HAZ is greater, and hence under-bead cracking is more likely to occur. Similar to the case of mild steels, the weld HAZ of a 1040 steel (the nominal carbon content of the steel is 0.40%) weld can be divided into three main

156　*English in Materials Science and Engineering*

regions: the partial grain-refining, the grain-refining, and the grain-coarsening regions. The microstructure in the grain-coarsening region is essentially martensite, with a relatively small amount of bainite* and pearlite present at the grain boundary. A relatively large amount of pearlite and a very small amount of ferrite and bainite are present at the grain boundary in the grain-refining region. The microstructure inside the grains is still essentially martensite.

In the grain-coarsening region, both the high cooling rate and the large grain size promote the formation of martensite. In the grain-refining region, both the lower cooling rate and the smaller grain size encourage the formation of pearlite and ferrite. The hardness profile of the HAZ is shown in Figure 3.30(a). When welded with preheating, the size of HAZ increases, but the maximum hardness decreases, as shown in Figure 3.30(b). Examination of HAZ microstructure near the fusion boundary reveals more pearlite and ferrite but less martensite, apparently because of the lower cooling rate caused by preheating*.

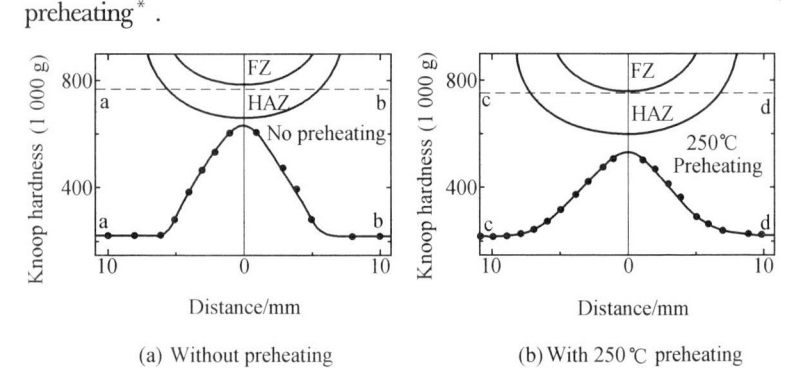

(a) Without preheating　　　　　(b) With 250 ℃ preheating

Figure 3.30 Hardness profile across the HAZ of a 1040 steel

Key words:
bainite [贝氏体]　　　　　preheating [预热]

3.2.3.3 HAZ *of Alloy Steels*

It is not intended here to give a complete discussion on the welding of various types of alloy steels. Instead, only two representative groups of alloy steels—quenched and tempered* alloy steels and heat-treatable alloy steels—are selected for discussion in this section. The welding of these three groups of alloy steels is quite different from that of mild steels and often requires special attention. Rolled and normalized low-alloy steels usually contain less than 0.25% carbon and have a yield strength level of 45 to 70 ksi. Microalloyed steels usually contain less than 0.15% carbon, with the addition of small amounts of Cb, V, Mo, and N as alloying elements. Both of these groups of low-alloy steels usually have good weldability, and the welding of them is similar to that of mild steels, though a higher hardenability is expected.

Quenched and Tempered Alloy Steels

The quenched and tempered alloy steels considered here as a group are those characterized by their high strength, remarkable toughness, and good weldability. Such alloys usually have low carbon contents (typically from 0.10% to 0.25%) and, therefore, are also called quenched and tempered low-carbon alloy steels. These alloys are relatively easy to weld; relatively low or no preheating is needed, and post-weld heat-treating is usually not required.

Low carbon content is desired in such alloys for two reasons—to minimize the hardness of the martensite, and to raise the M_s temperature so that any martensite formed can be tempered automatically during cooling.[1] Because of the formation of low-carbon autotempered* martensite, both high strength and good toughness can be obtained. The hardenability* of such alloys is ensured by alloying with Mn, Cr, Ni, and Mo. The use of Ni also significantly increases the toughness and lowers the ductile-brittle transition temperature in these alloys.

The welding of quenched and tempered alloy steels is described

158   *English in Materials Science and Engineering*

below using T-1 steel as an example. The continuous cooling transformation curves of T-1 steel are shown in Figure 3.31.

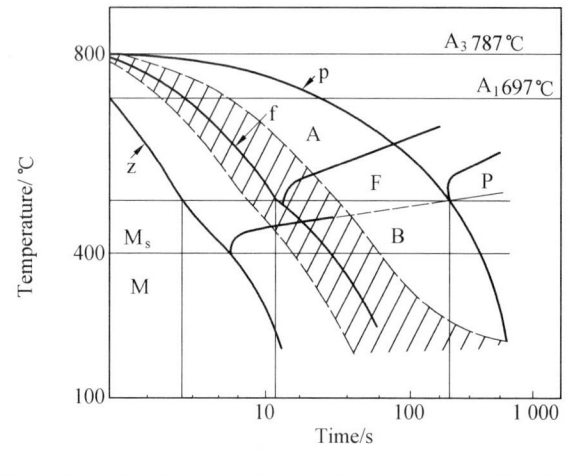

Figure 3.31 Continuous cooling transformation curves for T-1 steel

If the cooling rate during welding is too low, for example, between curve "p" and the hatched* area indicated in the Figure, a substantial amount of ferrite forms. This can in fact be harmful, since the ferrite phase tends to reject carbon atoms and turn its surrounding areas into high-carbon austenite. Such high-carbon austenite can in turn transform to high-carbon martensite and bainite during cooling, thus resulting in brittle weld HAZs. Therefore, the heat input and the preheating of the workpiece should be limited when welding quenched and tempered alloy steels.

On the other hand, if the cooling rate during welding is too fast (to the left of curve "z" in Figure 3.31), insufficient time is available for the autotempering of martensite. This can result in hydrogen cracking, if hydrogen is present. Therefore, low-hydrogen electrodes or welding processes are preferred, and a small amount of preheating is often recommended. The hatched area in Figure 3.31 represents the region of best cooling rates of welding T-1 steel. The amount of preheating needed for a given material increases with increasing plate thickness. This is because for a given heat input the cooling rate is higher in a thicker plate. In addition to the higher cooling rate, a thicker plate often has a slightly higher carbon content to ensure proper hardening during the heat-treating step of the steel making process.

To meet the requirements of both limited heat inputs and proper preheating, multipass welding is often used in welding thick sections of high-strength quenched and tempered alloy steels. In so doing, the interpass temperature is maintained at the same level as the preheat temperature. In fact, multipass welding offers another important advantage—bead tempering. In other words, the martensite in the HAZ of a weld pass is tempered by the heat resulting from deposition in subsequent passes. As a result, the overall toughness of the weld metal is enhanced. Figure 3.32 clearly demonstrates the effect of bead tempering. The HAZ of bead D, unlike that of bead E, was not quite tempered enough by bead F. As a result, the hardness of the HAZ of bead D was significantly higher than that of bead E.

Heat-treatable Alloy Steels

The heat-treatable alloy steels to be discussed here as a group refer to those that must be heat-treated after welding. Such alloys, usually have higher carbon contents (typically from 0.30% to 0.50%) and hence higher strength and lower toughness than the quenched and tempered alloy steels.

Heat-treatable alloy steels are usually welded in annealed* (or normalized) conditions. After welding, the entire weldment is then heat-treated in order to obtain the best combination of properties offered by the steel. For the weld metal to respond to the same postweld heat treatment, the filler metal should be similar to the base metal in composition.

Since high-carbon martensite is hard and brittle, proper preheating and low-hydrogen electrodes should be used to avoid underbead cracking. A convenient way of estimating the amount of preheating required is to use the so-called equivalent carbon content. The equivalent carbon content, or carbon equivalent, is intended among

160   *English in Materials Science and Engineering*

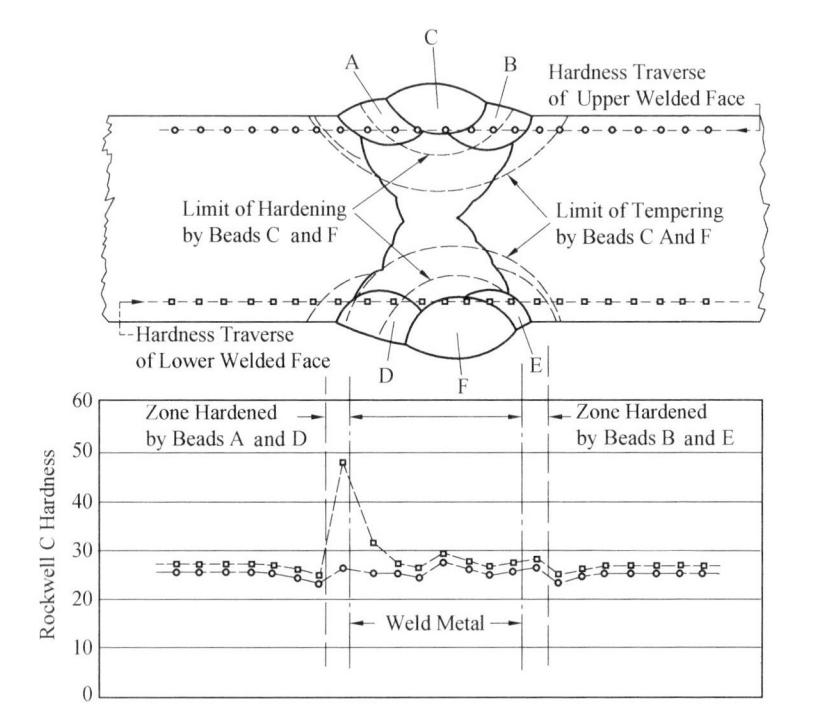

Figure 3.32 Tempering bead technique for multipass welding of a butt joint in a quenched and tempered alloy steel

other purposes to be used as a measure for the hydrogen-cracking sensitivity of a weld. For ordinary C-Mn steels, for example, the following equation for the equivalent carbon content has been used:

$$\text{Equivalent carbon content} = w_C + \frac{1}{4} w_{Mn} + \frac{1}{4} w_{Si}$$

The relationship between this equivalent carbon content and the average underbead cracking (one form of hydrogen cracking) sensitivity of C-Mn steels is shown in Figure 3.33.

A typical formula for determining the equivalent carbon content of a steel containing not more than $w_C = 0.5\%$, $w_{Mn} = 1.5\%$, $w_{Ni} = 3.5\%$, $w_{Cr} = 1\%$, $w_{Mo} = 0.5\%$ is given below:

$$\text{Equivalent carbon content} = w_C + \frac{w_N}{6} + \frac{w_{Ni}}{15} + \frac{w_{Cr}}{5} + \frac{w_{Cu}}{13} + \frac{w_{Mo}}{4}$$

Welding　161

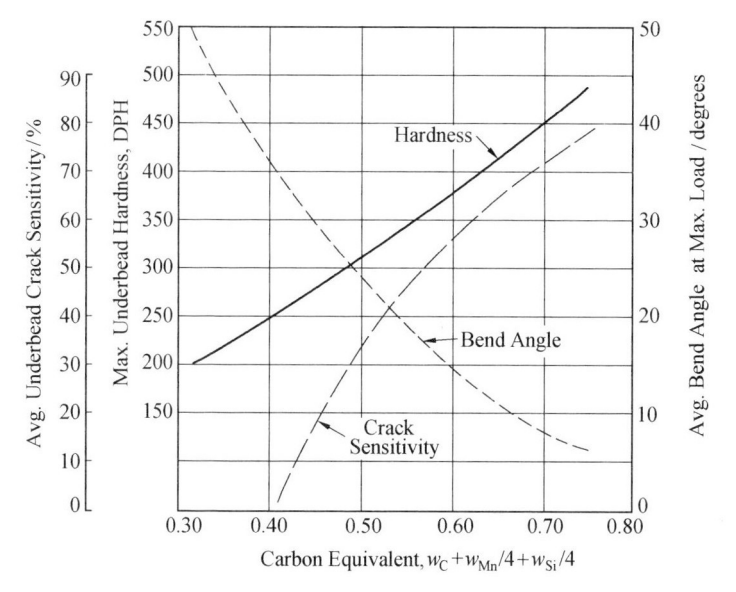

Figure 3. 33 Relationship between carbon equivalent and the underbead hardness, cracking sensitivity, and notch-bend angle for 1-in.-thick plates of C-Mn steels welded with E6010 electrodes

The preheat temperatures suggested for several ranges of the equivalent carbon content are:

Equivalent carbon content	Suggested preheat temperatures
Up to 0.45%	Optional
0.45% to 0.60%	100 to 200℃
Above 0.60%	200 to 350℃

The above suggested preheat temperatures are for arc welding processes. They may be affected by the thickness of the workpiece. For gas welding processes, however, preheating is usually not required owing to the slow cooling rates associated with such welding processes.

In addition to the use of preheating, the weldment of heat-treatable alloy steels is often immediately heated for stress-relief heat

162   *English in Materials Science and Engineering*

treatment, martensite is tempered, and the weldment can therefore be cooled to room temperature without danger of cracking. After this, the weldment can be postweld heat-treated to develop the strength and toughness the steel is capable of attaining. A sketch of the thermal history during welding and postweld stress relieving is shown in Figure 3.34.

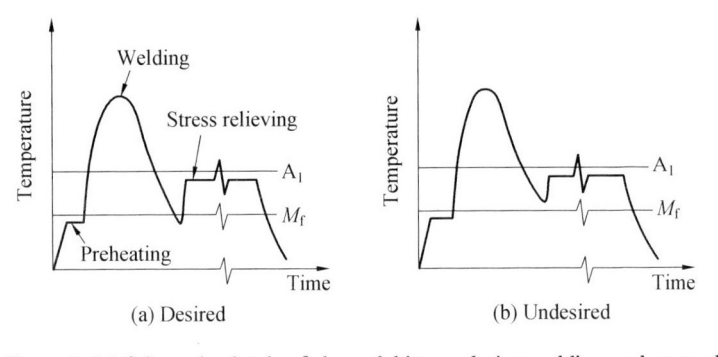

(a) Desired   (b) Undesired

Figure 3.34 Schematic sketch of thermal history during welding and postweld stress relieving of heat-treatable alloy steels

It should be noted that the weld heat-affected zone should be cooled down to a temperature slightly below the martensite-finish temperature M_f before being heated up for stress relieving. This is to prevent any untransformed austenite from decomposing into ferrite and pearlite during stress relieving to transforming to untempered martensite upon cooling to room temperature after stress relieving.

In cases where heat-treatable alloy steels cannot be postweld heat-treated and must be welded in heat-treated conditions, the softening, as well as the hydrogen cracking, of the HAZ can be a serious problem, as shown in Figure 3.35. To minimize the softening problem, lower heat input per unit length of weld should be employed, and the preheat, interpass, and stress-relief temperatures should be at least 50°C lower than the tempering temperature of the base metal before welding. Since postweld heat-treating of the weldment is not involved, the composition of the filler metal can be substantially different from that of the base metal, depending on the strength level of the weld metal required.

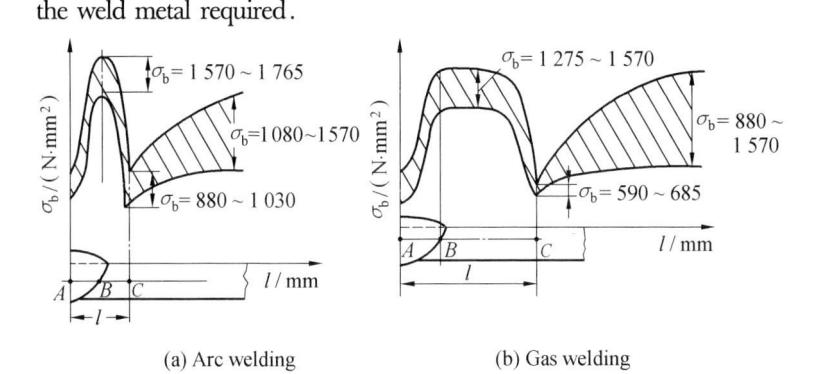

(a) Arc welding   (b) Gas welding

Figure 3.35 Variations in strength in the HAZ of 30CrMnSi steel

Key words:
temper［回火］   autotemper［自回火］   hardenability［淬透性］
hatch［画阴影线于］   anneal［退火］

Note:

［1］由于两方面的原因希望这些低合金钢中的含碳量低:第一,减小马氏体的硬度;第二,提高 M_s 点温度,使得形成的马氏体在冷却过程中能发生自回火。

Questions:

1) Why should the carbon content in quenched and tempered alloy steels be low?

2) Why should the cooling rate during welding of quenched and tempered alloy steels be neither too fast nor too low?

3) What can the carbon equivalent be used for?

3.2.3.4 *Hydrogen Cracking*

Hydrogen cracking occurs when the following four factors are present simultaneously: hydrogen in the weld metal, high stresses, susceptible microstructure (such as martensite), and relatively low temperature (between 200 and $-100℃$). High stresses can be induced by the heat input and constraints during welding. Martensite, especially hard and brittle high-carbon martensite, is susceptible to

164　*English in Materials Science and Engineering*

hydrogen cracking. Since the martensite formation temperature, M_s, is relatively low, hydrogen cracking tends to occur at relatively low temperatures. For this reason, it is often referred to as "cold cracking". It is also referred to as "delayed cracking*", owing to the incubation* time required for cracking development in some cases.

Figure 3.36 illustrates the diffusion of hydrogen from the weld metal to the HAZ during welding. As shown, the weld metal, being usually lower in carbon content than the base metal, transforms from austenite (γ) into ferrite and pearlite (α + Fe_3C) before the HAZ transforms from austenite into martensite (M). Because of the lower solubility of hydrogen in α-ferrite than in austenite, hydrogen is rejected into the α-ferrite near the γ/α + Fe_3C boundary of the weld metal. Because of the build up of hydrogen in the α-ferrite, it tends to diffuse into the HAZ austenite near the fusion boundary, as indicated by the short arrows in the Figure. This diffusion process is encouraged by the high diffusion coefficient of hydrogen in α-ferrite. On the contrary, because of the much lower diffusion coefficient of hydrogen in austenite, the hydrogen in this area does not have a chance to diffuse away (to the base metal) before the austenite/martensite transformation occurs, thus promoting hydrogen cracking.

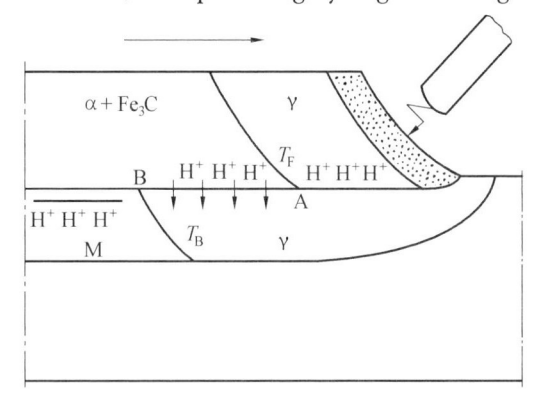

Figure 3.36 Diffusion of hydrogen from the weld metal to the HAZ during welding

Welding 165

There are various methods for testing the hydrogen cracking susceptibility of steels, such as the implant test. Figure 3.37 shows the schematic sketch of the implant test. In this test, a cylindrical specimen is notched and inserted in a hole in a plate made from similar material. A weld run is made over the specimen, which is located such that its top becomes part of the fusion zone and the notch lies in the HAZ. After welding and before the weld is cold, a load is applied to the specimen, and the time to failure is determined. A plot of stress against time to failure gives an assessment of hydrogen-cracking susceptibility.

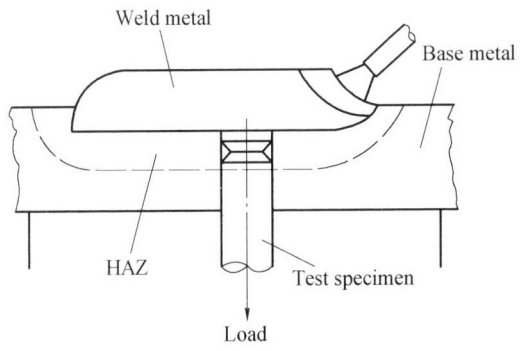

Figure 3.37 Schematic sketch of the implant test[*] for hydrogen cracking

Hydrogen cracking can be reduced in the following two ways.

◆ Control of Welding Parameters

Preheating

The use of the proper preheating and interpass temperature can help reduce hydrogen cracking. In general, the greater the equivalent carbon content and thickness of the workpiece, the higher the preheat and interpass temperatures required.

Postheating

Postweld heat treatment can be used to stress-relieve the weld before it cools to room temperature. In the event that stress-relief heat treatment cannot be carried out immediately upon completion of welding, the completed weldment can be held at a proper temperature to allow austenite to transform into a less susceptible microstructure

166   *English in Materials Science and Engineering*

than martensite. Of course, postweld heating alone can also help hydrogen diffuse out of the workpiece.

Bead Tempering

Bead tempering in multipass welding can also be effective in reducing hydrogen cracking.

◆ Use of proper welding processes and materials

Use of Low-hydrogen Processes And Consumables

The amount of hydrogen present in the welding zone can be minimized by avoiding high-hydrogen welding processes (such as gas welding processes) or materials that tend to produce hydrogen during welding (such as cellulose* -type electrode coverings, and fluxes or electrode coverings containing moisture).

Use of Lower-strength Filler Metals

The use of filler metals of lower strength than the base metal can help reduce the stress levels in the HAZ and, hence, the chance of hydrogen cracking.

Use of Austenitic Stainless-steel Filler Metals

Austenitic stainless steels have been used as the filler metal for welding heat-treatable alloy steels as well as other steels in which cracking induced by hydrogen is of concern. Austenite (γ) can absorb about 6-10 ml hydrogen per 100 g, which is significantly higher than what can be absorbed by ferrite (α). Therefore, the amount of hydrogen evolved from normal dry basic-coated electrodes, which is about 4 to 8 ml/100 g, can be readily dissolved in the weld metal. As a result, susceptibility of hydrogen cracking can be reduced. Furthermore, the good ductility of austenitic stainless-steel weld metal tends to prevent the buildup of excessively high residual stresses in the HAZ. This also helps reduce the susceptibility of hydrogen cracking. Of course, the composition of the austenitic stainless steel used should be properly chosen to avoid weld metal solidification cracking. Also, the difference between the thermal expansion coefficient of the austenitic stainless-steel weld metal and that of the base metal should also be considered, if high-temperature applications of the weldment are

Welding 167

expected.

    Key words:
    delayed cracking [延迟裂纹]   incubation [酝酿,潜伏]
    implant test [插销试验]   cellulose [纤维素]

Questions:

1) What are the factors that promote cold cracking?

2) Why can austenitic stainless-steel electrodes be used to weld heat-treatable alloy steels?

3.3 Some New Developments in Welding

3.3.1 Fusion Welding

3.3.1.1 *Tandem* MIG/MAG *Welding**

In the tandem MIG/MAG process, shown in Figure 3.38, two wires are fed into a single molten pool through the same torch, but they are electrically isolated from each other and connected to two separate power sources.

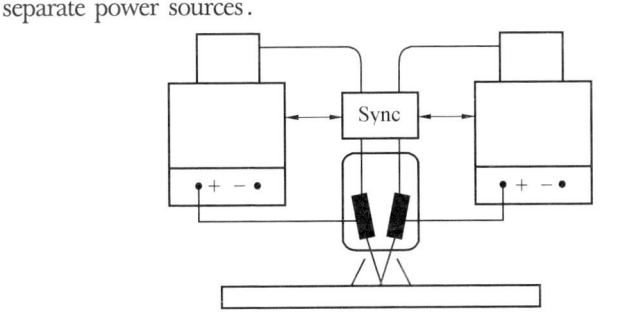

Figure 3.38 Tandem MIG/MAG welding

The main advantages of the process are claimed to be increased welding speed, deposition rate and penetration, reduced porosity and better tolerance to variations in fit-up* compared with conventional single wire MIG/MAG welding.[1] Travel speeds and deposition rates are typically 2 ~ 3 times higher than for conventional single wire MIG/MAG welding.

168 *English in Materials Science and Engineering*

A butt joint of 10 mm thick plate was completed in two passes, as shown in Figure 3.39. The same preparation required five single wire passes to fill in this work, shown in Figure 3.40.

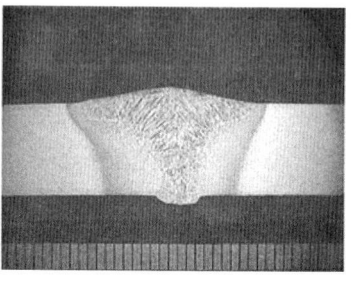 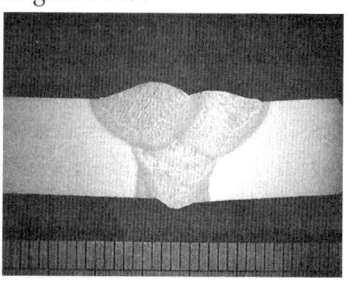

Figure 3.39 A 2-pass tandem wire 10 mm butt weld

Figure 3.40 A 5-pass single wire 10 mm butt weld

The process has been chiefly applied to steels, and some aluminum alloys with thickness in the range 1.5 to 25 mm for steel, and 2 to 6 mm for aluminum.

Key words:
tandem MIG/MAG welding [双丝熔化极惰性/活性气体保护焊]
fit-up [装配]
Note:
[1] 和传统的单丝 MIG/MAG 焊相比,该工艺的主要优点有:焊接速度高、熔敷效率高、熔深大、气孔少、对装配间隙变化的适应性强。

3.3.1.2 *Magnetically Impelled Arc Fusion* (MIAF) *Welding**

Magnetically impelled arc fusion (MIAF) welding, shown in Figure 3.41, is a variation on MIAB (magnetically impelled arc butt welding) which is widely used to join steel pipes and tubes. In MIAB, an arc is struck between the two components to be joined. MIAF uses a non-consumable electrode as an arc initiator.

Figure 3.42(a) and 3.42(b) show a MIAF set-up for edge-welding the periphery of a flat, circular component.

Welding 169

Figure 3.41 Magnetically impelled arc fusion welding

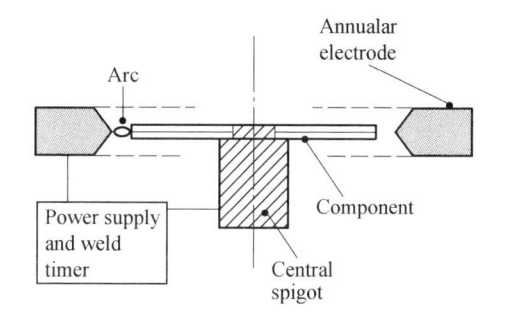

(a) Cross-sectional view

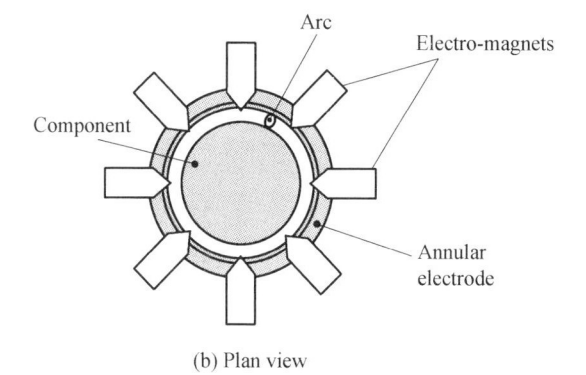

(b) Plan view

Figure 3.42 MIAF welding set-up

170　*English in Materials Science and Engineering*

The component to be welded is located on a central spigot* that is connected to a pulsed arc welding power supply, similar to that used for micro-TIG welding. The annular electrode* completes the electrical circuit.

When the power supply is activated, an arc is struck between a point on the annular electrode and the edge of the component. The arc is then propelled around the annular electrode by a series of electromagnets which are switched on and off in a high-speed sequence.[1]

Rotation of the arc continues for a pre-set period until the edge of the component is fusion welded. No additional filler material is used.

Pressure or temperature (as used in thermostatic heating controls) transducer bellows* are typical applications of MIAF welding. Formed (dished) washers* have been edge welded to form a compressible assembly for pressure measurement. The capping of tubes is also feasible.

Candidate applications need to incorporate a defined point for the arc to target, otherwise arc wander can cause melting adjacent to the joint line.

> Key words:
> magnetically impelled arc fusion (MIAF) welding [磁驱动电弧焊]
> spigot [插头,塞子]　　　　annular electrode [环形电极]
> bellow [波纹管]　　　　　washer [垫圈]
> Note:
> [1] 电弧在一系列高速通断的电磁铁的驱动下绕环形电极旋转。

Question:

1) What is the relationship and difference between MIAF welding and MIAB welding?

3.3.1.3 *A-TIG Welding**

Activating fluxes to improve the performance of the TIG process were first reported by the Paton Welding Institute (PWI), Ukraine, in the 1960's. More recently, the Navy Joining Center (NJC)/Edison Welding Institute (EWI), US, has developed an alternative range of fluxes. The principle of the technique is that by applying a thin coating of the flux to the surface of the material, the arc is constricted which increases the current density at the anode root and the arc force acting on the weld pool.[1] The characteristic appearance of the constricted arc compared with the more diffused conventional TIG arc is shown in Figure 3.43. As demonstrated in welding 6mm thick stainless steel, arc constriction significantly increases weld pool penetration producing a deep narrower weld compared with a wide, shallow weld bead with the conventional TIG process.

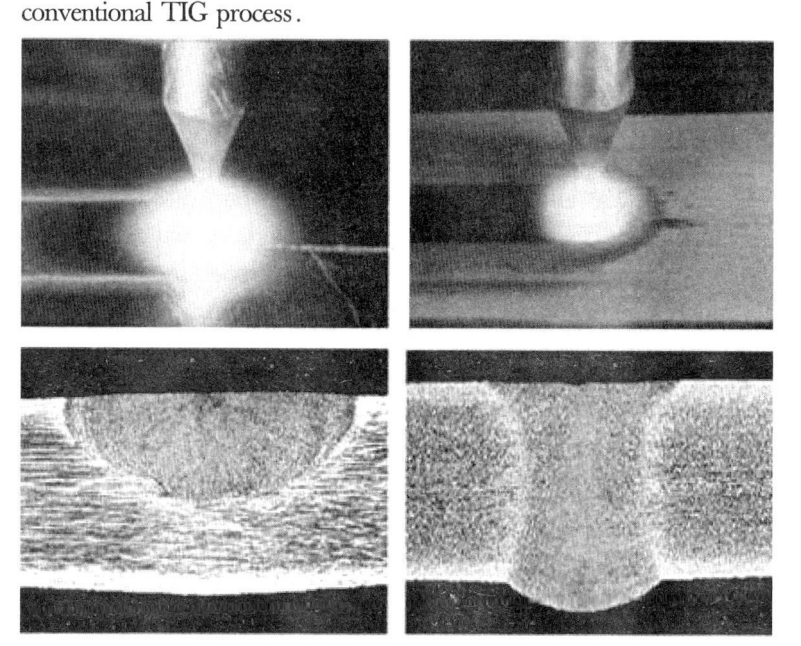

Figure 3.43 A-TIG process compared with conventional TIG process

Activating fluxes* have led to a dramatic improvement in the operating characteristics of the TIG process notably a greater depth of penetration, higher welding speed and a reduction in the sensitivity to cast to cast material variation.

The activating flux process can be applied in both manual and mechanized welding operations. However, because of the need to maintain a short arc length to achieve deep penetration, it is more often applied in mechanized applications.

Specific advantages claimed for the activating flux process, compared with the conventional TIG process, include:

(1) Increases depth of penetration e. g. up to 12mm thick stainless steel can be welded in a single pass compared with typically 3mm with conventional TIG.

(2) Overcomes the problem of cast to cast variation e. g. deep penetration welds can be produced in low sulphur (less than 0.002%) content stainless steels which would normally form a wide and shallow weld bead with conventional TIG.

(3) Reduces weld shrinkage and distortion e. g. the deep narrow weld in a square edge closed butt joint will produce less distortion than a multi-pass weld in the same thickness material but with a V-joint.

The claims for a substantial increase in productivity are derived from the reduction in the welding time either through the reduction in the number of passes or the increase in welding speed.

Disadvantages of using a flux include the rougher surface appearance of the weld bead and the need to clean the weld after welding. In mechanized welding operations, the as-welded surface is significantly less smooth than is normally produced with the conventional TIG process but in manual welding operations, the surface roughness is similar. On welding, there is a light slag residue on the surface of the weld that often requires rigorous wire brushing to remove.

Key words:
A-TIG welding [活性 TIG 焊]   activating flux [活性剂]
as-welded surface [焊后未经处理的表面]

Note:

[1] 该技术的原理是,在材料表面涂上一薄层活性剂,电弧会受到压缩,从而提高了阳极区电流密度和作用在熔池上的电弧力的大小。

Question:

What are the main advantages of A-TIG welding?

3.3.1.4 *Electron Beam Welding*

◆ Improvement of the Electron Beam Gun

Directly heated triode* guns can be prone to give various problems such as short filament life, beam voltage and current ripple*, poor beam reproducibility and a tendency to gun discharge, particularly when welding light alloys.[1] In the mid 1980s it was recognized that there was a requirement for an indirectly heated diode* gun, and Sanderson et al reassessed both the gun and power source approach and designed a unique indirectly heated gun and switch mode power source without the need for conventional auxiliary* power supplies, thus simplifying the system and overcoming the problems noted above.

The heart of the development is the use of RF excitation in the gun cartridge* (typically 84MHz). A single turn winding collects the RF power and produces a high current in a ribbon filament. Electrons are drawn from the filament every half cycle producing a beam that then heats the main cathode. This is shown in Figure 3.44(a). The gun is shown in Figure 3.44(b).

◆ Reduced Pressure Electron Beam Welding (RPEBW)

Out of vacuum EB welding is a well-recognized technology and has been employed widely in the automotive sector for thin component manufacture in the USA for several decades. In 1992, TWI demonstrated that very narrow satisfactory electron beams, shown in Figure 3.45, could be produced at 5 mbar, and that it was difficult to distinguish welds made in this pressure regime from those produced at 5×10^{-3} mbar. Welds in C-Mn steel of 100 mm thickness were soon being made reliably at pressures of ~ 1 mbar.

These achievements were made possible by the development of a 200kV, 100kW EB system which could operate over the pressure range 1000 mbar to 0.01 mbar, using differentially pumped stages in the beam transfer column. At the extremity of the gun column, an over-pressure stage was added through which Helium was bled, which

174   *English in Materials Science and Engineering*

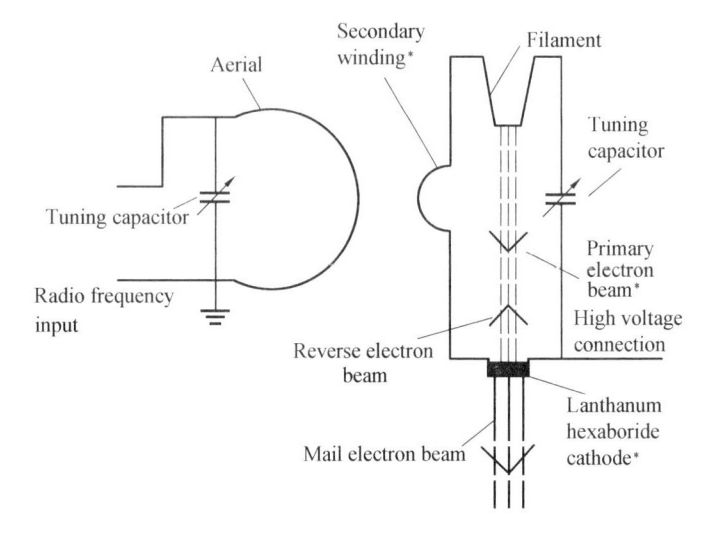

(a) Circuit diagram and principles of operation of an RF excited filament and indirectly heated cathode

(b) RF excited 150kV, 100kW in-chamber mobile gun—covers removed

Figure 3.44 RF excited electron beam welding system

helped to minimize beam scattering and reduced the risk of metal vapour entering the gun housing, held typically at 10^{-6} mbar.

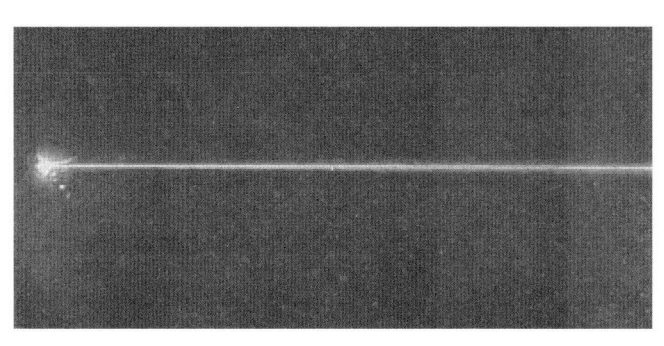

Figure 3.45 200kV, 300mA electron beam in helium atmosphere at 5mbar pressure

It was quickly seen that this development could do away with large vacuum chambers and the worry of leaks and seals. With the new system, pressures of ~ 1 mbar could be achieved with simple mechanical pumps and crude local seals. It was also shown that the system was very tolerant to fluctuations in working vacuum pressure, gun to work distance and workpiece cleanliness. These advantages led to the development of systems for two large scale applications (i) the use of RPEBW for steel pipeline girth welds*, and (ii) the use of RPEBW for sealing of copper canisters* to contain high level nuclear waste.

◆ Non Vacuum Electron Beam Welding (NVEBW)

In non vacuum electron beam welding, the electron beam was generated in a high vacuum envelope, as usual, but emerged from the gun column via a series of differentially pumped vacuum stages separated by small diameter orifices*[2]. This allowed the system to be used for welding at atmospheric pressure, thereby eliminating the need for a vacuum chamber.

It has been reported that NVEB welding was identified in a comparative study to be the optimum method for manufacture of a structural beam in 2.5 mm thick AlMg₃ aluminum alloy, shown in Figure 3.46, for the VW/Audi group and has since been adopted for production. The process is used to produce edge welds at a welding speed of 12m/min.

176   *English in Materials Science and Engineering*

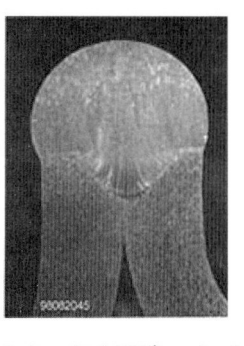

Figure 3.46 Macro section of NVEB weld (12 m/min, 19.3 kW) at the flange of 2 × 2.5 mm AlMg₃ deep-drawn shells

The parts require two welds of 1359mm in length and in excess of 2 000 parts per day are required making a high productivity welding process essential. The system illustrated in Figure 3.47 has been engineered to permit production of two fully welded parts every 65 seconds.

Figure 3.47 The production NVEB welding machine for structural beam production

The welding time in the production sequence is 7 seconds per seam. The high welding speed is made possible by the high power output available from the electron beam generator (19.3 kW). Current research at TWI is examining the performance of an NVEB welding system with a maximum power of 150 kW which, it is hoped

Welding　177

would extend the performance capability of this welding method further.

Key words:

triode [三极管]
diode [二极管]
cartridge [管壳]
secondary winding [次级线圈]
lanthanum hexaboride [六硼化镧]
canister [罐]

ripple [波动]
auxiliary [辅助的]
aerial [天线]
mail electron beam [主电子束]
girth weld [环形焊缝]
orifice [孔]

Notes:

[1] 直接加热的三极管电子枪存在灯丝寿命短、电子束电压和电流波动、电子束重现性差、电子枪放电等问题,特别是在焊接轻合金时。

[2] 在非真空电子束焊接中,电子束和通常情况下一样,还是在高真空室中产生的,但它通过一系列有压差的真空室从电子枪中穿出,这些真空室中间由小直径孔道分隔。

Questions:

1) What is advantage of RPEBW?

2) In NVEBW, the electron beam is generated in vacuum. (T/F)

3.3.1.5 *Laser Welding*

◆ Clearweld®

An extension of the transmission* laser welding process allows completely clear or similarly coloured components to be welded by using an infrared* absorbing medium, clear in the visible range of the spectrum, but tailored to absorb heavily the specific wavelength of the laser beam being used.[1]

The nature of the infrared absorbers, means that it is possible to tailor the absorber to the wavelength of light being used to absorb energy efficiently. Thus only relatively small amounts of absorber at the interface between the two components to be welded are required. The absorber can be introduced as a discrete layer at the interface (in a film, as a coating, or in an absorber rich surface layer of the component), or incorporated into the bulk of the polymer of the

178　*English in Materials Science and Engineering*

underlying component. Development work on this process, which has the trademark Clearweld®, at TWI, was mainly carried out using polymethylmethacrylate* (PMMA) test specimens. An example of an overlap weld made by applying a painted layer of absorber to the joint region between two transparent sheets of 3mm thick PMMA can be seen in Figure 3.48.

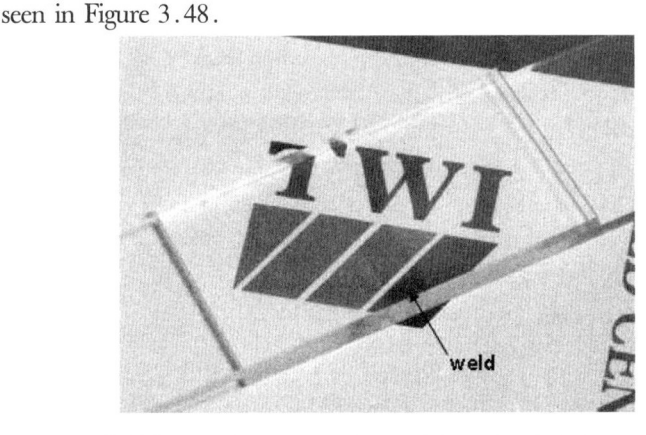

Figure 3. 48 Transmission laser overlap weld in clear PMMA made with an infrared impregnated film interlayer

One of the obvious advantages of this technique is that almost any colour of plastic material can be used on either side of the joint.

◆ Hybrid Laser-arc Welding*

Hybrid laser-arc welding refers to the coupling of the two welding processes into a single process area or weld pool, as depicted in Figure 3.49. Figure 3.50 is a laboratory demonstration of hybrid Nd:YAG laser/GMA welding for pipelines. The options available include combining either CO_2 or Nd:YAG laser welding with an arc welding process such as gas metal arc welding, gas tungsten arc welding or plasma arc welding.

Welding 179

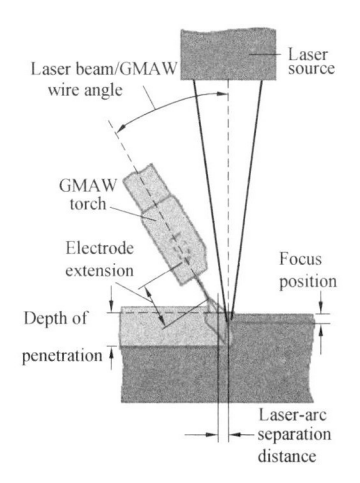

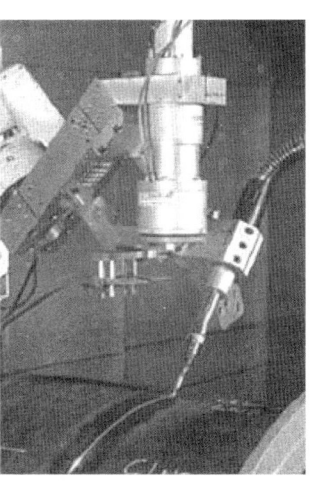

Figure 3.49 Hybrid laser-arc welding

Figure 3.50 Laboratory demonstration of hybrid Nd: YAG laser/GMA welding for pipelines

Compared with the use of laser power alone, hybrid laser-arc welding offers the following benefits:

⊙ increased travel speed or penetration

⊙ improved tolerance to fit-up gap

⊙ ability to add filler material to improve weld metal microstructure, joint quality and properties

⊙ potentially improved energy coupling

⊙ increased heat input, and reduced hardness

There are, however, some drawbacks which include increased process complexity ("more things to go wrong"); additional welding parameters to be defined; and the requirement to define the process parameters anew* as these cannot simply be determined from the two separate processes.[2]

◆ Direct Metal Deposition (DMD)

Metal may be melted onto a surface to build 3D shapes or as a method of surfacing. If a laser is used to do this, the process is termed Direct Metal Deposition or DMD. Figure 3.51 shows DMD in action.

180   *English in Materials Science and Engineering*

Figure 3.51 DMD in action

There is currently considerable interest in DMD for repair and prototyping applications. The process provides rapid, accurate placement of material at low heat input allowing the use of crack-sensitive alloys such as nickel-based alloys of particular interest to gas turbine manufacturers and repairers.

The benefits of DMD include minimal post-process machining, negligible distortion and significant cost saving on high cost repairs.

The first laser Direct Metal Deposition system of its kind in the UK is housed in a unique facility at TWI Yorkshire in Sheffield, shown in Figure 3.52. The system comprises a 2kW CO_2 laser and a patented deposition nozzle attached to a 5-axis gantry[*], controlled by 3D CAD software. Powder is melted onto a substrate using the laser and nozzle, allowing material to be built up in a controlled and accurate manner. Lasers are used because of their accuracy and low heat input allowing fully dense, defect free deposits to be made. The equipment is capable of carrying out a number of operations, such as cladding, but will perform two main functions at TWI Yorkshire; repair and original part build. Figure 3.53 and Figure 3.54 show the thick and thin DMD parts, respectively.

Welding   181

Figure 3.52 DMD505 Laser deposition system installed at TWI Sheffield

Figure 3.53 Thick DMD deposit

Figure 3.54 Thin DMD deposit

182　*English in Materials Science and Engineering*

Key words:
transmission [透射]　　　　infrared [红外的]
polymethylmethacrylate [聚甲基丙烯酸甲酯,有机玻璃]
hybrid laser-arc welding [激光 – 电弧复合焊接]
anew [重新]　　　　　　gantry [台架]
Notes:

[1] 透射激光焊接工艺的一种扩展技术,利用红外吸收介质,可以对全透明的或相同颜色的部件进行焊接,这种红外吸收介质在可见光谱范围是全透明的,但对所采用激光的特定波长有很高的吸收率。

[2] 但是,存在一些缺点,包括工艺复杂性提高("出问题的东西更多")、要确定额外的焊接参数,以及要重新确定工艺参数,因为这些工艺参数无法从两个单独的工艺中确定。

Questions:

[1] What does Clearweld(r) mean?

[2] What are the advantages of hybrid laser – arc welding?

[3] What are the benefits of DMD?

3.3.2 Welding with Pressure

3.3.2.1 *Conductive Heat Resistance Seam Welding* (CHRSEW)

Conductive heat resistance seam welding (CHRSEW), shown in Figure 3.55, was developed at the Edison Welding Institute (EWI). This process takes advantage of a range of physical phenomena in aluminum and steel using conventional resistance seam welding equipment.

In CHRSEW, aluminum sheets to be joined are positioned in a butt configuration. Then, steel cover sheets are placed on the top and bottom surfaces of the joint, and conventional resistance seam welding is applied along the joint at the end of the process, the cover sheets are removed revealing the completed joint.[1] The resulting full-penetration welds consist of overlapping fusion zones originating from the top and bottom cover sheets. Cover sheets also shield the aluminum from the environment eliminating the need for shielding gases, which often are required for arc welding processes.

CHRSEW offers the potential to create continuous, autogeneous, leak-tight welds at very high speeds (up to 4 meters per minute), without any external shielding on a range of aluminum alloys. Because it is accomplished with conventional resistance seam welding equipment, the process could be used in many manufacturing environments, including:

⊙ Coil joining for continuous processes

⊙ Tailor-welded blank applications

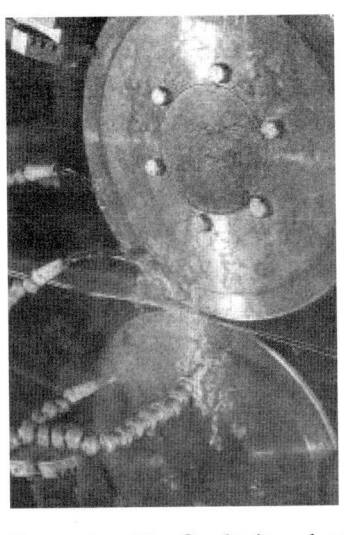

Figure 3. 55 Conductive heat resistance seam welding

⊙ Aluminum container vessels

⊙ Aluminum wheel rims

The basic characteristics of melting under high hydrostatic forces allow high-speed CHRSEW of a range applications not widely considered joinable. One area in which considerable success has been achieved is joining alloys that are sensitive to weld cracking, such as 7075, 6061, and 2219. These metals typically are susceptible to liquation-related weld cracking particularly when welded without filler metals. However, they readily can be joined with CHRSEW.

Key words:
conductive heat resistance seam welding (CHRSEW)［导热电阻缝焊］
Edison welding Institute(EWI)［爱迪生焊接研究所］

Note:
［1］然后,在接头的上下表面盖上钢片,对接头进行传统的电阻缝焊,最后,将钢片去除,即获得完整的接头。

184 *English in Materials Science and Engineering*

3.3.2.2 *Diffusion Bonding*

Diffusion bonding is a solid-state joining process capable of joining a wide range of metal and ceramic combinations to produce both small and large components. The process is dependent on a number of parameters, in particular, time, applied pressure, bonding temperature and method of heat application.

Diffusion bonding itself can be categorized into a number of variants, dependent on the form of pressurization, the use of interlayers and the formation of a transient liquid phase. Each finds specific application for the range of materials and geometries that need to be joined.

In its simplest form, diffusion bonding involves holding pre-machined components under load at an elevated temperature usually in a protective atmosphere or vacuum. The loads used are usually below those which would cause macrodeformation of the parent material(s)* and temperatures of $0.5 \sim 0.8 T_m$ (where $T_m =$ melting point in K) are employed. Times at temperature can range from 1 to 60 minutes, but this depends upon the materials being bonded, the joint properties required and the remaining bonding parameters. Although the majority of bonding operations are performed in vacuum or an inert gas atmosphere, certain bonds can be produced in air.

◆ Solid Phase Diffusion Bonding

Bonding in the solid phase is mainly carried out in vacuum or a protective atmosphere, with heat being applied by radiation, induction, direct or indirect resistance heating. Pressure can be applied uniaxially or isostatically. In the former case, a low pressure ($3 \sim 10$ MPa) is used to prevent macrodeformation of the part (i.e. no more than a few percent). This form of the process therefore requires a good surface finish on the mating surfaces as the contribution to bonding provided by plastic yielding is restricted. Typically surface finishes* of better than $0.4~\mu m~Ra$ are recommended and in addition the surfaces should be as clean as practical to minimize surface contamination.

In hot isostatic pressing, much higher pressures are possible (100 ~ 200 MPa) and therefore surface finishes are not so critical, finishes of 0.8 μm *Ra* and greater can be used. A further advantage of this process is that the use of uniform gas pressurization allows complex geometries to be bonded, as against the generally simple butt or lap joints possible with uniaxial pressurization.

Where dissimilar materials need to be joined in the solid phase (and in particular metal to ceramic joints), it is possible to introduce single or multiple interlayers of other materials to aid the bonding process and to modify post-bond stress distribution.[1]

◆ Liquid Phase Diffusion Bonding/Diffusion Brazing

This technique is applicable only to dissimilar material combinations or to "like" materials where a dissimilar metal insert is used. Solid state diffusional processes lead to a change of composition at the bond interface and the bonding temperature is selected as the temperature at which this phase melts.

Alternatively, with the dissimilar metal insert, it melts at a lower temperature than the parent material. Thus a thin layer of liquid spreads along the interface to form a joint at a lower temperature than the melting point of either of the parent materials. A reduction in bonding temperature leads to solidification of the melt, and this phase can subsequently be diffused away into the parent materials by holding at temperature, shown in Figure 3.56.

The technique has been used particularly for the bonding of aluminum alloys where eutectics can be formed with copper, silver or zinc to assist in the break-up of the stable aluminum surface oxide.

◆ Superplastic Forming/Diffusion Bonding

This technique has been developed specifically within the aerospace industry, and its industrial importance is such that it should be considered separately here. The process is used commercially for titanium and its alloys, this material being one that exhibits superplastic properties at elevated temperatures within defined strain rate conditions. These conditions of temperature and pressure coincide with

186　*English in Materials Science and Engineering*

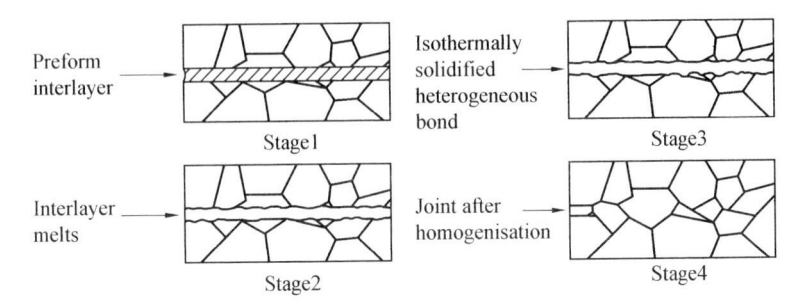

Figure 3.56 Schematic illustration of the steps involved in making a diffusion-brazed joint

the conditions required for bonding, and therefore the two processes have been combined into one manufacturing operation either in sequence or together. The process (known as SPF/DB or more correctly DB/SPF) is used to produce stiff sandwich structures for airframe parts, or the wide chord, hollow fan blades for aeroengines. Both these involve skins with internally bonded structures as reinforcing elements.

　　Key words:
　　parent material [母材]　　　　　　surface finish [表面光洁度]
　　Note:
　　[1] 当需要对异种材料进行固态连接时(特别是连接金属和陶瓷时),可以加入其他材料的单层或多层中间层,以帮助连接过程的进行,并改变焊后的应力分布。

Question:

　　What is the difference between solid phase diffusion bonding and liquid phase diffusion bonding?

3.3.2.3 *Friction Pulse Bonding* (FPB) *

　　Friction pulse bonding (FPB), shown in Figure 3.57, is a process that uses the principles of friction welding to produce a seam weld in thin plate (< 2mm thick). A non-consumable wheel (made from hardened steel) is rotated at high speed and brought into contact with the components to be joined. The heat generated by friction and by a secondary ultrasonic pulsing effect combine to cause material movement and diffusion at the interface. The FPB process can produce lap seam welds in a variety of materials.

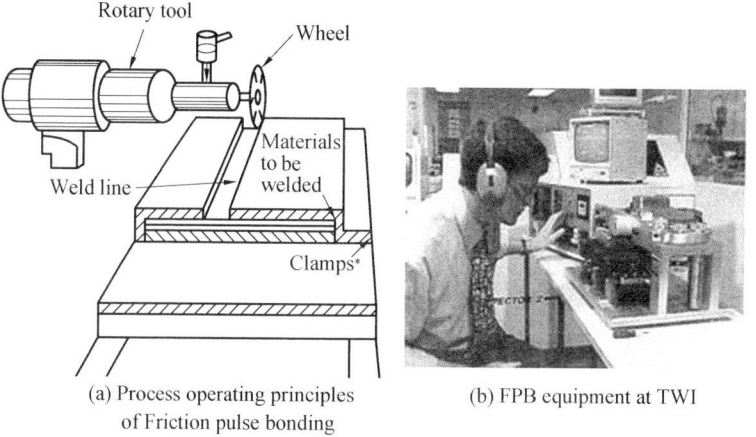

(a) Process operating principles
of Friction pulse bonding

(b) FPB equipment at TWI

Figure 3.57 Friction pulse bonding

Key words:
friction pulse bonding (FPB) [脉冲摩擦焊]   clamp [卡具]

3.3.2.4 Friction Stir Welding (FSW)*

Friction stir welding (FSW), shown in Figure 3.58, is invented and developed at TWI. FSW is a technique which allows aluminum, lead, magnesium, steel and copper to be welded, continuously, with a non-consumable tool*. The technique brings the benefits of solid-phase friction welding to certain materials regarded as difficult to weld by fusion processes.

◆ Tool Design

Early on in the development of FSW it was realized that the detailed form of the welding tool was critical in achieving sound* welds with good mechanical properties. Some of the most recent developments at TWI are those of the Whorl™, shown in Figure 3.59, and MX Triflute™ tools, shown in Figure 3.60. In general terms, the tool comprises a shoulder and a probe. The shoulder

188　*English in Materials Science and Engineering*

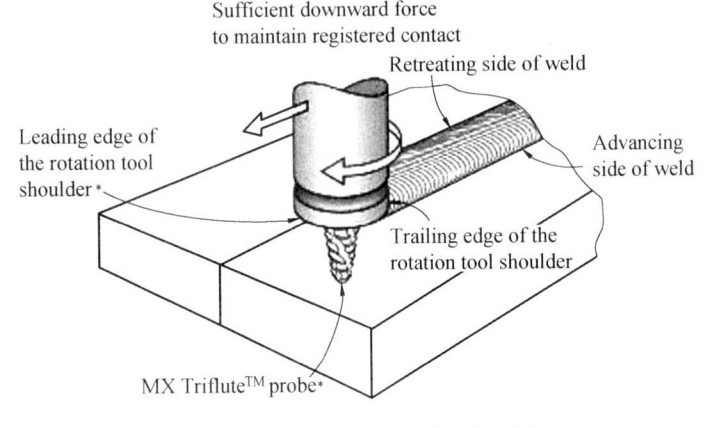

Figure 3.58 Friction stir welding (FSW)

compresses the surface of the workpiece and contains the elasticized weld region. Heat is generated on the surface by friction between the rotating shoulder and the workpiece surface and, when welding comparatively thin sheets, this is the main source of heat. However, as the workpiece thickness increases, more heat must be supplied by friction between the rotating probe and the workpiece. In addition to this, the main functions of the probe are to ensure sufficient working of the material at the weld line and to control the flow of the material around the tool to form a satisfactory weld.[1]

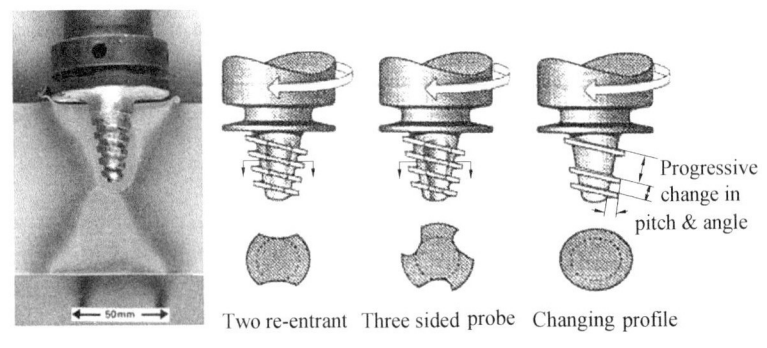

Figure 3.59 Whorl[TM]

Welding 189

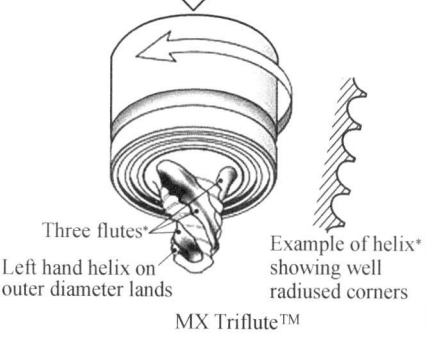

Three flutes*

Left hand helix on outer diameter lands

Example of helix* showing well radiused corners

MX Triflute™

Figure 3.60 MX Triflute™

◆ Materials

Friction stir welding can be used for joining many types of materials and material combinations, as shown in Figures 3.61, 3.62 and 3.63, if tool materials and designs can be found which operate at the forging temperature of the workpieces.

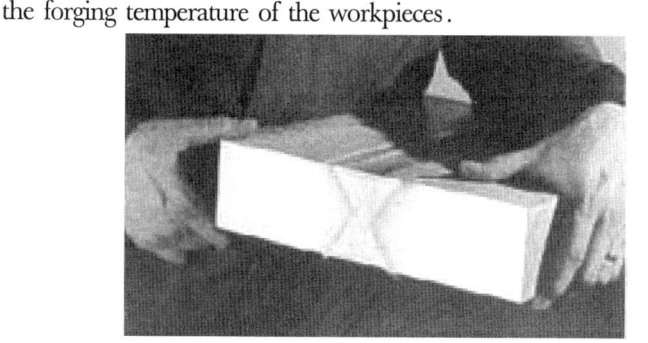

Figure 3.61 Double sided friction stir weld in 75mm thick aluminum extrusions produced at TWI

For aluminum alloys, the following alloys are easily welded. Maximum thickness in a single pass is dependent on machine power, but values ≥ 50mm are achievable.

* 2000 series aluminum (Al-Cu)
* 5000 series aluminum (Al-Mg)
* 6000 series aluminum (Al-Mg-Si)
* 7000 series aluminum (Al-Zn)

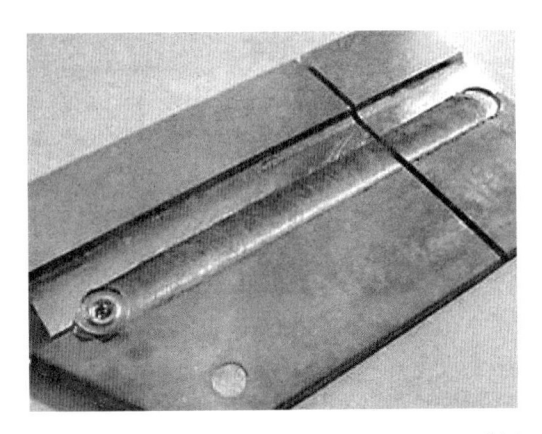

Figure 3.62 Friction stir weld between an aluminum extrusion (AA2219) and a 3mm thick die cast magnesium alloy AZ91

Figure 3.63 Pilot trial on friction stir welding aluminum to a mild steel plate comprising a mechanical interlock.

    * 8000 series aluminum (Al-Li)

    * MMCs based on aluminum (metal matrix composites)*

Other aluminum alloys of the 1000 (commercially pure), 3000 (Al-Mn) and 4000 (Al-Si) series, aluminum castings.

Other materials successfully welded include:

    * Copper and its alloys (up to 50mm in one pass)

    * Lead

    * Titanium and its alloys

* Magnesium alloys
* Zinc
* Plastics
* Mild steel
* Stainless steel (austenitic, martensitic and duplex[*])
* Nickel alloys
◆ Equipment

TWI installed an ESAB SuperStir[TM] machine, shown in Figure 3.64, in its friction welding laboratory, for confidential[*] studies. The machine has a vacuum clamping table and can be used for non-linear joint lines.

* Sheet thickness: 1 ~ 25 mm aluminum
* Work envelope: Approx. $(5 \times 8 \times 1)$m
* Maximum down force: Approx. 60 kN (6t)
* Maximum rotation speed: 5000rev/min

Figure 3.64 ESAB SuperStir[TM] machine FW28

◆ Applications

The first commercial application of friction stir welding concerned the manufacture of hollow aluminum panels for deep freezing of fish on fishing boats (Figures 3.65, 3.66). These panels are made from friction stir welded aluminum extrusions. The minimal distortion and high reproducibility make FSW both technically and economically a

192   *English in Materials Science and Engineering*

very attractive method to produce these stiff panels.

Figure 3.65 FSW panel for pre-pressing of fish blocks before quick freezing. The panel is welded from both sides

Pre-fabricated wide aluminum panels for high-speed ferryboats[*] can be produced by friction stir welding and are commercially available, shown in Figure 3.67. The panels are made by joining extrusions, which can be produced in standard size extrusion presses. Compared to fusion welding, the heat input is very low and this results in low distortion and reduced thermal stresses.

Figure 3.66 Joint design of freezer panels (weld penetration 4.5mm, total weld length 16m)

Nippon Sharyo use friction stir welded panels produced by

Figure 3. 67 FSW catamaran* side-wall with cut-out sections for windows at Marine Aluminum in Haugesund, Norway

Sumitomo Light Metal Industries for the floor panels of the new Shinkansen, shown in Figure 3. 68. Some of these trains operate at speeds up to 285 km/h. Nippon Light Metal Co. has also made use of friction stir welding for subway rolling stock. The weld quality was confirmed to be excellent based on microstructural, X-ray and tensile test results.

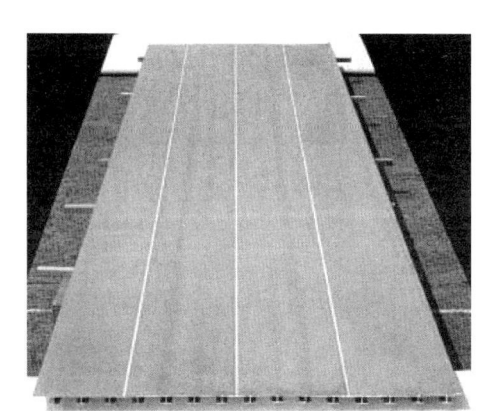

Figure 3.68 Friction stir welded floor panel produced by Sumitomo Light Metal for Shinkansen trains

In Norway, an innovative technique of joining two parts of a car wheel by FSW has been invented and successfully demonstrated by

194　English in Materials Science and Engineering

Hydro Aluminum in Håvik for the manufacture of prototype parts, shown in Figure 3.69. Optional design concepts have been developed to either butt or lap weld cast or forged centre parts to rims that are made from wrought alloys. Branched designs of the centre part are possible by providing two parallel friction stir welds per wheel, which run along a cavity to achieve good load transfer and weight reduction.[2]

Figure 3.69 Hydro Aluminum's light alloy car wheel, where the rim was friction stir welded to the hub

Key words:
friction stir welding (FSW) [搅拌摩擦焊]　　　tool [搅拌头]
shoulder [搅拌头轴肩]　　　probe [搅拌针]
sound [良好的]　　　flute [槽]
helix [螺旋线]　　　die cast [压铸]
metal matrix composite [金属基复合材料]　　　duplex [双相的]
confidential [机密的]　　　ferryboat [渡船]
catamaran [双体船]

　Notes:
　[1] 除此以外,搅拌针的主要作用是保证对焊缝处的材料提供充分的搅拌,并控制搅拌头周围材料的流动,以形成满意的焊缝。
　[2] 对每个车轮在一个空腔上用搅拌摩擦焊焊两条平行的焊缝,从而使得中间的部件可以采用树枝状设计,既可以有效承载,又可以大幅度减重。

Questions:

1) What is the tool's main function?
2) What are the advantages of FSW?
3) What kind of materials can FSW be used to join?

3.3.2.5 *Electrostatic Bonding**

Electrostatic bonding is also known as anodic or field assisted bonding. The technique is used to join glass to metals and semiconductors at temperatures well below the softening point of the glass. The components to be joined are polished to a smooth, flat surface finish (e. g. 50 μm rms) then heated to a temperature below the softening point of the materials, but sufficiently high for ionic conduction to occur (200 ~ 600°C for glass). A d.c. voltage is applied across the components such that the metal (or semiconductor) is at a positive potential with respect to the glass. The voltage applied can vary from a few hundred volts to three thousand volts, for bonding times of 10 seconds to several hours. A bond is formed as a result of the joint interfaces being brought into intimate contact by the electrostatic forces generated by ion migration in the glass.[1] No external pressure is applied other than that required to hold the components in contact.

Figure 3.70 shows the electrostatic bonding machine, and Figure 3.71 shows the electrostatic bonded silicone to glass pressure sensor array.

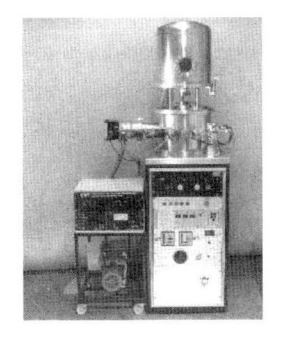

Figure 3.70 The electrostatic bonding machine

196　*English in Materials Science and Engineering*

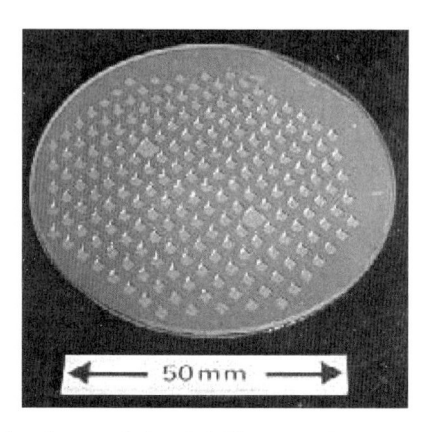

Figure 3.71 The electrostatic bonded silicone to glass pressure sensor array

Key words:
electrostatic bonding [静电连接] rms [均方根]
　Note:
　[1] 玻璃中离子的迁移产生的静电力使连接界面紧密贴合,从而形成接头。

Question:

What is the difference between electrostatic bonding and solid phase diffusion bonding?

3.3.3 Ceramic Joining

The ceramic joining technologies used today—few of which have been developed specifically for this class of materials—range from simple mechanical attachment, through liquid phase processes such as adhesive bonding* and brazing*. However, there are problems associated with these processes, including processing considerations (such as component size, joining atmosphere), time constraints and costs. It is for these reasons that new ceramic joining technologies, such as the ones described below, are under development.

3.3.3.1 *Ultrasonic Joining**

Ultrasonic joining (used extensively in the plastics industry) has

Welding 197

been applied to such ceramic-metal combinations as alumina[*]-aluminum, alumina-stainless steel, zirconia[*]-steel and glass-ceramic (cordierite[*] based)-copper. Typical applications include batteries, thread guides, textile cutting equipment and heavy-duty electrical fuses. The advantages of the process are the very fast joining times (less than 1 second), surface preparation is not critical (which is contrary to almost every other ceramic joining process) and the lack of melting and intermetallic formation. However, for joining of hard metals such as steel, soft, deformable interlayers are needed. A limitation of this technique as applied to ceramics is that only films/thin sheets of metal can be joined to a ceramic.

Typically, the technique employs a transducer[*] assembly operating at ~ 20kHz, which is the source of the ultrasound, coupled to a sonotrode[*][1]. The sonotrode tip is placed in contact, (usually under a clamping load of $1 \sim 10 \ N/mm^2$) with the workpiece, shown in Figure 3.72. The heat generated is localized at the interface (up to 600°C when using aluminum interlayers).

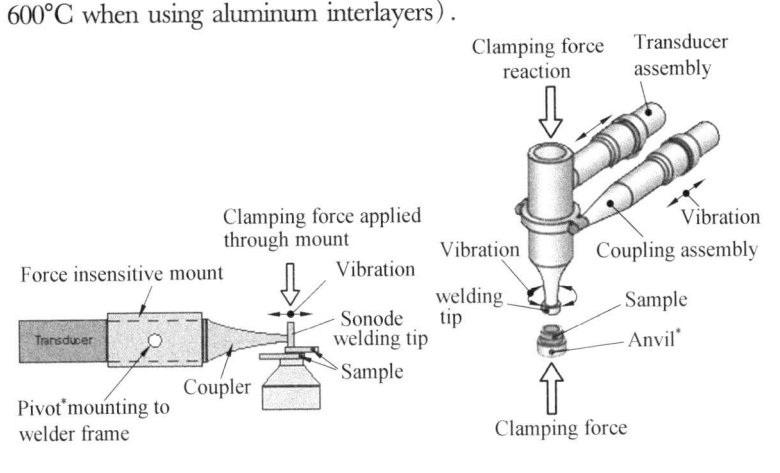

Figure 3.72 Set-up for ultrasonic welding

The bonding mechanism relies on the vibratory shear stress of the metal exceeding its elastic limit, coupled with the breakdown of surface oxide films, thus exposing atomically clean metal. The clamping force

198   *English in Materials Science and Engineering*

exerts plastic deformation on the metal, which increases the interfacial contact between the metal and ceramic. Then, mechanical keying occurs across the interface and the joint is formed, perhaps with a contribution from chemical interactions.

Key words:
adhesive bonding [胶接]   brazing [硬钎焊]
ultrasonic joining [超声连接]   alumina [氧化铝]
zirconia [氧化锆]   cordierite [堇青石]
transducer [换能器]   sonotrode [变幅杆]
pivot [心轴]   anvil [铁砧]

Note:
[1] 典型情况下,这种技术采用一套工作在 20kHz 左右的换能器作为超声波源,换能器和变幅杆相连。

Question:

Is the surface preparation critical for ultrasonic joining?

3.3.3.2 *Transient Liquid Phase Bonding* (TLPB)*

TLPB has the ability to produce a bond at a lower temperature than that at which it will be ultimately used. The technology is currently being adapted for a number of ceramics using "interlayers" based either on glasses, (such as oxynitrides* for joining SiAlON) or pure metals or alloys, (such as Ge and Ge-Si for joining SiC and SiC/SiC composites). The schematic representation for bonding in the SiAlON system is given in Figure 3.73. A mixture of silicon nitride, yttria*, silica* and alumina are applied (by spray coating) to one surface of the joint. As the samples are heated to 1 600°C, a load of 2 MPa is applied. Joint formation occurs at this temperature over a period of 10 to 80 minutes. At about 1 400°C, the oxide components react to form a Y-Si-Al-O liquid phase. This leads to densification and sintering. The silicon nitride then dissolves into the liquid, boosting both Si and N contents and altering the composition to Y-Si-Al-O-N. At the same time, beta-SiAlON grains grow and form an interlocking network.

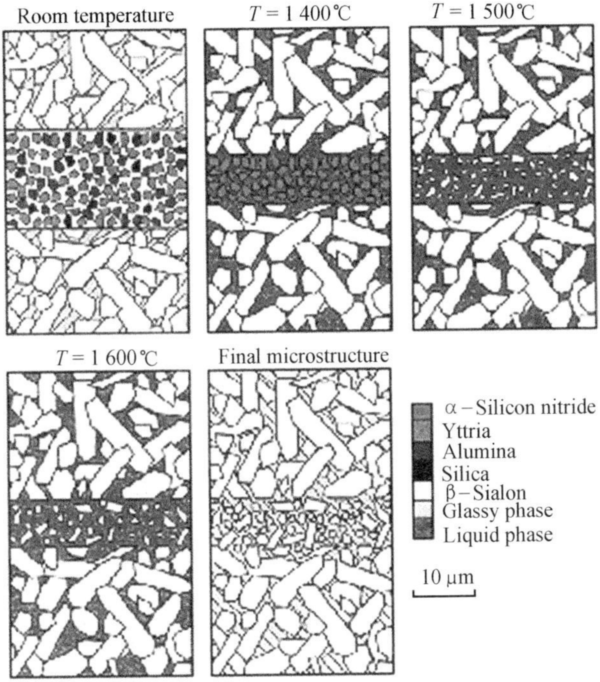

Room temperature $T = 1\ 400\ ℃$ $T = 1\ 500\ ℃$

$T = 1\ 600\ ℃$ Final microstructure

α − Silicon nitride
Yttria
Alumina
Silica
β − Sialon
Glassy phase
Liquid phase

10 μm

Figure 3.73 Transient liquid phase bonding process

Key words:
transient liquid phase bonding（TLPB）[瞬间液相扩散连接]
oxynitride [氮氧化合物]   yttria [氧化钇]
silica [二氧化硅]

3.3.3.3 Infiltration* Processes

High strength, high temperature capability materials for operation in excess of 1 000°C, such as SiC based composites, are required for structural applications, including heat exchangers and gas turbine components. The substitution of these materials is in recognition that traditional stainless steels and superalloys have reached their operational limits. There is a demand from industry to develop a robust joining process suitable for both SiC monolithic* and composite materials. The use of polymers which react with and infiltrate into the bulk material offer a potential solution.

A mixture of polymer precursor (a source of carbon), aluminum, boron and silicon is applied to the joint surfaces (in a tape, paste or slurry) and then heated (generally to 1 200°C) in an inert atmosphere and/or air (using a propane* torch, or furnace). The joint forms through polymer pyrolysis* of the precursor material which subsequently reacts with the added elemental Si (in the presence of sintering aids of Al and B), to form in-situ*, high density SiC. Strengths have ranged from ~ 95 MPa for air-joined samples, to ~ 40 MPa for argon atmosphere samples. The very fact that the joint can be produced using a simple gas torch could have a large impact on the repair, or on-site production of ceramic-ceramic joints. To date various grades of SiC, SiC/SiC and C/SiC composites have been joined using this technique.

Key words:
infiltration [渗透]   monolithic [整体的]
propane [丙烷]   pyrolysis [热解]
in-situ [原位的]

3.3.3.4 Microwave Joining of Ceramics

Microwave energy is already being applied to the drying/firing of refractories and whiteware; however, it has recently been considered as an energy source for joining ceramics such as alumina, zirconia, mullite*, silicon nitride and silicon carbide. The direct coupling of the microwave with the ceramic results in volumetric heating, hence there is a great potential to heat large sections uniformly. Control of the location of maximum electric and magnetic fields also enables precise, selective heating. Conventional diffusion bonding techniques use radiant heating methods and therefore the time to reach temperature and the time at bonding temperature can be up to 8 hours. This is particularly so for materials such as alumina, which are diffusion bonded at temperatures approaching 1 600°C. By use of a microwave heat source, these bonding times can be reduced by an order of magnitude.

Very high purity aluminas are difficult to heat, due to low inherent dielectric properties, making joining difficult. However, relatively impure 85% alumina is joined with little difficulty. The inability to produce joints between the high purity alumina has led to investigations on the use of interlayers including sealing glasses and alumina gels* . The latter of these offers the advantage that, at the joining temperature, the gel transforms into colloidal* alpha alumina which subsequently sinters to provide a homogeneous interface. Joints produced between 85% alumina have shown bond strengths equivalent to that of the parent material. The mechanism of joint formation has been studied and a number of possible mechanisms have been identified, depending on the material. For impure aluminas, the glassy grain boundary phase softens and assists in the bonding process, whilst for zirconia, a solid state process has been identified.

Key words:

mullite [莫来石]　　　gel [凝胶]　　　colloidal [胶体的]

Question:

What is the advantage of microwave joining comparing to diffusion bonding?

3.3.3.5 *Ceramic-modified Braze Alloys*

Whilst work at TWI is focused on the more traditional methods of joining ceramics, such as brazing, diffusion bonding, glasses and adhesives; current development programmes are investigating the modification of braze alloys by the addition of a ceramic reinforcement. This will provide a joining medium with a coefficient of thermal expansion (CTE) intermediate to that of ceramics and metals and also give the joint improved strength due to the introduction of a second phase, i.e. an in-situ metal matrix composite. Whilst the additional joint strength is, in effect, a bonus, it is the ability to tailor the CTE of the joining medium that is of interest, since this raises the possibility of designing the braze to accommodate thermal stresses which would otherwise build up during the joining process.

3.3.3.6 *Novel Polymer Adhesives*

For low temperature applications, novel, organic based adhesives reinforced with nano-sized ceramic particles are being fabricated at TWI using sol-gel* chemistry (a liquid phase process). The use of this technique allows intimate mixing of the ceramic and organic constituents (on a molecular scale) and this produces materials with high purities and a high level of homogeneity. This process provides a joining medium, which is tough and yet flexible and can be designed to be hydrophobic* and self-repairing. Applications for these strong, modified adhesives may be found in the optical, biomedical and defence industries.

Key words:
sol-gel [溶胶 – 凝胶]   hydrophobic [疏水的]

Question:

Which method do you think will find wide industrial application in ceramic joining? Why?

4

Casting

4.1 Metal Flow in Die Casting*

Die casting is the infant of modern metal casting methods. Its use is largely limited to the non-ferrous metals. The rapid chilling of the metal by its injection into bare* steel molds provides for rapid production cycling but at the same time presents severe challenges to orderly mold filling. [1] Only the advent of industry sponsored research in the past 10 years has brought any effective degree of understanding of what happens in the one fiftieth of a second or so available for mold filling. From this research has come a practical system for preengineering fill time and gate area in relationship to metal temperature, die temperature, and casting configuration. The management of metal flow has provide benefits to the die caster and user alike. These systems, too, have provided the springboard* for further industry supported research to reduce the minimum wall thickness possible in large zinc* die casting. Research on this subject continues with the help of modern instrumentation and high speed photography.

204　*English in Materials Science and Engineering*

Key words:
die casting [压铸]　bare[裸露的]　springboard[跳板]　zinc[锌]

Note:

[1]金属注入裸露的钢模时产生快速激冷,从而获得快速的生产周期,但同时也对有序的铸型填充提出了严重的挑战。

Questions:

1) What kind of mold is used in the die casting?

2) What kind of materials can be cast with the die casting method?

4.1.1 Introduction

Die castings are important components in thousands of industrial products such as automobiles, home appliances, electrical products, office equipment, small tools, hardware, plumbing* goods, photographic equipment, toys, etc. In fact, die casting applications cover a broader range of usage than almost any other metal form.

The die casting process is believed to have started with die casting of type for printing as early as 1849. The earliest commercial applications were said to have been for phonograph* and cash register parts in the 1890s. Mass product ion practice was evident with the die casting of connecting rod bearings* by the Franklin Motor Car Co., shortly after the turn of the century.

The first metals used for die casting were tin and lead, but their cost and limited mechanical properties limited their application. With the development of zinc base alloys before the first world war, the significance of tin and lead declined. Aluminum alloys were first used for commercial die casting about 1914 and magnesium and copper alloys followed later. Recent figures indicate that around 1 500 000 tons of die castings are produced by U.S. industry annually.

Die casting is a process distinguished by its low labor content. It provides accurate dimensional control with tolerances* closer than those possible by any other foundry process. With long mold life and rapid production, die casting makes possible many high production application.

Casting 205

Key words：
plumbing[铅工业、管道]   phonograph[留声机]
rod bearings[滚柱轴承]   tolerance [公差]

Questions：

1）What are the first two materials which were cast with die casting method?

2）There are about 1 500 000 tons of die castings produced by U. S. industry, among which most are lead and zinc product. (T/F)

4.1.2 Terminology*

At the outset* it might be well to get some definitions and terminology clear to ensure that we are talking the same language. First, die casting, as its known in this country, is a process by which liquid metal is injected under high pressure into a closed metal mold. By "high pressure" is usually meant pressures of several hundred psi or more. In contrast, "die castings" in Europe are what we know as permanent mold castings. In between these lies the process variously known as the Schmidt or low pressure permanent mold casting process. The distinction is the ability of the mold to retain an insulating wash coating on its surface for a number of cycles. This is not possible at this time in die casting.

Special terms and phrases have been used to describe parameters of the die casting process. The term "shot speed" is used to describe the velocity of the metal injecting plunger, expressed in feet per minute or inches per second. The " shot plunger" is a piston* operating in the "shot sleeve*" or "shot cylinder" to constitute the metal pump. The "die cavity" is the open space in the mold which forms the casting. "Fill time," as we use the term, denotes* the time in seconds or milliseconds required for the cavity, including overflows*, to fill completely. "Vents*" are the thin recesses* in the die parting face which permit air but not metal to escape from the cavity. Another term

206　*English in Materials Science and Engineering*

is "gate velocity," by which is meant the calculated rate of liquid metal flow through the gate orifice*, expressed in feet per second. "Die temperature" is the temperature of the surface of the mold cavity, usually just before the metal is injected. The term "temperature gradient" refers to the difference between the surface and subsurface die temperature.

Key words:
terminology[术语]　　　　outset[开头]　　　　piston[活塞]
sleeve[套管]　　　　　　denote[表示]　　　　overflow [溢流]
vent[排气口]　　　　　　recess [深口]　　　　orifice[孔口]

Questions:

1) How high is the pressure usually adopted in die casting?

2) List some of the terminology used in the die casting industry.

4.1.3 The Process

Three basic types of casting machines are used in die casting. Almost non-existent now are those using high pressure air to "blow" the metal into the mold. Later came the plunger* gooseneck machines for zinc, lead, and tin alloys. In this, a submerged plunger and cylinder is used to pump the liquid metal directly into the mold. More recently, the cold chamber process utilizes a piston and cylinder into which the metal charge for each cycle is ladled.

As with any other process, die casting has its limitations as well as its advantages. For one thing, it is rarely economical to use multiple part cores such as are normal in the permanent mold casting of auto pistons. Further, in considering what alloys are castable, the piston cylinder fit* and also the temperatures involved must be taken into account. For this latter factor, copper and iron alloys pose serious economic obstacles in terms of die life.

Key words:
plunger[柱塞]　　　　　　fit[配合]

Questions:

1) If die casting technology is selected to cast copper or iron, a big problem would emerge with the life of the mold, since _____ .

2) The second paragraph of this passage is talking about both the advantage and the limitations of die casting. (T/F)

4.1.4 Empirical Gating Approaches

Almost since the beginnings of the process, engineers and practitioners* have wondered, conjectured*, and guessed at what was happening as the die cavity filled. In essence*, they were using a process successfully without understanding the mechanics involved. Around 1933, two German die casting engineers named Frommer and Brandt tried to depict what they believed took place as the cavity filled. They were hampered* by the relatively crude* instrumentation and simulation possibilities available to them. The result was two diametrically opposing concepts. Frommer visualized the metal as shooting from the gate orifice in a jet like stream, striking the far wall of the cavity, then sliding back along the side walls to meet the ingoing stream at the gate.[1] This would create a "bow-tie" metal path, trapping air in the two loops. Brandt, on the other hand, depicted the mold as filling by a mode now called solid front flow. He thus did not think that the metal stream jumped away from the gate. It is most interesting that high speed movies taken of water injected into plastic molds a few years ago confirm Frommer's concept.

Since the early thirties, many investigators have attempted to correlate production experience with gate size. The objective was to systematize metal flow into empirical gating formulas without yearly studying what was going on.

Key words:
practitioner[从业者]   conjecture[推测]   essence[本质]
hamper[阻碍]   crude[粗糙]
Note:
[1]弗罗姆想像液态金属像一束射流从浇道口喷射而出,撞击型腔远处

的型壁,然后顺着侧壁滑下来与内浇道处进入的液流汇合。

Questions:

1) At the early thirties the scientists did know what was going on after the metal was shot into the mold. (T/F)

2) The investigators did not have instruments good enough to do the experiment that they were interested in. (T/F)

4.1.5 Organized Research

Real scientifically based research on metal flow in die casting did not move forward until researchers at now introduced the concept of water analogy of metal flow. They used clear plastic molds and shot sleeves to study the action of the water with high speed photography. Their calculations, confirmed later by researchers at Case, demonstrated that, aside* from thermal factors, the behavior of water would be very similar to that of molten aluminum.[1] These first studies at Dow were later continued at Case by the Die Casting Research Foundation in cooperative efforts with the International Lead Zinc Research Foundation and the American Foundrymen's Society. These systematic and carefully guided researches started about 10 years ago and continue at the present time.

The water analogy studies confirmed that the metal stream, in virtually* all instances, did leap from the gate orifice as a jet, as Frommer had predicted. This served to explain why porosity is frequently trapped in the middle of a casting. It can thus be seen that the most generous venting* of the mold will not ensure completely sound castings if the metal does not cross the cavity as a solid front.[2]

Later work at Case, taking into account some thermal considerations and making some heat transfer assumptions, suggested the beginnings of a sleeve, in the runner channels* and finally in the cavity, the time required for the metal to freeze could be predicted. Assuming that the mold must be completely filled with molten metal before major solidification takes place, a systematic relationship may be established among the pertinent* factors. These include the freezing point of the metal, the mold surface and metal heat transfer rates, the casting thickness, and the original metal temperature. The resulting value is maximum allowable fill time. Equating fill time, cavity volume, and a chosen gate velocity gives gate area.

One controversial* question entered into the considerations at this point: Does the metal heat up markedly, as indicated in the literature, fundamental energy conservation calculations had demonstrated that the work involved precluded* heating of the metal by more than a few degrees. Thus, this factor will be ignored as being of minor importance.

Key words:
aside[除了]   virtually[事实上]   venting[排气口]
runner channels[浇道]   pertinent[有关的]   preclude[妨碍]
controversial[有争议的]

Notes:

[1]凯斯的研究者们后来证实,他们的计算表明除了热因素以外,水和熔融铝液的流动行为非常相似。

[2]因此可以看出,如果液态金属不能以固态前沿方式通过型腔,那么无论铸型有多大的排气口,都不可能保证生产出完全致密的铸件。

Questions:

1) Why the scientists study the movement of water with high speed photography?

2) Since so many factors are involved, the freezing time of metal could not be predicted. (T/F)

4.1.6 Using the Die Casting Research Foundation System

So, with 10 years of concentrated research on the subject of metal flow, the Die Casting Research Foundation (DCRF) was able to develop a viable* system of gate sizing. It is in extensive use and works well when coupled with good judgment in the placement and aim

210 *English in Materials Science and Engineering*

of the gate. The factors that are "plugged in" to the DCRF system include: (1) casting configuration in terms of relative thinness, expressed as pounds per square foot of total surface area; (2) the average temperature of the mold cavity surface (that experienced by the entering liquid metal); (3) the temperature of the metal in the holding furnace*.

To simplify the multiplicity* of nomography* that would otherwise be needed, our work sheets have been designed for the predominantly popular alloys of zinc, aluminum, and magnesium.

It should be pointed out that the DCRF gate sizing nomographs provide a quick solution of the gate area for "mechanical" finish castings of "normal" size. Members who produce plating quality zinc die castings have found by experience that they must make an adjustment to about 60 percent of the fill time is determined by incorporating the factors listed above. This figure is then transposed* to the back side of the sheet. Here, the fill time is related to the amount of metal through the gate, gate velocity, gate area, plunger size and plunger velocity. The nomograph that constitutes the back side was developed by F. C. Bennett of Dow Chemical Co., in 1961. Supplies of the DCRF nomograph work sheets are avail able to member companies in pad form.

The value of this system to the members of DCRF has been tremendous. It has provided them with a tool to shorten greatly the time and expense needed to tune up each new die. Equally valuable has been its use in debugging old jobs.

One thing that has been found to be helpful is that once the fill time has been established, the mathematical relationship to the plunger size and speed is forcefully brought to the user's attention. It illustrates with no mystique* that to achieve a certain, limiting fill time we must use a shot plunger of a certain size and move it at a definite minimum speed, all wishful thinking notwithstanding.[1] How many die casters have, in years past, selected a plunger/sleeve size because it held sufficient metal, then made defective* shot after shot, not realizing that the limited plunger speed would never produce a quality part?

Permit the writer to draw on his own in plant experience to illustrate the effectiveness of the system on a first person basis. One particular two cavity die for an electric motor end frame was particularly troublesome. It had been gated in the typical old seat of the pants manner. Even after several years of welding and regating, it still had a 40 ~ 45 percent reject rate. My engineers agreed to start over on the entire gating system, so we welded up everything on the die face except the cavity proper. Back we went to the drawing board* and, using the DCRF system, designed new gates, runners, and vents. The drawing was executed in the die without any personal flourishes* by the die maker or casting foreman*. The reborn* die was mounted, preheated, and, with our fingers crossed, the first shots were made. Within three cycles, once the excess* lube was expelled*, the castings were beautiful. A number of subsequent production runs confirmed a reject rate of less than 5 percent.

Key words:

viable[可行的]	holding furnace[保温炉]	multiplicity[多样性]
nomograph[图解法]	transpose[调换]	mystique[奥秘]
defective[有缺陷的]	drawing board [绘图板]	flourish[华饰]
foreman[工头]	reborn[再生的]	excess[过剩]
expel[排出]		

Note:

[1]尽管都是异想天开,但它很清楚地表明:要想获得一个确定的、有限的填充时间,必须使用具有一定尺寸的柱塞,并以一个确定的最小速度移动。

Questions:

1) Die casting is a successful technology according to the passage. (T/F)

2) What does the sentence "with our fingers crossed" mean?

4.1.7 Gate Placement

Industry has not yet conducted sufficient systematic research to be able to predict where to place the gate or how to distribute the gate area. This is where the "marriage" comes into play—the bringing together of technology and hard won experience. The variety of sizes and shapes of parts desired is infinite. Each new job is a challenge to the mold designer as to where to place the gate and how to aim it to provide proper metal distribution. This is a fruitful field for research.

We must not leave the impression, however, that we are completely at sea with regard to gate placement. Accumulated experience has shown that certain "standard" shapes are best gate in this or that way. Open frames, for example, should be gated from the inside (center gated). Rings or frames that must be gated on the periphery should be fed in such a manner that a pool of metal which would be expected to expand is created at the gate.[1] The use of a fan gate in such instances encourages the metal to follow the outer perimeter* of the part, closing of fall opportunity for venting. Boxes with flanges* are subject to similar problems. It is surprising to some that the most difficult shape to fill with good surface finish is a flat plate. In this observation we may have a clue that the concept of a back pressure at the gate may be desirable.

In recent years, die construction techniques that permit "pin" gates, remote from the parting plane, have been perfected. Even multiple pin gates are occasionally seen. Most "mag" style auto wheels are gated into the center hub* by way of a three part mold. This provides ideal metal flow: center to rim where good venting is available.

With the advent of industrial research in metal flow, the nature of metal flow and die filling is becoming better understood. With this better understanding in hand, the die caster is becoming more adept* at directing the gate stream logically and scientifically.

Key words:
perimeter[周长]　　flange[凸缘、法兰]　　hub[轮毂]　　adept[熟练的]
Note:
[1]必须在周边设置内浇道的环或框架使得以这样一种形式填充,即在

Casting   213

浇道口处形成一个要膨胀的金属熔池。

Questions:

1) Why is the gate placement so important?

2) What does the sentence "we are completely at sea" mean?

4.1.8 The Velocity Dilemma

Another aspect of the gating picture that needs and is receiving attention is gate velocity. Until the advent of electronic instrumentation, little thought is given to this parameter in most die casting shops. Some students of the process are vaguely aware that there is not complete freedom to roam up and down the gate velocity scale at will. Die casting engineers have often told of grinding the gate to change its direction only to find the casting quality deteriorating*. What was happening was that as they enlarged the gate area they reduced the gate velocity, virtually canceling the possible benefits of their efforts at redirection.[1]

A survey and analysis of hundreds of gating systems in successful production dies showed a peak in the velocity distribution curve in the range of 100 ~ 150 ft/sec for aluminum and 80 ~ 120 ft/sec for zinc. Researchers who have explored the influence of gate velocity at some length have frequently reported a "no man's land" in the velocity scale. This slump* in casting quality may occur in one range with one casting and in another range with a different casting. Generally, however, it is seen most often in the 30 ~ 50 ft/sec range.

In an effort to understand further the role of gate velocity, the DCRF is currently sponsoring additional work under Wallace at Case Western Reserve University. By means of high speed photography(5 000 frames/sec), the influence of velocity on the nature of the metal stream emerging from the gate orifice is being studied. At this time several things have been learned.

True solid front flow is a myth. Velocities as low as 15 ft/sec were seen to produce a fanlike spray. At higher velocity, the streamers tend to break up into strings of coarse discrete* globules*. At still higher velocity, the particles become very fine. This may be the sort of flow referred to by die casters as "fog," "atomized," etc. After the nature of the stream with respect to velocity is established and the boundary zones of these modes are determined, these factors will be correlated, with casting quality. Internal and surface quality optima may very possibly occur at quite different gate velocity ranges. The reader should keep in mind that we have been referring to the nature of the metal stream immediately after it emerges from the gate orifice and leaps into the open space of the mold cavity. It is clear that in actual practice the stream that starts out as a spray may very well be slowed to a small fraction of its original velocity by impinging* on as few as one or two successive* walls of the die's convolutions* [2]. Thus, those who have observed clearly round nosed, solid stream fronts after the metal has progressed some distance from the gate were not dreaming. In fact, it is probable that as the stream is bounced from one wall to another, it could not possibly retain sufficient velocity to remain a spray of liquid metal particles.

Why, some foundrymen ask, doesn't the die caster fill the mold cavity right from the outset with a solid front flow of metal? There are two reasons. First, since initial solid front flow is clearly a matter of gate velocity, the area of the gate required would be so large as to preclude* its economical removal in cleaning. The cost of sawing off a heavy gate is many times the cost of die trimming* on a power press. Also, the unsightly appearance of the gate area is difficult to camouflage*. In decorative parts such as in plated zinc, shrinkage* porosity, such as occurs with gates thicker than about 0.04, would make smooth polishing all but impossible. In die casting, as noted above, the rapid chill of the uninsulated mold surface precludes attaining a low gate velocity with a small gate area, as the limiting fill time would be grossly violated.

Key words:
deteriorate[恶化]   slump[剧降]   discrete[不连续的]

Casting 215

globule[液珠]　　　　impinge[撞击]　　　successive[连续的]
convolution[回旋体]　　preclude[预先排除]　　trim [清理]
camouflage[伪装]　　　shrinkage[收缩]

　Notes:

　[1]发生的事情就是当他们扩大内浇道面积时,内浇道填充速度减小,实质上也就是消除了他们在改变方向上的努力可能带来的益处。

　[2]很明显,在实际的浇注过程中,以喷射流形式开始的液流在与一个或两个连续的模具回转壁面碰撞后,其速度将降低很大幅度。

Questions:

1) What is the best gate velocity for most aluminum castings?

2) By what means did the researchers study the gate velocity?

4.1.9 The Air Problem

In the current research project at Case, in addition to the change in the basic form of the metal stream with respect to velocity, random anomalies* in the metal have been observed. These take the form of explosions or eruptions* of air entrapped* in the metal charge as it emerges from the gate in a manner reminiscent*, when seen in high speed motion pictures, of a volcanic* eruption.[1] These eruptions are observed to disturb the orderly flow of metal, and are very probably one source(of several) of random defects in die castings. Attempts by the researchers to eliminate these eruptions by filling the shot sleeve to 80 percent and then to 100 percent full failed to eliminate the condition completely. The question remains: how to eliminate this patently* damaging problem? Sheptak has shown, through water analogy studies of the fluid behavior in a shot sleeve, that tipping* the sleeve upward at an angle helps to prevent the wave from breaking ahead of the plunger. From a practical standpoint this, though not impossible, would mean installing the casting machine at an angle or, alternatively, mounting the shot sleeve at an angle to the die face.[2] A method that has been employed to attempt to minimize this air entrainment in the shot sleeve is to connect the runner channel to the shot sleeve at the bottom. This is on the unconfirmed premise* that any entrained air in

216 *English in Materials Science and Engineering*

the sleeve will be at the top. This runner configuration has been seen in Czechoslovakian papers, and the General Motors Vega engine block dies appear to have been designed in this manner. The tendency of the metal charge to freeze in the runner loop before the plunger begins its advance might create problems in the case of smaller dies.[3]

At this point in the discussion, those engineers who are devotees of the vertical injection cold chamber machine are sure to make their point. It is generally acknowledged that this concept has merit* from a foundry viewpoint. Over the years, however, such vertical plunger machines have failed for a variety of reasons to attract the popularity enjoyed by the horizontal plunger machines. Commercial activity is currently under way that may change that picture, however.

Key words:

anomaly[异常]   eruption[爆发]   entrap[陷入]
reminiscent[使人想起的]   volcanic[火山]   patently[明显地]
tip [倾斜]   premise[前提]   merit[优点]

Notes:

[1]当金属料像火山喷发那样从内浇道填充时,这些异常现象以金属料中卷入气体的爆炸或喷发形式出现,就像高速摄影所看到的那样。

[2]从实际观点来考虑,这尽管不是不可能,但却意味着以一定倾斜角度安装铸造设备,或是将冲头衬套以一定角度安装在铸模表面。

[3]在更小的压铸模中,金属炉料在冲杆开始前进之前就在环形浇道中凝固的倾向可能会带来问题。

Questions:

1) During casting the air can't be entrapped since it is too light compared with metal.(T/F)

2) The horizontal plunger machines are better than the vertical plunger machines.(T/F)

4.1.10 The Runner

Up to this point we have been speaking largely of the influence of the gate orifice and the shot sleeve on casting quality. Obviously, we cannot ignore the design of the runner system; the channels in the die

face that communicate the sprue* or shot sleeve to the gate orifice.
With the advent of some early DCRF sponsored and jointly sponsored
work at Case, the design of the runner system began to receive its
proper attention. Water analogy studies in which no gate restriction
was incorporated demonstrated that the runner when it changes
direction must do so smoothly.[1] Otherwise the metal stream breaks
free from the inside of the carve, causing turbulence. Later work which
incorporated gate area restrictions, in the range of 65 ~ 85 percent of
the runner area, showed no serious corner turbulence. This made it
practical to design runner systems that were simple to machine into the
die. It further demonstrated that gate/runner system management was
simplified if the system were gate controlled, in contrast to runner
control which occurs if there is no gate restriction.

Several important design criteria were established from this
research and are in general use by the die casters today.

(1) Design the runner system to provides a definite restriction at
the gate.

(2) Maintain a constant or slightly increasing velocity in the
runner system as the metal charge progresses from the starting point to
the gate orifice.

(3) Reduce runner areas arithmetically as they divide.

(4) Make the runner area reduction halfway between the
branches. This will provide equal flow and flow initiation in each of
the branches.

(5) Exercise care in the runner/in-gate transition design to
provide a gradual changes in area. To permit a reduction and then an
increase in velocity at this important point is not good practice.

When these runner design factors are incorporated, the overall
mass of the runner system usually proves to be less than would be the
case in a seat of the pants designed system, thus providing further
economies.

218　*English in Materials Science and Engineering*

Key words:

sprue[浇道]

Note:

[1]没有内浇口限制的水模拟研究表明,横浇道改变方向时必须很平滑。

Questions:

1) The runner will cause turbulence in casting. (T/F)

2) The thickness of the runner should keep constant. (T/F)

4.1.11 Porosity in the Casting

The preceding observations lead us to a discussion of the forms and causes of porosity in die castings. As you who are foundrymen know, the absolutely perfect casting has probably never been, and may never be made. The same is true in die casting. Even though the industry has come a long way, it has a long way to go toward consistently making die castings with few or no internal and external imperfections. Imperfections and defects should be differentiated as the terms are used here, a defect is an imperfection that makes a casting unsuitable for its intended role. Thus an imperfection may or may not be a defect.

Rarely is porosity, in the foundry sense, looked upon as anything but undesirable. There are several sources of porosity in die castings. Each has its own distinctive appearance and cause, though they may at times be coincident. The most familiar type is that of entrapped air. These defects, logically, look like bubbles and may be either rounded or greatly elongated. This is the type of defect that prompted a flurry[*] of inventiveness about 15 years ago that led to numerous patents for vacuum venting. It was widely thought that if there was no air in the cavity none could be trapped. What was quickly learned was that in the die casting process, conditions are such that we could do a fine job of entrapping no thing; a void without air. In fact, some die casters found occasional castings made with vacuum which were so porous that they could float on water. Thus, vacuum was not the easy answer to the porosity problem. Effective vacuum venting does, however, provide the die caster with a tool to help fill castings with hard to vent sections such as deep, blind bosses. If gross porosity can occur in the absence of air(or other cavity gases), we must assume that such voids are the result of the metal's freezing while in a swirling*, turbulent state. Gating techniques are frequently used that provide a minimum of turbulence in the cavity. Such methods can produce castings that are substantially devoid of bubblelike porosity in specified critical areas. It is then that solidification shrinkage porosity becomes evident. The management of this type of defect is often quite difficult for the die caster. He is limited in his part design flexibility, his parting line placement, his gate thickness, and the inability of solid steel molds to accept such expediencies* as blind risers*, etc. It is probable that the existence of bubblelike porosity often masks shrinkage voids, i.e., provides a hiding place for them.

The die casting, being made with high metal injection pressure, has the capability of compressing all types of porosity into a smaller space than it might otherwise occupy.[1] This has led die casters to resort* to higher and higher pressures in order to produce castings with minimum visible porosity. On occasion, these pressures have approached 50 000 psi(plunger force/plunger area). Obviously, such extreme pressures are detrimental* to dies and also necessitate more powerful and massive casting machines. The economics of operating huge casting machines, compounded by the auxiliary facilities needed, are staggering*. Little wonder, then, that the die caster often feels like a man who has painted himself into a corner. It is to be hoped, therefore, that research sponsored by DCRF, the International Lead Zinc Research Organization(ILZRO) and others may soon lead to the knowledge needed to produce sounder* die castings through technology rather than bruteforce*.

Before leaving the subject of porosity, we would be remiss* if we failed to mention two rather recent developments which seek to reduce porosity in die castings. The first is the ACURAD process developed by General Motors Corp. This is a four cornered concept:

(1) Use of electrically resistive paper to create a thermal analogy of the freezing pattern that would exist in the actual mold.

(2) Use of thermal information developed in (1) to design the mold and its cooling passages to promote directional solidification of the casting.

(3) Use of thick, large area gates to provide low gate velocities and to permit feeding of the solidification shrinkage.

(4) Use of a compound, coaxial injection plunger to "wring" the last vestiges* of liquid metal out of the biscuit and thereby to feed the shrinking casting through the thick gate openings. ACURAD is frequently misunderstood and misrepresented because Corners (1), (2) and (3) are overlooked in discussing it.

The other technique that has received coverage in the technical press is the one patented by ILZRO as the Gas Pore Free process. Its operation is based on the principle of flushing* the die cavity with oxygen which reacts with the incoming metal and is thus consumed. The execution of the technique, however, requires complex equipment for flushing the mold and lubricating the mold and shot plunger with dry(non-oxidizable) lubricant films. To date, a few installations have been made in Japan, but none in the U.S., The process has not yet been applied to the hot chamber die casting of zinc or to magnesium or copper alloys.

It would certainly be unfair, too, to close our discussion of this subject leaving the reader with the impression that all die castings produced today contain gross voids. Such is not the case when many thousands of parts are produced daily to stringent* soundness specifications. Intelligent gating, generous venting, and the aid of powerful, modern die casting machines make it possible for the technically knowledgeable die caster to produce parts that are quite sound. Certainly, such demanding applications as automotive transmission parts would not be possible if the castings were very porous or otherwise lacking in integrity.

Casting 221

Key words:

flurry[阵风]	swirl[旋涡]	parting line[分型线]
expediency[方便]	riser[冒口]	resort[采取]
detrimental[有害的]	staggering[惊人的]	sound[致密的]
brute force[强力]	remiss[疏忽的]	vestige[残余]
flush[冲洗]	stringent[严格的]	

Note:

[1]因为有高的金属注射压力,压力铸造具有将各种气孔压缩得比其他任何铸造方法都小的能力。

Questions:

1) What is the difference between the terms Imperfection and Defect according to this passage?

2) All the porosities were generated due to air entrapping. (T/F)

3) There are defects in any casting product. (T/F)

4) With powerful modern die casting machines one can produce casting products which are free of defects. (T/F)

4.1.12 Venting the Mold

Over the years the die casting industry has either concentrated on or ignored cavity venting. Perhaps the dilemma results in part from the influence of cavity back pressure on the mature and the flight of the metal stream. The use of vacuum to try to extract the cavity gases ahead of the entering metal has been discussed above, and it was mentioned that the simple addition of vacuum to a die that had been gated for conventional venting actually made the casting more porous. In commercial practice today, the use of vacuum occupies a small but valuable niche*.

The relationship between gate and vent area was examined as a part of DCRF sponsored research at Case Western Reserve University. It was determined that the influence of the placement of the vent slot was greater than that of its size. Also, a device for venting the cavity at a point other than the parting plane was perfected. Similar devices made of commercially available porous metal inserts have been employed since as early as 1944, both here and in Russia.

The DCRF owns a patent on a venting device that has been found to be effective for many applications. It consists of a labyrinth* die section that is heavily water cooled. This configuration permits a vent area many times that otherwise possible, while still preventing the exit of the molten metal. The overflow pocket is usually considered as a part of the venting system. This consists of a pocket or numerous pockets in the die face outside of the cavity but close to it. These serve to accept the damaged metal at the front of the entering stream. A further function is to add heat to the die in preferred locations to achieve uniform mold temperature distribution. This latter role of the overflow is increasingly being recognized and exploited.

Key words:
niche[适当位置]   labyrinth[迷宫]

Questions:

1) Venting the mold is to pump the air out of the mold before casting. (T/F)

2) The molten metal may exit during venting if no proper device is employed. (T/F)

4.1.13 Other Efforts

ILZRO has for several years sponsored massive research work at Battelle Memorial Institute. The thrust of this program has been to identify the factors required to permit the economic production of large, thin wall zinc die castings. In large measure this aim has been achieved, though further refining working remains to be done. The successes to date are reflected in the reduction in the nominal* wall thickness of a 21 inch TV bezel basting from 0.06 to 0.036, briefly, this has been accomplished by:

(1) Meticulously* controlling mold temperature, developing automatic control equipment for the purpose.

Casting 223

(2) Employing gate and runner designs based on DCRF developed principles. Additionally, it was found effective to match the gate thickness at any one point to distance that the metal must flow to reach the overflow pocket.[1]

(3) Employing massive overflow volumes(100 to 200 percent of casting weight). The objective here is to create a momentarily high surface temperature on the mold. By scrubbing* the mold surface with this large amount of extra metal, a die temperature gradient is provided. The DCRF patented labyrinth chill plug was employed to seal off the massive overflow and to contain the metal within the die.

ILZRO has also sponsored extensive research at the British Non-Ferrous Metals Research Organization(BNF). This work has been more in the direction of developing process control techniques and equipment.

The International Copper Research Association (INCRA) has sponsored research work in the fields of die material and gating. These efforts are aimed at widening the markets for brass die castings.

Major custom and captive* die casters have facilities for die casting research. General Motors Corp., Western Electric Co., Bell Telephone Laboratories, Parker White Metal Co., and others have made major contributions to our storehouse of knowledge of the technology of die casting.

Key words:
nominal[名义的]   meticulously[仔细地]
scrub[冲刷]   captive[被迷住的]

Note:
[1]另外,据发现在任何一点匹配内浇道尺寸与金属必须流动到溢流槽的距离都是有效的。

Questions:

1) There are a few organizations which studied the die casting technology.(T /F)

2) Cu is also the kind of material often used in die casting.(T/F)

4.2 Optimization of Properties in Aluminum Casting

To achieve optimum properties in aluminum castings, basic theoretical considerations must be translated into commercial practice. Controls are required over various factors including microstructure, alloy chemistry, gas content, mode of fluid flow, and feeding. These points are discussed in terms of specific castings whose case histories illustrate the operation of the relevant factors under commercial conditions.

4.2.1 Introduction

In the past, the use of aluminum castings for aerospace and other critical applications was viewed with considerable caution. Minimum mechanical properties given by the standard specifications, were so low that the use of aluminum castings was not worthwhile where weight was an important consideration.

When specification MIL-A-21180 for high strength castings was issued in 1958, it was a challenge to the commercial industry. Although the principles for making high quality aluminum castings were known, it was necessary to translate these principles into workable commercial techniques. The innovations introduced by MIL-A-21180 included these points:

(1) Minimum mechanical properties at least 50% higher than previously specified.

(2) Properties determined from test bars machined from the casting rather than separately cast test bars.

(3) Molding technique to be chosen by the producer.

In these passages, the applications of important theoretical principles in a commercial foundry are illustrated by actual case histories of specific castings. Although the foundry is an investment casting[*] facility, the points made should be applicable to sand foundry molds or other ceramic mold techniques.

4.2.2 Chemistry Control

At present, the most widely used high strength alloys are of the aluminum silicon magnesium type. Strengthening* is accomplished by the controlled precipitation* of the magnesium silicate compound. The degree of strengthening is related to the amount of precipitate. This, in turn, is determined by the magnesium content of the alloy because the silicon content is well in excess of the amount required to react with the magnesium.

In general, yield strength is the property* most sensitive to the magnesium level. For high yield strengths, magnesium is held in the range of 0. 4% ~ 0. 7% (357 alloy). Lower yield strengths are obtained by holding the magnesium in the range of 0.2% ~ 0.4% (356 alloy).

With increasing matrix strength, there is an inevitable decline in ductility. However, this relationship can be easily overlooked because ductility is also very sensitive to soundness* and the morphology* of the silicon phase.

Specifications for high strength aluminum castings are difficult to satisfy by merely controlling the magnesium within the specified range. It is necessary to hold magnesium within closer limits, depending upon the balance desired between yield strength and elongation*.

Key words:
investment casting[熔模铸造]　strengthen[强化]　precipitation[沉淀]
property[性能]　　　　　　　soundness[致密性]morphology[形态]
elongation[延伸率]

Questions:

1) By what means can you strengthen the aluminum casting?

2) There are the elements of _____ in most aluminum castings.

3) The mold is not necessary if you want to make an aluminum casting. (T/ F)

226 *English in Materials Science and Engineering*

4.2.3 357 Alloy Casting

As an example, 357 alloy castings were experimentally produced at two levels of magnesium content: 0.42 and 0.58 percent. Other than magnesium, the remaining elements were the same.

Mechanical properties were determined from specimens machined from the castings. Locations 1 and 2 are on the base plate supporting the yoke* configuration. Properties show that at both specimen locations, the elongation is one third higher at the lower magnesium level. Also, the yield strengths are lower with lower magnesium specimens.

The 356 alloy castings were experimentally produced at two levels of magnesium content: 0.31 and 0.40 percent. Other than magnesium, the remaining elements were the same.

Mechanical properties were determined from specimens machined from four locations in the castings. Location 1 is on the long edge of the casing perimeter*; Location 2 is on the short edge; Location 3 is from an interior blade segment; Location 4 is from a diagonal* rib* stiffener. The results show that the mechanical properties vary with specimen location because of local solidification conditions. However, it is clear that higher elongations are achieved at the lower magnesium level. Conversely, yield strengths are higher with higher magnesium level.

Key words:
yoke[轭铁]   perimeter[周长]   diagonal[对角线]   rib[肋]

Questions:

1) What is the relationship between the magnesium content and the property of elongation for the aluminum alloy castings?

2) If lower yield strength is needed, more magnesium should be added into the 356 alloy. (T/F)

4.2.4 Degassing*

High quality aluminum castings cannot be produced from melts containing appreciable amounts of dissolved* hydrogen. Since the dissolved hydrogen is substantially insoluble* in the solidified metal, the gas tends to promote unsoundness*. The gas released from solution during solidification forms bubbles that block the channels by which feed metal flows to make up the volumetric* liquid to solid shrinkage.[1]

X-ray examination results show that the same section of two castings produced under different conditions of pouring*: poured before degassing with gas content of 0.026cc/100g, and poured after degassing with gas content of 0.001cc/100g. The porosity characteristic of the gassy* melt casting and the soundness of the degassed melt casting are self-evident*.

In order to achieve a reliable freedom from hydrogen in the melt, it is necessary to have an accurate and dependable method of measuring the gas content. It is essential to use the test to determine the end point of the degassing procedure, and also to perform the test at intervals as the melt is tapped* for pouring into molds to assure that no gas pickup occurs during this time.

In the authors' plant, the test method used is patterned after the method described by Sulinsky and Lipson. A 20 cc sample of liquid metal is solidified in a vacuum chamber at approximately 0.1 atmospheric pressure. From the measured density of the specimen, the gas content can be deduced.

Key words:

Degas[除气]   dissolve[溶解]   insoluble[不可溶解]
unsoundness[不致密]   volumetric[体积的]   pour[浇注]
gassy[含气的]   tap[排放]   self-evident[不言而喻的]

Note:

[1]凝固过程中从溶体里排出的气体形成气泡,阻塞了凝固收缩时补缩金属液流的通道。

228   *English in Materials Science and Engineering*

Questions:

1) Why must the aluminum melt be degassed before being poured into the mold?

2) Most gas dissolved in the aluminum melt is _____ .

3) Hydrogen can also be dissolved in the solid metal. (T/F)

4.2.5 Modification[*]

In the aluminum silicon type of alloys, the silicon has negligible solubility[*] in the aluminum. In the silicon range of the 356 and 357 alloys, the silicon phase is formed by a eutectic[*] reaction. If untreated, the silicon phase is acicular[*] and, because of its shape, has a detrimental effect on ductility. A number of substances, when added in small amounts, have the ability to modify the shape of the silicon phase. These addition agents are normally used for the eutectic and hypereutectic[*] aluminum silicon alloys.

Sodium[*] is the best known modifying agent and is used routinely for the eutectic type alloys containing about 12 percent silicon. However, in the hypoeutectic[*] alloys such as 356 and 357, the value of sodium additions is controversial. Melts made from virgin ingot normally have sodium present because it is a natural impurity from the aluminum refining process.

Since sodium is a volatile[*] element, it is easily lost from the melt. Thus the sodium additions have a limited life in the melt, and the modifying effect is known to "fade[*]" after extended holding periods. The melting of revert[*] adds to the danger that the melt will be depleted[*] of its sodium content.

The presence of adequate sodium is easily determined from a check of the microstructure. It is therefore good practice to make such checks routinely to determine when a modifying agent should be introduced to the melt.

A 356 alloy casting was used to determine experimentally the effect of modification. The sodium addition in this instance was 0.05

percent, and was added as a capsule* encased* in an aluminum cartridge. The microstructure before modification and after modification were checked.

Test bars were machined from the casting. Location 1 is in the midsection area while location 2 is in the extremity* of the casting. It can be concluded from both the mechanical properties and the microstructure that the modification effect represents a definite improvement.

Key words:
modification[变质]	solubility[溶解度]	eutectic[共晶]
acicular[针状]	hypereutectic[过共晶]	sodium[钠]
hypoeutectic[亚共晶]	volatile[不稳定的]	fade[减弱]
revert[返料]	deplete[耗尽]	capsule[胶囊]
encase[装入]	extremity[末端]	

Questions:

1)After modification, the silicon phase has an acicular structure. (T/F)

2)What is the best known modifying agent for the eutectic type Al-Si alloys?

4.2.6 Metal Flow

Aluminum castings are prone* to have oxide inclusions because molten aluminum forms an oxide skin that is insoluble in the liquid. Detached oxides may be floating or submerged in the melt. Gravity pouring tends to transfer these oxides into the casting. In addition, gravity pouring of aluminum produces oxides on the surface of the stream as well as in the metal as it cascades* through the ga ting system and mold cavity.

An effective method for avoiding oxide inclusions is to force the metal to flow into the mold cavity from a molten metal reservoir positioned below the mold. An effective method for accomplishing this is described by Lipson and Ripkin. In the method described, air

230   *English in Materials Science and Engineering*

pressure acts on a ceramic piston to force the metal upward into the mold cavity.

Castings produced by upward flow exhibit a much reduced incidence[*] of oxide defects as detected by X-ray technique.

4.2.7 Feeding

Feeding of castings is facilitated by upward flow both for chilled and unchilled castings. For unchilled castings, the feeding is enhanced by the forceful injection of the liquid into the solidifying semisolid casting. In chilled castings, the absorption of heat by the chill is increased by the minimizing of heat conduction losses at the chill casting interface.

The effectiveness of the chills in pressurized upward flow is explained by the loss of heat conduction experienced when an air gap is formed between the chill and the casting.[1] Reynolds has shown that the coefficient of heat transfer at the metal chill interface can be an order or magnitude greater if air gap is avoided. Reynolds' results are corroborated[*] in the paper by Levy, et al.

Savchenko, et al, have shown that aluminum castings poured under low pressure into chill molds solidify more rapidly than those gravity poured into the same chill mold. A 1.5 lb casting solidified in about 0.5 sec under pressure as compared to 2.5 sec for solidification by gravity pour.

A 355 alloy shrouded impeller[*] casting made without chills by upward flow under the pressure of 5 ~ 6 psi illustrates the fact that feeding is facilitated by forcing liquid into the solidifying mushy[*] metal. Five psi is the equivalent of a metallostatic pressure exerted by a 50 inch high liquid metal column.

It can be seen from examining the properties that the shroud and vane areas have the best properties, followed by the properties in the massive hub[*]. Except for the hub, Class 11 properties would be easily met. For the hub, Class 12 properties can be specified.

Casting 231

Key words:

prone[易于]   cascades[喷流]   incidence[发生率]
corroborate[确证]   shrouded impeller[闭式叶轮]
mushy[糊状的]   hub[轮毂]

Note:

[1]当在激冷铸型和铸件之间形成气隙时所经受的热传导损失说明了在加压情况下向上流动补缩时激冷铸型的效果。

Questions:

1) Why the inclusions are prone to be produced during casting?

2) Is the feeding method important to the properties of the castings?

3) In order to achieve optimum properties in aluminum castings, what methods shall we take into consideration?

4.3 Precision Casting* Process

Metal casting has a historic pedigree* as the manufacturing process first used by man to produce intricate metal articles and art objects. It played a major role in the industrial revolution and remains the basis of current manufacturing equipment and manufactured goods. The process plays an important part in aerospace component production and, as such, remains at the leading edge of technology development. Despite the competition from plastics and ceramics, metals still remain the dominant materials in the production of capital equipment and manufactured goods. Metal casting will continue to play a major role, as a manufacturing process of considerable versatility, for the foreseeable* future.

In common with other manufacturing processes, metal casting has not remained static and there have been significant developments in both the metallurgy of cast alloys and in casting processes. It is the developments in processing, and particularly those devised* to improve precision, which is the focus of this pass age. The objectives of these introductory passages are to establish the context within which precision casting processes are operated. This requires a definition and

232   *English in Materials Science and Engineering*

description of metal casting, a consideration of the attributes of metal casting in relation to other manufacturing processes, a summary of the structure of the foundry industry, and a definition of the term precision in the context of metal casting.

Key words:
precision casting [精密铸造]   pedigree[谱系]
foreseeable [可预见的]   devise[设计]

Questions:

1) The main purpose of this passage is to describe the casting processes of the parts for aerospace components. (T/F)

2) The role that the casting technology plays now is not so important as it did before. (T/F)

4.3.1 Metal Casting

In the metal casting process a metal, or more commonly an alloy, is heated until it is molten, whereupon it is poured into a mold or die that contains a cavity which represents the shape of the component or casting to be produced. In the case of a mold the cavity is produced by a pattern which is a replica* of the component required, whereas in the case of a die the cavity replicating the shape of the component is produced by machining.[1] Molds are invariably* expendable, being destroyed when the casting is removed. Dies, on the other hand, are permanent and may be used to produce a succession* of castings. Patterns may also be permanent or expendable. A permanent pattern is reusable, whereas an expendable pattern is consumed during the process of mold or casting production.

Key words:
replica[复制]   invariably[总是]   succession[连续]
Note:

[1] 一般铸型的型腔是通过一个铸模造型出来的,这个铸模和所需零件外形一致;而在压铸模中,具有零件外形的型腔是通过机械加工而成。

Questions:

1) What is the difference between the mold and the die?
2) Many products can be produced with a single mold. (T/F)

4.3.2 Sand Casting

In the traditional sand casting process, sand is mixed with clay and water to produce a moldable mixture. The moistened clay provides the bonding agent* which binds* the sand grains together when the molding sand is compacted around a pattern to produce a mold.[1] In order that the pattern may be removed from the mold, to provide the cavity into which the metal will be poured, the mold must be made in at least two parts. These mold parts can be separated for removal of the pattern and joined again to receive the metal.

4.3.3 Gating and Feeding

The metal enters the mold cavity through a system of channels referred to as the running or gating system. The gating system transports the liquid metal from the pouring ladle to the mold cavity and it has an important influence on the quality of a casting. Metal, like most materials, expands when it is heated and contracts when it cools. Contraction has a major effect on casting quality. During the melting stage the metal is heated to a temperature above its melting point to ensure that it will flow readily and completely fill the mold cavity before solidification commences*. When this superheated liquid metal is poured into a mold it will lose heat and contract as it cools, this is referred to as liquid state contraction. With further cooling, and the loss of latent* heat of fusion, the atoms of the metal lose energy and become closely bound together in a regular structure. A significant decrease in volume accompanies the change of state from liquid to solid and this is referred to as phase change or solidification contraction. If no attempt is made to compensate for these two forms of contraction then the casting will show signs of shrinkage, either in the form of surface sinks* or as internal voids*. To overcome this problem feeder heads* are provided and act as reservoirs which feed liquid metal into the casting as it solidifies, thus compensating for the shrinkage. When the entire system is solid it will cool down to ambient temperature and contract as it does so, this is referred to as solid state contraction. As a consequence of this form of contraction the casting will clearly be smaller than the pattern from which it was produced.

Key words:

agent[剂]   bind[束缚]   commence[开始]
latent[潜伏的]   sink[陷坑]   void[空洞]
feeder heads [冒口]

Note:

[1]当用紧实铸模周围的型砂来造型时,湿粘土提供粘结剂把砂粒粘结起来。

Questions:

1) How is the sand mold made?

2) How many kinds of contraction are there in the casting process? What are they?

3) What is the function of the gating system?

4.3.4 Pattern Features

Solid state contraction is, in principle, predictable because it is a function of the metals coefficient of thermal expansion (CTE). Consequently, it is possible to produce a pattern which is oversize by the predicted solid state contraction so that the casting produced will be of the required size.[1] It can be seen that a pattern is not an exact replica of the component to be produced. It is over size to compensate for solid state contraction. The pattern will be oversize for another reason, which is the provision* of a machining allowance*. This assumes that the casting cannot be produced to the precise dimensions required by the component and that machining will therefore be necessary.

Casting 235

4.3.5 Expendable* Patterns

When an expendable pattern is used to produce a mold there is no requirement for a joint in the mold or, consequently, taper on the pattern. The casting produced more closely resembles the final dimensions and shape of the component required. Not surprisingly, therefore, less machining is required and the casting can be considered to be more precise. Expendable* patterns are used in the lost-wax, investment casting process and the lost-foam, evaporative pattern casting process.

Key words:
provision[供应]   allowance[余量]   expendable[消耗的]
Note:
[1]因此,可以按照已知的固态收缩率来加大铸模尺寸,从而生产出符合尺寸的铸件。

Questions:

1)The size of the pattern should be larger than that of the casting. (T/F)

2) The castings produced with the expendable pattern is more precise than those with permanent patterns. (T/F)

4.3.6 Die Requirements

As indicated, metal may be poured into a metal die within which the cavity has been machined. Although no pattern is used the die, like an expendable mold, must have a joint line, in this case to enable the casting to be extracted. The die cavity, like a permanent pattern, must incorporate contraction and machining allowances and, to aid extraction of the casting. Castings produced in dies may not be quite as precise as those produced by the lost-wax process, but they are noted for a high degree of precision and consistency. [1]

236 *English in Materials Science and Engineering*

4.3.7 Cores

Internal features or external features that cannot readily be molded, can be provided in castings by the use of cores*. Collapsible* cores are made in bonded sand, plaster* or ceramic materials are expendable. Separate equipment, termed a core box, is required for the production of cores and special processes have been developed for their production. Cores are located in core prints in the mold or die and these prints are formed as features of the mold or die. Permanent metal cores can be used in the die casting process, especially pressure die casting for which collapsible cores are not currently suitable.

This preliminary consideration of the casting process has provided a basis for process classification according to the permanent or expendable nature of the pattern and/or mold.

Key words:
core[芯]　　　　　collapsible[组合的]　　　　　plaster[石膏]
core print[芯座]
Note:
[1]压力铸造生产的铸件或许没有熔模铸造生产的铸件精度高,但它们却是以高精度和一致性著称的。

Questions:

1)What is a die?
2)The die is a expendable mold. (T/F)
3)Why are the cores used in the casting processes?

4.3.8 The Advantages of the Metal Casting Process

Metal casting competes against several alternative manufacturing processes in the production of shaped metal components, they are Forming, Fabrication, Machining, and Powder Metallurgy etc, each of these processes has its advantages and disadvantages but none can match the sheer* flexibility of metal casting in respect of design

Casting 237

versatility, alloy range, shape, size and order quantity.

4.3.9 Casting Size and Weight Range

Components ranging in size from those used to produce a zip*
fastener, produced as zinc alloy in pressure die castings weighing a
fraction of a gramme, to steel mill housings, produced in sand molded
steel and weighing 200 tons, can be produced by metal casting.[1] No
single process meets the entire size and weight range, but there is a
process to meet every requirement.

4.3.10 Design Versatility

The foundry maxim* if you can design it, we can cast it holds
true, with the provision that design modifications should be considered
when they can reduce production costs and improve casting quality!
However, the designer has almost unrestricted freedom when casting is
chosen as the principal manufacturing process. Complex contours, thin
sections, ribs, and cast holes can be specified. Internal features such as
hollow shapes, volute* forms, water jackets and oil galleries* can be
accommodated through the use of cores. However, the versatility is
process specific and an appropriate process must be chosen to provide
the principal design features required. Generally, the refractory mold
aggregate and sand casting processes provide the greatest versatility and
the permanent mold processes the least.

4.3.11 Alloy Compatibility

All metals and alloys in common use pass through a melting and
casting stage, even when they are subsequently shaped by forming,
fabrication or machining. Even the alloy powders for powder
metallurgy can be produced by atomising a liquid melt. Some alloys
may only be processed by the casting route, the major examples being
the range of cast irons. While metal casting is generically suitable for
processing the whole range of commercial metals and alloys, this does

not imply that each specific casting process is suitable for every alloy. Constraints may be imposed* by the melting temperature of the alloy or by its reactivity with certain mold materials. Nevertheless, by careful selection a process can be chosen to be compatible with a specific alloy system.

4.3.12 Production Quantities

The metal casting process is as suitable for one-off production as it is for one million-off.[1] This versatility is only restricted by the production methods employed by a foundry and the tooling requirements of a particular process. In vestment in specialist equipment and tooling usually requires appreciable order quantities to justify it. Sand casting is the most versatile process and is suit able for the economic production of any order quantity. On the debit* side, the metal casting process requires specialist plant and tooling and is energy intensive because of the requirement to melt the metal. Although castings are produced to shape and therefore minimize the amount of material removed by machining, the yield of the casting process itself can be low as 50%. The waste material, in the form of the gating and feeding system, can be recycled, but there is an additional cost associated with this. Critics of the process will argue that castings are prone* to defects such as shrinkage and gas porosity, non-metallic inclusions, distortion and cracking. However, the causes of such defects are well understood and careful attention to process control can eliminate them.

Key words:
sheer[绝对的]   zip[拉链]   maxim[格言]
volute[涡形]   oil gallery[油沟]   impose[加上]
debit[借方]   prone[倾向于]

Notes:

[1]从小到拉链扣等只有几分之一克重的锌合金压铸件,到大如轧钢机机架等重达 200 吨的砂型铸造零件都可通过金属铸造工艺生产。

[2]金属铸造工艺既适合于单件生产,也适合于大批量生产。

Casting 239

Questions:

1) What are the advantages of the metal casting process?

2) What kinds of defects will be there in the castings if the process is not controlled precisely?

3) What is the difference between the sand casting processes and the permanent mold processes?

4) What is the most versatile process in the production of shaped metal components?

5) Which is suitable for the economic production of any order quantity?

(a) Permanent mold casting.   (b) Continuous casting.

(c) Squeeze casting.   (d) Sand casting.

4.3.13 Structure of the Foundry Industry

The foundry industry has evolved to the extent that individual companies tend to specialize in particular processes, alloys and type of production. This is a general rule to which there are, of course, exceptions. The major division within the industry is based upon whether the companies produce ferrous or nonferrous alloys. The ferrous sector of the industry is the larger, both in terms of the tonnage output and the number of companies engaged in it. The method of melting and the metallurgy of steels is quite different to that for cast irons, so that most foundries specialize in one of the two ferrous groups. Within the ferrous sector iron founding predominates and this industry features. Some quite large production units which specialize in the mass production requirements of the automotive industry. The sand molding processes are predominant within the ferrous foundry sector, with green sand the most widely used mold material, although there is significant and widespread use of the cold set processes. The requirements for making one-off, large castings are quite different from those for making repetition automotive castings, so that companies tend to specialize either as jobbing or repetition founders.[1]

240　*English in Materials Science and Engineering*

4.3.14 Refractory Metals

In the non-ferrous sector of the industry the differentiation between jobbing and repetition founders still exists. The size of the foundries in this sector is generally smaller than those in the ferrous sector. Although foundries may specialize in one alloy group, for example aluminum base, a significant proportion will produce more than one alloy group. The range of processes available to non-ferrous founders is extended beyond those available to the ferrous sector, primarily because they are able to use the die casting processes. While non-ferrous foundries successfully exploit a range of casting processes there is a tendency towards specialization, especially where pressure die casting is employed. The cost of capital plant and the specialist engineering skills required in die design and production encourages this specialization.

Investment casting is also highly specialized and represents a distinct sector of the foundry industry. Within this sector of the industry foundries tend to specialize in one of three principal alloy groupings which are superalloys, steels and aluminum alloys. The investment casting industry has shown steady growth for many years and this growth is predicted to continue world wide. The pressure die casting sector is also growing. In this case the automotive industry is the driving force as it substitutes aluminum alloys for cast iron in its bid to reduce the weight of cars and improve their fuel efficiency.

Note：
[1]单个大铸件生产和重复自动化生产的要求差别很大,因此铸造厂家要么专门单件生产要么专门批量生产。

Questions：

1)What is the tendency of the development of foundry industry?
2)Which is not the principal casting process for aluminum alloys?
（a）Continuous casting.　　　（b）Sand casting.

Casting   241

(c) Die casting.   (d) Investment casting.
3)What is investment casting?

4.3.15 Precision in the Context of Metal Casting Processes

If asked to define the attributes they expect of a precision casting, most people would start by stating that the casting must be dimensionally accurate. By this they mean that it should conform as closely as possible to the required dimensions of the final component. Associated with this will be the requirement for consistency, which is an attribute that is especially valued by the customer. Dimensional accuracy is directly related to surface smoothness, so that the attribute of a good surface finish is important in a precision casting. The ability to produce thin sections over comparatively large areas is an attribute much sought after by designers seeking to minimize component weight or achieve consistent heat transfer properties.[1] This is a feature not generally attributed to sand castings but expected in precision castings.

The ability to produce intricate shapes and reproduce fine details is expected of precision castings. While the metal casting process is generically capable of producing complex shapes, the replication of fine detail is the province of the specialist precision casting processes. This capability for detail can be extended to the provision of as cast holes, not necessarily round, which in the best of the precision casting processes may be produced without the need to resort to machining.[2] The final expectation of a precision casting is that it should demonstrate the attribute of metallurgical integrity. The casting should be free from shrinkage and gas porosity, non-metallic inclusions and other casting defects. It should demonstrate, as a consequence, improved mechanical properties and performance in service.

Notes:
[1]生产大型薄壁铸件的能力是设计者们所努力追求的目标,设计者们希望能使零件重量最小化或获得均匀一致的热传导性能。
[2]生产精密铸件的能力可以延伸到提供铸造孔洞等,在铸孔要求不高

242 *English in Materials Science and Engineering*

的情况下,最好的精密铸造工艺可直接铸出孔洞而不用机械加工。

Questions:

1)What are the attributes of a precision casting?

2)What does the term "metallurgical integrity" mean?

4.3.16 Factors Influencing the Attainment of Precision in Casting

Several stages are involved in the production of a casting, each of which can exert an influence on precision.

◆ Tooling

A casting cannot be produced to a higher standard of dimensional accuracy or surface finish than the pattern or die from which it is produced. It is essential that the highest standard of tooling in a material appropriate to the process is used. This equipment must be maintained regularly and inspected for damage or wear that might impair the precision of the casting.

◆ Mold Production

In the permanent pattern, expendable mold processes the extent to which the mold conforms to the pattern shape is extremely important. Poor conformity at this stage negates[*] the advantage of accurate tooling. Separation of the mold from the pattern is a critical stage in that damage of the mold is possible. The expendable pattern, expendable mold processes are not susceptible[*] to this problem but the process must still ensure that the mold conforms to the pattern. For the permanent mold processes, mold production implies die production and the requirements here are similar to those highlighted under tooling.

◆ Mold Materials

The material chosen for the mold has a direct influence on both the dimensional accuracy and surface finish of the casting. It may also affect the metallurgical integrity of the casting by influencing the formation of shrinkage, gas porosity, non-metallic inclusions and metal penetration defects.

◆ Mold Location

Processes employing permanent patterns or permanent molds require a joint line in the mold or die. Joint lines are invariably associated with a reduction in accuracy. Dimensions across a joint line are never maintained to the same tolerances as those within a single mold or die half. This problem is compounded by multiple joints and by the requirements for core location. Further inaccuracies may arise from the need to locate the mold or die halves to one another. The pin and bush method of location is most frequently employed and inaccurate machining or wear of the pins and bushes can contribute to inaccurate matching of the mold or die halves, with a consequent mismatch showing on the casting.[1] Apart from locating to each other mold halves, when produced in molding boxes, must locate to the pattern equipment, so this aspect must also be considered.

◆ Pouring Stage

The principal requirement at this stage is that the metal should completely fill the mold and die and replicate its shape and detail. This is related to the concept of metal fluidity which is a technological rather than a physical property. Several factors influence metal fluidity. A high metal pouring temperature promotes fluidity, so too does a preheated mold or die. Alloy composition plays an important role and near eutectic alloys such as cast iron and certain aluminum silicon alloys are especially good in this respect. Smooth mold surfaces aid metal flow but if this is achieved at the expense of a loss in permeability* , then the back pressure exerted because air cannot readily escape from the mold will in turn restrict the inflow of metal. A second cause of concern is the effect of heat on the mold or die material. This will clearly expand, enlarging the mold cavity and consequently the casting. For those materials which expand in a predictable manner, an allowance can be made in much the same way as the allowance for contraction. However, silica* , which is the most common mold material, does not expand in a uniform manner, so that castings produced in this material are the most prone to inaccuracy.

244　*English in Materials Science and Engineering*

◆ Casting Contraction

Although the value of the CTE is a constant for a given material and is used as the basis for incorporating a contraction allowance in the tooling, casting contraction is unfortunately not so predictable in practice. This lack of predictability arises because castings are complex shapes with section variations and, therefore, do not cool or contract uniformly. In addition, the mold or die may exert a constraint* to contraction, building in residual stresses that may lead to distortion. The combination of these factors conspires* against accurate prediction of, and allowance for contraction and therefore contributes to dimensional variations.

◆ Casting Finishing

After separation from the mold or die castings progress through a series of finishing stages which typically consist of shot blasting*, degating*, feeder head removal and grinding. Heat treatment may also be required and, in the absence of controlled atmospheres, a separate post heat treatment shot blasting operation may be necessary. The nature of these activities is such that if they are not practised with care they can impair the precision of the castings.

Key words:
negate[否定]　　　susceptible[易受影响的]　　permeability[渗透性]
silica[硅土]　　　constraint[约束]　　　　　conspire[凑合起来]
shot blasting[喷砂/喷丸]

Note:
[1]插销和衬套定位法是最常用的铸造定位法。插销和衬套的不精确加工或磨损能导致铸型或压铸模分型面的错位,从而导致铸件误差。

Questions:

1)List some factors that affect the precision of the castings.

2) In order to obtain a precise casting, some post casting technologies should be adopted.(T/F)

3) The precision of the casting is not decided by the mold material.(T/F)

4.3.17 Measures Available to Improve the Precision in Castings

Clearly, attention to detail in respect of each of the aforementioned factors will maximize the potential for improving the precision of a casting, independently of the process chosen. However, it is generally recognized that special measures must be taken to optimize precision and some of these measures are introduced here.

The sand molding processes are considered to produce the least precise castings. However, the standards of precision have improved with developments in machinery and processes. In the case of green sand molding, improvements have been obtained through an understanding of the inter relationship between clay and moisture content, mold compaction and dimensional accuracy. Molding machines have been developed which achieve consistently high mold densities and this has resulted in an improvement in dimensional accuracy and consistency. The introduction of the cold setting processes(inorganic and organic) revolutionized the jobbing a nd short run production of castings. Hardening of the sand in contact with the pattern is also a feature of the shell molding process. The process also provides an improved casting surface finish through the use of a fine sand, without the adverse effect on permeability that this usually implies.[1] The development of the unbonded sand processes has also provided improvements. Reduced machining requirements are a feature of the castings produced by both the V-process and lost- foam process. The absence of water or binders form these sands mold material related casting defects and results in improved metallurgical integrity.

Silica sand is the common feature in the sand casting processes and its use legislates* against the highest standards of precision in most cases. Substitution of silica by zircon* is practised to a limited extent in the shell molding process and the Cosworth process, with improved dimensional accuracy as a benefit. However, zircon sand is expensive and this has prevented its widespread use.

The elimination of silica sand as the mold material is a feature of

246   *English in Materials Science and Engineering*

the plaster mold, investment casting, ceramic mold and die casting processes, so that these processes can be expected to demonstrate improved precision. Precision is improved still further in the investment casting process because an expendable pattern is used there is no mold joint line. With the exception of die casting, these processes also use very fine refractory particles and so provide improved casting surface finishes.

Mold preheat, as an aid to improved metal fluidity and mold or die filling characteristics, is featured in investment casting and is an option in the ceramic mold and plaster mold processes, where it improves thin section capability and detail replication*. Die preheat confers* the same advantages, but it is the almost instantaneous pressurised filling associated with pressure die casting which makes that process unique in its thin section casting capability.[2] Pressure displacement of metal into molds or dies is featured in a number of counter gravity casting processes. However, the pressure difference is small by comparison with pressure die casting and its primary objective is to provide quiescency*, that is non-turbulent, filling of the cavity. This reduces the generation of non-metallic inclusions, thereby improving metallurgical integrity. The maintenance of the pressure difference during solidification of the casting enhances casting soundness and this is used to advantage in such processes as low pressure die casting, the counter pressure process, the Cosworth process and the Hitchiner CLA and CLV processes. Vacuum melting and casting is an essential requirement for the production of nickel base superalloy castings. Under the condition of vacuum, oxidation and gas absorption are eliminated, with a consequent improvement in metallurgical integrity. Vacuum suction may also be used to improve mold filling by removing the air, and thus the back pressure it creates, from the mold or die cavity. In die casting the removal of air from the cavity reduces the occlusion* of gases during turbulent* filling.

It can be seen from the foregoing comments that there are a number of measures which can be adopted by metal founders to improve the precision attainable in castings. Further details of these measures and other process developments are provided in subsequent passages.

Key words:
legislate[制定法律]　　zircon[锆石]　　replication [复制]
confer[赠与]　　　　　quiescency[静止]　occlusion[封闭]
turbulent[紊乱的]

Notes:

[1]使用细砂,也可以提高铸件表面精度,而不会带来常见的对渗透性的不利影响。

[2]压铸模预热具有同样的优点,但它是对压力铸造件的近乎瞬时加压填充,从而使压铸工艺在薄壁铸件生产能力上有着独特的优势。

Questions:

1)List some measures by using which the precision of the casting can be increased.

2)List several materials that can be used to make the mold.

4.3.18 Cost Implications of Precision Casting

Precision castings are invariably more expensive than standard castings. This arises because of the more expensive plant and processes required to produce precision castings and through the need for improved standards of process and quality control. The increased cost of precision castings is justified when there is simply no suitable alternative manufacturing route or when the savings which accrue from the reduced requirement for machining outweigh the additional cost of the casting.[1]

Significant cost savings may also occur when precision casting is used to produce components previously produced by an alternative manufacturing process. Regan and Fleck have reported that significant cost savings arose when investment castings were used to replace forgings and/or fabricated assemblies and that this was achieved without a compromise* in design function or component integrity.

248 *English in Materials Science and Engineering*

Pressure die castings can provide similar benefits and may even be competitive on a weight saving basis when compared with plastics.

4.3.19 Near Net Shape Capability

Manufacturing processes that produce components to net or near net shape and size with the minimum number of processing steps and with as little waste as possible have the potential to reduce manufacturing costs and improve manufacturing efficiency. This concept is being applied in metal forming processes such as flashless forging* and fine blanking*, and in the powder metallurgy route. The metal casting process has an inherent near net shape capability and the precision casting processes can produce castings which come close to meeting net shape and size requirements. With the continuing process development and improved process control, castings are being produced closer to shape and size to the benefit of the industry's customers.

Key words：
compromise[妥协]　　　　　flashless forging [无飞边锻造]
fine blanking[精密冲裁]
　Note：
[1]精密铸件的高成本在下列两种情况下是值得的：一是没有其他合适的替代加工方法；二是因降低铸件要求引起的后续加工成本超过了精密铸件的附加成本。

Questions：

1）The higher the precision of a casting, the higher the cost of the product.（T/F）

2）The cost of the high precision castings can not be lowered.（T/F）

5

Forming

5.1 Fundamentals of Metal Forming

5.1.1 Metal Forming Processes as a System

The term metal forming refers to a group of manufacturing methods by which the given shape of a workpiece(a solid body) is converted to another shape without change in the mass or composition of the material of the workpiece.

Classification of manufacturing processes: Metal forming is used synonymously* with deformation or deforming and comprises the methods in group II of the manufacturing process classification shown below. The manufacturing processes are divided into six main groups:

Group I —Primary forming: Original creation of a shape from the molten or gaseous state or from solid particles of undefined shape, that is, creating cohesion* between particles of the material.

Group II —Deforming: Converting a given shape of a solid body to another shape without change in mass or material composition, that is, maintaining cohesion.

Group Ⅲ—Separating: Machining or removal of material, that is, destroying cohesion.

Group Ⅳ—Joining: Uniting of individual workpieces to form subassemblies*, filling and impregnating* of workpieces, and so on, that is, increasing cohesion between several workpieces.

Group Ⅴ—Coating: Application of thin layers to a workpiece, for example, galvanizing*, painting, coating with plastic foils, that is, creating cohesion between substrate* and coating.

Group Ⅵ—Changing the material properties: Deliberately* changing the properties of the workpiece in order to achieve optimum characteristics at a particular point in the manufacturing process, These methods include changing the orientation of microparticles as well as their introduction and removal, such as by diffusion, that is, rearranging, adding, or removing particles.[1]

In manufacturing technology, particularly in groups Ⅰ to Ⅳ, we are continually faced with the problem of how to manufacture most economically a particular technical product with specific tolerance requirements, surface structure, and material properties.

Key words:
synonymously[同义地] cohesion[结合，凝聚] subassembly[部件]
impregnate[使充满] galvanize[电镀] substrate[底层，下层]
deliberately[有目的地，故意地]
Note:
[1]这些方法包括改变微粒的取向，以及通过扩散产生或消除这些微粒，或者说是重排，增加或减少微粒。

Question:

Which group do the casting, forging, welding and heat treatment process belong to respectively?

Forming 251

◆ Characteristics of Deformation Methods

In contrast to the very large group of methods of shaping parts by means of separation (group Ⅲ), metal forming methods have the following characteristics:

(1) The loads and stresses required for deformation are very high. The stresses vary between 50 and 2 500 MPa, depending on the method and material concerned. Since usually the entire workpiece, or at least a major part of it, is to be deformed, the loads can also be very high. In forging presses, for example, they may reach 750 MN.

(2) The majority of the parts are completely deformed. Because of the high loads involved, the tools are generally very large, heavy, and correspondingly expensive. The manufacture of metal forming tools requires well-equipped workshops and highly skilled workers since the tolerances required approach[*] those of precision engineering and gauge[*] making. Thus metal forming technology is closely associated with machining through the manufacture of metal forming tools. However, only small batches, or even a single set, are the rule.[1]

(3) Because of the high costs of machinery and tools, certain minimum quantities are a prerequisite[*] for production to become economical. When minimum quantities are assured, the advantages of the deformation methods are (a) high productivity and short production times, (b) high accuracy, within particular tolerances, with regard to dimension and shape, and (c) good mechanical properties of the manufactured component.

Key words:
approach[接近]　gauge[量规,量表]　prerequisite[先决条件;首要的]
Note:
[1]然而只是小量的,甚至是单件(单套)的(工具设备)才是这样的。

Question:

Comparing with other groups of methods, what characteristics do

252　*English in Materials Science and Engineering*

the metal forming methods have?

◆ Technical And Economic Significance of Metal Forming

The following list outlines the most important areas of application of workpieces produced by deformation, underlining their technical significance:

(1) Components for automobiles and machine tools as well as for industrial plants and equipment. Here metal forming is a vital link in the development of modern design in light alloys.

(2) Hand tools, such as hammers, pliers*, screwdrivers, and surgical instruments.

(3) Fasteners*, such as screws, nuts, bolts, and rivets.

(4) Containers, such as metal boxes, cans, and canisters*.

(5) Construction elements used in tunnelling, mining, and quarrying* (roofing and walling elements, pit props*, etc.).

(6) Fittings* used in the building industry, such as for doors and windows.

With regard to the variety of materials to be deformed, the 1970s brought about continued diversification, corresponding to higher demands for strength, and resistant to fatigue, heat, and corrosion by the users of such workpieces. Besides steel (carbon and alloy steels, including stainless and heat-resistant steels), nonferrous light and heavy alloys, such as aluminum, zinc, and copper and their alloys, may be shaped by deformation. Furthermore, metals such as titanium* and its alloys are in increasing demand, as are heat-resistant nickel-based materials and metals such as tungsten*, molybdenum*, and zirconium* and their alloys, as well as other similar materials. Strong impetus* for the development of the latter materials has come from the fields of aerospace and reactor technology.

The great economic significance of metal forming to modern

industrial states can be only briefly outlined here. Both ferrous and nonferrous metals—unless cast directly in their final shapes—pass through either rolling mills or extrusion presses. This creates a so-called "semifinished" product. In the subsequent step from semifinished to finished product, the significance of sheet-metal working has tended to increase proportionally with the improvement in the standards of living. If one accepts that from 20% to over 40% of all rolled steel production (depending on the standard of living) is in the form of sheets and coils, it is clear that many millions of tons of steel go on to be worked by metal-forming processes. In the manufacture of bulk-metal components, hot forging of steel and nonferrous materials—as used for high-strength temperature-resistant workpieces for aircraft and engine components—as well as cold extrusion and upsetting in conjunction with other processes are of major importance for the manufacture of shaped components and fixtures [*].

Key words:

pliers[钳子, 老虎钳]   fastener[扣件, 紧固件]   canister[小罐, 筒]
quarrying[采石]   pit props[坑道支架]   fitting[部件,配件]
tungsten[钨]   molybdenum[钼]   zirconium[锆]
fixture[固定设备, 装置, 工作夹具]

Question:

What kind of things can be produced by deformation?

◆ Methods Used in Metal Forming

The following classification of the deformation methods into five groups is based mainly on the important differences in effective stresses. No simple descriptions of stress states are possible since, depending on the kind of operation, different stress states may occur simultaneously, or they may change during the course of the deforming operation. Therefore, the predominant stresses are chosen as the classification criteria. The five groups of metal-forming processes may then be defined as follows:

(1) Compressive forming (forming under compressive stresses): German standard covers the deformation of a solid body in which the plastic state is achieved mainly by uni- or multiaxial compressive loading.

(2) Combined tensile and compressive forming (forming under combined tensile and compressive stresses). German standard covers the deformation of a solid body in which the plastic state is achieved mainly by combined uni- or multiaxial tensile and compressive loading.

(3) Tensile forming (forming under tensile stresses): German standard covers the deformation of a solid body in which the plastic state is achieved mainly through uni- or multiaxial tensile stresses.

(4) Forming by bending (forming by means of bending stresses): German standard covers the deformation of a solid body in which the plastic state is achieved mainly by means of a bending load.

(5) Forming by shearing (forming under shearing stresses): German standard covers the deformation of a solid body in which the plastic state is achieved mainly by means of a shearing load.

Within these groups, further subdivision is possible on the basis of kinematic* considerations (a relative movement between tool and workpiece), of tool geometry and workpiece geometry, as well as of the relationship between the two. However, these aspects are not necessarily of the same importance in the different groups.

The classification of metal forming methods intentionally* leaves open* the question of whether a process is carried out without preheating, that is, at room temperature, or after heating to a higher temperature. Up to now, the recrystallization* temperature has been taken by metallurgists as the boundary between cold and hot forming.

Forming   255

However, although this undoubtedly influences the behavior of the workpiece material during forming, it is widely recognized today that spontaneous* recovery plays a far greater role in rapid forming operations. In addition, this terminology* leads to a confusing situation with the wide variety of materials now in use. For example, the deformation of lead at room temperature should be termed "hot forming" while that of molybdenum at 800° C would be "cold forming". For this reason German standard makes a distinction between deformation performed at room temperature and deformation performed on a workpiece heated above room temperature.

The classification system chosen has the great advantage that each process appears only once. It permits, at least in groups 1 to 3 of the metal forming methods, to draw qualitative conclusions as to what changes in shape may be aimed at by means of the methods belonging to these groups. It is well known that formability (a measure of the shape change that a workpiece can withstand) decreases until external or internal damage occurs. This happens when the stress state in the deformation zone changes from multiaxial pressure through combined tensile and compressive stresses to tri-, bi-, or uniaxial tension. Examples of this are extrusion, upsetting, deep drawing, and stretch forming. The process boundary, that is, the degree of deformation attainable, depends either on the load that the tool will withstand (as in cold extrusion) or on the loading of the workpiece (as in stretch forming).

The five groups of metal forming methods may further be divided into 18 subgroups, and these subgroups comprise a total of about 230 basic methods of which special applications exist, in particular where rolling is concerned. Furthermore, innumerable combinations of these methods are used in industry.

256 *English in Materials Science and Engineering*

Key words:

kinematic[运动学的]　　facilitate[推动,使容易]　inclusion[包含]
intentionally[有意地,故意地]　　　　　　　open[未决定的]
recrystallization[再结晶]　spontaneous[自发的]　terminology[术语]
allocate[分派,分配]

Question:

How many different stress states can you tell us?

5.1.2 Fundamentals of Technical Plasticity Theory

Plasticity theory is the foundation for the numerical treatment of metal forming processes. The use of its fundamental equations, though, often results in mathematical difficulties when applied to practical problems. This led to the development of solution techniques which today collectively carry the name of elementary* plasticity theory. In this theory, the mathematical difficulties are circumvented* by making simplifying assumptions regarding the deformation and stress states occurring in the workpiece. As a result, one obtains an approximate quantitative description of a metal forming process.

Materials science and metallurgy can explain the origins of the plastic state of metallic bodies and its dependence on various parameters, such as process speed, prior history, temperature, and so on. The essentially older plasticity theory deals with the calculation of stresses, forces, and deformation. Its formulation does not directly incorporate the body of metallurgical* knowledge, even though the accuracy of the description of metals undergoing plastic flow could thereby be increased.

Plasticity theory is rather based on macroscopically* observed phenomena, in other words, on the properties of materials which can be observed and measured directly in deformation processes, such as the tension and compression tests. This leads to the following simple

Forming   257

description of the plastic state.

Plasticity is the capacity of a material to change its shape permanently under the action of forces when the corresponding stress state reaches a material-dependent critical magnitude called yield strength or initial flow stress. As seen from the results of the tension test, when the stress is below the yield strength, the deformation disappears upon unloading: the material behaves elastically. If the stress exceeds the yield strength, permanent deformation results. Upon unloading, the workpiece has a form that is different from its initial one. It is then said to have been plastically or permanently deformed, or, if a definite final shape was sought, it has been (trans)formed. Materials which behave in an elastic-plastic manner can, after having been permanently deformed, again be loaded until the flow stress is reached (it now has a magnitude larger than the initial one) without additional permanent deformation setting in. This increase in the flow stress as a result of prior deformation is called strain hardening.

Key words:
elementary[基本的]   circumvent[智取]   metallurgical[冶金学的]
macroscopically[宏观上]

Question:

What is the difference between elastic deformation and plastic deformation?

◆Finite-Element Method

The finite-element method has been used extensively for elastic problems. The method is a powerful one and is reserved* for problems that can be programmed and solved by computer techniques. The literature* over the last 20 years abounds with references to finite-element development and application, and many all-purpose finite-

258   *English in Materials Science and Engineering*

element codes are now commercially available.

As the name implies, the basic building block is an element of finite dimensions. The object to be analyzed is divided into a number of these small elements. These elements are joined at corners, and it is usually assumed that the stress is uniform throughout the element. The element distortions* are computed by conventional theory. The total behavior of the structure depends on the integrated effects of each of the parts. Thus since a part is usually divided into a multitude of elements, a solution is possible with the help of a computer. The accuracy of the finite-element method depends on both the type of problem and the number and type of elements selected.

In the late 1960s the success of the finite-element problems stimulated the work of extending the application of the method to the area of plastic deformation. It was originally applied to elastic-plastic problems, ones in which the plastic strain is of the order of the elastic one. Here the strain is separated into an elastic part and a plastic part. The elastic part is governed by Hooke's law, while the plastic part used the Prandtl-Reuss equations. The nonlinearity in the constitutive equations is satisfied iteratively*. This can be accomplished by either the initial-strain method or the initial-stress method. Of these two methods, the initial-stress method has found increased favor. With this method, the deformation zone can be very accurately determined.

It needs to be pointed out that the finite-element method is not geometry-dependent. Rather, with this technique one can analyze arbitrary geometrically complicated structures.

For large deformations it is generally not necessary to consider elastic deformations. In fact, in the analysis of most metal forming operations, as a rule one can neglect them and employ the rigid-plastic material model. An exception to this rule is that it is generally mandatory* to utilize elastic-plastic analysis in order to be able to predict forming defects. Defects comprise* the initiation and growth of internal or surface cracks in the deforming metal or the localization of deformation through plastic instability, which could impair the dimensional accuracy of the finished workpiece. Similarly, residual stresses in the unloaded workpiece cannot be evaluated using a rigid-plastic model.

Key words:
reserved[专用的]   literature[文献]   distortion[扭曲, 变形]
iteratively[迭代]   mandatory[命令的, 强制的]
comprise[包含, 由…组成]

Question:

What kind of finite element codes do you know? What kind of problems can these codes solve?

◆ Friction Measurement in Metalworking Processes

Most experimental and much production equipment is equipped with force-measuring instrumentation, and the efficiency of a lubricant and the magnitude of friction can then be judged by comparing forces. Sometimes the value of friction coefficient is calculated from measured forces with the aid of a suitable theory. However, variations in the flow stress of the material may make the calculated values unreliable. The value of friction coefficient can be determined without resorting to theory and without the need of knowing the flow stress of the material by suitable instrumentation. Thus in drawing a strip the die can be instrumented to give both frictional and normal force readings, and similar provisions* can be made, often with the aid of ingenious* die design and instrumentation, in some other processes. Even more detailed information may be gained by building pins that bear on small load cells into the die surface. A pin oriented normal to the surface gives the normal stresses, and an obliquely* embedded* pin the shear component. The technique is laborious and subject to errors, but it is still one of the few that can give detailed information on the distribution of normal and shear stresses along the die surface.

It is obvious that the universal friction test has not been and will never be found. In view of the very great variety of process conditions that a lubricant may have to contend with, there is thus some merit* in evaluating lubricants by a number of techniques.[1] Because of their simplicity, ring compression and wire (bar) or sheet drawing are usually chosen, supplemented by plain-strain and twist compression or deep drawing and back extrusion, depending on the intended range of applications.

A further problem with all laboratory tests is that scaling up to production can be difficult. Even if the process geometry is appropriately scaled and surface finishes are representative of full-scale operation, production speeds and temperatures are sometimes difficult to maintain. The resulting change in lubricating mechanisms then makes the results questionable. Nevertheless, if a systematic correlation is established between laboratory behavior and plant performance, valid lubricant evaluation becomes possible,

Key words:
provision[装置]   ingenious[机灵的, 精制的]   obliquely[偏斜地]
embedded[植入的]   merit[优点, 价值]
Note:
[1]润滑剂能使加工条件产生很大变化,这有助于利用一些技术方法对润滑剂(的作用)进行评估。

Question:

Friction plays important role in metal forming process. (T/F)

5.1.3 Machine Tools for Metal Forming

◆ Hammer

Hammers* are the cheapest metal forming machines from the point of view of generating a large force and transmitting a definite energy, as long as the high contact velocities, which are normally between 3 and 8m/s, do not cause damage to the workpiece. The design features of hammers are relatively simple, and the forces resulting from forming need not be transmitted through the drive and frame system* as is the case with mechanical presses. Therefore the hammer cannot be overloaded. Hammers are flexible, that is, for increased energy requirements one or more additional blows can be used.

Hammers still occupy a leading position in hot forging in spite of increased press applications in this area in recent times. Major areas of application of hammers are open-die forging and die forging. In special cases, hammers are also used for coining*, hot extrusion, and sheet forming.

◆ Screw Presses

Screw presses* are generally built as double-column presses. The frame can be of either a single-piece (welded steel construction) or multipiece (cast steel with tie rods and bolts) design.

The major characteristic of these presses is the drive. The motor drives a flywheel* which is either directly connected or can be connected as necessary to the screw spindle*. The screw spindle transmits the rotary motion through the threads* (multiple start), which have pitch angles between 13° and 17°, to a linear movement of the main ram*. On contact with the workpiece the complete kinetic energy of the flywheel and the ram is transformed into useful work and losses (elastic deformation work and frictional). The elastic deformation work results in a reaction force in all the press parts lying in the force transmission path. The elastic deformation force stored in the frame and the drive causes a reverse acceleration of the flywheel. By proper reversal of the drive control, the ram is brought back to its initial position. This forms the complete cycle of a working stroke* .

◆ Hydraulic* Presses

The possibility of generating large forces with high-pressure fluids was recognized very early (Pascal, 1662). A patent in the year 1795 by the Englishman Bramah was given for a hydraulic press with hand pump drive. In 1860 Haswell, also from England, built a water hydraulic open-die forging press which was put to use in Austria.

Force generation and the movements in hydraulic presses are achieved using fluids under pressure.

Fluids are pumped with high pressure into one or more cylinders in hydraulic presses to convert the hydraulic energy to mechanical work. Based on the type of energy source for the fluid, hydraulic flow in forming machines can be classified into two groups:

(1) Hydraulic circuit with flow source;

(2) Hydraulic circuit with pressure source.

An ideal flow source supplies the hydraulic cylinders* with a constant fluid flow whose magnitude is independent of the system. Correspondingly the ideal pressure source has a constant pressure which is independent of the flow extracted from the pressure source. The systems in the hydraulic presses are in practice only approximately ideal sources.

◆ Mechanical Presses

The machines which belong to the category* of presses controlled by stroke are generally called mechanical presses.

This group of presses is probably the one used most frequently in batch forming. Based on the application requirements, several designs

Forming   263

are available. A classification according to the type of drive will provide useful information on the working of presses belonging to this category.

Two major groups of mechanical presses are:

(1) Presses with crank* drive;

(2) Presses with cam* drive.

Crank presses may have either simple or extended crank drives. Conventional crank presses (the total stroke cannot be varied) and eccentric* presses (the total stroke is variable) belong to the simple drives. If either a knuckle* or a lever is used to extend the crank drive, the designs are called knuckle joint or link drive presses. Multipoint presses are those in which two or more cranks are used to drive the same ram.

◆ Other Methods of Classification

Frame type: C or closed frame;

Number of useful motions: Single or more;

Location of drive: Top drive (connecting rod subjected to compression) and bottom drive (connecting rod subjected to tension);

Positioning of drive shaft: Longitudinal or cross shaft;

Number of connecting rods: One-, two-, or four-point drive.

Key words:

hammer[锻锤]	drive and frame system[传动及框架系统]	
coin[压印,精压]	flywheel[飞轮]	spindle[螺旋杆]
thread[螺纹]	ram[锤头]	stroke[行程]
hydraulic[水压的,液压的]	cylinder[缸]	category[种类]
crank[曲柄]	cam[凸轮]	eccentric[偏心的]
knuckle[关节]		

Question:

Have you ever seen other kinds of machines for metal forming process from TV or movie?

264　*English in Materials Science and Engineering*

5.2 Bulk-metal Forming

5.2.1 Upsetting*

Upsetting is defined as "free forming, by which a workpiece segment* is reduced in dimension between usually plane, parallel platens* ". It also includes coining and heading*. Closed-die forming, shape upsetting, or die heading involve tools which contain the intended shape wholly or in part.

Upsetting is of interest for theoretical studies as a model process. Among the processes of metal forming it represents a basic process which can be varied in many ways. A large segment of industry depends primarily on the predominant application of upsetting processes. Parts produced are screws, nuts, rivets, nails, and bolts*.

Although upsetting has great significance for metal forming, research remains to be done with regard to stresses and deformation which occur during the process. This is due to significant difficulties which result from the transient* nature of the process and the difficulty of defining friction conditions between tool and workpiece.

Upsetting is a transient forming process, that is, streamlines and flow lines do not coincide* during forming. Material flow, characterized by streamlines and flow lines, can be made visible through grid* lines or photos of light dots. Both the state of motion and the deformation distribution are affected more profoundly by friction than by temperature and strain rate. The severity* of friction increases for large reductions and for workpiece with initially high diameter-to-thickness ratios. For such cases good lubrication becomes especially important,

Deformation distribution can be determined by micro-hardness scanning. A distribution is obtained which had previously been provided qualitatively by Siebel: deformation is concentrated on an area, which extends diagonally* outward from the center of the sample. In hot upsetting, the distribution of local deformation becomes more uniform with increasing tool contact speed [0.445 m/s]. This is indicated by diminishing bulging of the peripheral surface. However, cold upsetting with high tool contact velocities [0.144 5 m/s] results in a deformation distribution which is less uniform in the upset direction, but more uniform perpendicular to it.

The contact areas expand by both sliding and fold-over of parts of the free surface onto the die face. By choosing the inclination* of the platens sliding can be influenced, resulting in a change of the relative amounts of sliding and fold-over. In hot upsetting the increase in tool-workpiece contact area of cylindrical samples is greatly dependent upon work material, tooling, initial diameter-to-length ratio, and strain.

Key words:
segment[段,部分]　　　platen[模板]　　　　　heading[顶锻]
screws, nuts, rivets, nails, bolts[螺丝钉,螺母,铆钉,钉子,螺栓]
transient[瞬时的]　　　coincide[一致,符合]　grid[格子]
severity[严重]　　　　diagonally[对角地]　　inclination[倾斜,弯曲]

Question:

Why is upsetting of interest for theoretical studies as a model process?

5.2.2 Forging

◆ Advanced Forging Techniques

The term advanced forging techniques is used here to describe processes which either produce a much more accurate surface finish or aim at achieving special mechanical properties. In many cases the processes discussed aim at making improvements in both of these

266   *English in Materials Science and Engineering*

directions. Particular impetus for the development of advanced techniques and processes in the areas of primary forming and forging has come from the aerospace industry and its rapid development over the past 40 years. The need to manufacture highly stressed airframe and engine components led very rapidly to the combination of specific primary forming and forging processes. In particular, spectacular[*] advances have been made through the combination of powder metallurgy and forging processes. Exactly how many "new techniques" have been created in this way is difficult to estimate, but it is true to say that more and more applications are now being found in other fields too, such as in automobile and machine tool manufacture, as a result of the increasing pressure to save time, material, and energy.

◆ Precision and High-Precision Forging

The term precision forging is used to describe closed-die forging processes in which manufacturing accuracy with regard to shape and dimensional tolerances as well as surface finish exceeds the normal standards by such an amount that at least one finish-machining operation can be saved.

Precision forgings differ from conventional forgings in the following respects: the draft[*] angle is 0° or close to this value, tolerances are narrower, length and width tolerances including offsetting are typically only half those of conventional forging, and thickness tolerances are reduced to about two-thirds of their former values.

The manufacturing processes used in conventional and precision forging are similar in principle. Precision forging may be considered as an intermediate stage between closed-die forging with and without flash. In order to reduce the die load, provision has been made for flash on the web, although the flash thickness must be kept to a minimum. This may be achieved by accurately controlling the weight of the intermediate forging. The flash is subsequently removed by sawing[*].

A kind of precision forging without side draft is a part of an aircraft window made of aluminum alloy. The component is subjected to a complex system of tensile and torque stresses corresponding closely to the stresses in the fuselage[*] shells of the aircraft. A conventional forging requires almost complete machining on all sides. Value analysis showed the great economic savings of using a precision forging which eliminates all the machining required except for the machining of the fixing holes. Furthermore the elimination of surface machining improves the mechanical properties of the component with respect to fatigue and stress corrosion since the grain flow is not interrupted. Draft on precision forgings is reduced from 5° to 1.5°, the minimum web thickness being 3.05 instead of 6.35 mm, and the transition radii and part thicknesses are also smaller. The length and width tolerances, on the other hand, are the same as with conventional forging, although offsetting is reduced and the demands on flatness are higher. A further consideration is the need for exact and even trimming, since no residual flash is permissible either on the outside or on the inside of the part.

High precision forging may be considered a special case of precision forging. Through high-precision forging components can be produced ready for assembly to an accuracy normally only achieved by machining. High demands are made not only on dimensional and shape accuracy, but also on surface finish, and this not just with respect to individual dimensions or surfaces, but with regard to the entire workpiece or a major part of it, as in the case of turbine blades. Thus it is possible to make a distinction between precision and high-precision forging, even though the boundary is blurred[*].

In high-precision forging the conditions must be respected even

268　*English in Materials Science and Engineering*

more closely than with precision forging. In particular, the following points must be observed:

(1) High-quality finish of the die cavity, corresponding at least to ISO quality IT 8.

(2) Reduction of tool wear through suitable choice of die material. Avoidance of scale formation through rapid heating of the workpiece, heating in an inert atmosphere, or forging in the warm condition (i.e., at reduced temperature). Attention must be paid to good agreement between intermediate and final shapes.

(3) Precise control of both die and workpiece temperatures.

(4) Precise control of the volume of the starting material. In addition, the material should be clean and free of surface defects. In some cases this may necessitate machining prior to forging.

It is necessary to avoid oxidation and decarburization as far as possible during heating, forging, and heat treatment. In order to improve surface finish after forging and heat-treatment operations, parts are usually pickled* and then polished.

Key words:
spectacular[壮观的]　　draft[拔模斜度]　　sawing[锯]
fuselage[机身]　　　　blur[界限模糊]

Question:

Why do precision forgings differ from conventional forgings?

5.2.3 Rolling

The rolling process belongs to the compressive deformation processes, and has been classified based on kinematics, tool geometry, and workpiece geometry.

Rolling can be defined as a compressive deformation process in which there is either a continuous or a stepwise* deformation with one or more rotary tools (rolls). Additional tools, such as mandrels*, guide blocks*, and support bars, may also be used in the rolling process. The force transmission is achieved either by power-driven rolls or by the workpiece transport.

Based on kinematics, the rolling process can be classified as follows: longitudinal*, cross*, and skewed*. In longitudinal rolling the rolled workpiece moves through the rolling gap perpendicular to the axis of the rolls, without rotation about the workpiece axis. Cross rolling is characterized by a rotary movement of the workpiece without translational* motion. In skewed rolling a combination of both rotary and translational movements of the workpiece occurs.

The tool geometry is another characteristic that can be used to classify the rolling process. The process of rolling where the rolls have along their contact surfaces either a cylindrical or a conical* form in the rolling gap is termed flat-rolling*. If the contact surface of the rolls deviates* from the cylindrical or conical form, the process is called profile rolling*.

The rolling process can be further classified depending upon whether a solid or a hollow workpiece is rolled.

The process of sheet rolling is convenient for defining the various basic parameters. Furthermore the sheet is the form of starting material that is used for many processes of tensile, compressive, and combination forming. The characteristics (dimensional accuracy, forming behavior, and surface quality) and thus the manufacturing conditions of the sheets are very important for their optimum use in the various deformation processes.

Key words:
stepwise[逐步的]   mandrel[心轴]   guide block[导板]
longitudinal[纵向的]   cross[横向的]   skewed[斜向的]

270 *English in Materials Science and Engineering*

translational[平移的] conical[圆锥形的] flat-rolling[平辊轧制]
deviate[偏离] profile-rolling[孔型轧制]

Question:

Rolling method is mainly applied in metallurgy industry. (T/F)

5.2.4 Extrusion*

Owing to the fibrous* structure developed in the extrusion direction, the mechanical properties of extruded products are directionally oriented (mechanical anisotropy*). The anisotropy may be caused in different ways, such as a straight-line arrangement and linking of the heterogeneous* structural elements in the extrusion direction (geometric anisotropy), banding of the structure, or the creation of preferential* orientation in the crystals (texture*). The practical consequence* of mechanical anisotropy is generally a reduction in strength at a right angle to the extrusion direction, which, however, is unimportant in most cases.

Recrystallization plays an important part in determining the structure of extruded products, not only in materials that recrystallized during deformation (e.g., copper, brass), but also in those subject to dynamic* recovery during extrusion (e. g., aluminum and aluminum alloys). Recrystallization may in part be superimposed* on the recovery processes during extrusion. It may, on the other hand, only begin after deformation when the deformation rate is greater than the rate of the recovery and recrystallization processes, thus causing no major reduction in work hardening.

The grains formed by recrystallization may vary considerably in size, both in the direction of extrusion and at a right angle to it. The size depends on the type of material, the strain imparted*, and the temperature. Large strains lead to a smaller grain size, high temperatures during deformation tend to increase grain size. This

Forming 271

results in an irregular structure and thus variations in the mechanical properties. This takes the form of an increase in strength from the center to the edge of the cross section and from the beginning to end of the extrusion (assuming no subsequent heat treatment is performed). Variations in strength across the cross section can mostly be overcome by the use of larger strains.

Coarse grains may be found in the boundary layer of the extrusion when a critical* value of residual* stress still remains after recovery or recrystallization. Above all, this has often been observed in aluminum-copper-magnesium and aluminum-magnesium-silicon alloys after solution heat treatment. The coarsely recrystallized layer is thinnest at the beginning of the extrusion and thickens toward the end. The material properties are very different in the coarse-grain zone from those in the extrusion core. Thus, for example, corrosion resistance is less, and the strength in the extrusion direction is also reduced. In contrast to the typical characteristics of extruded products (anisotropy), extrusions with coarse-grain zones may exhibit higher strength in the transverse direction than in the direction of extrusion, even though the structures in the coarse-grain zone may have grains parallel to the extrusion direction. Coarse-grain zones tend to cause surface roughening during subsequent forming operations and to lead to the formation of cracks during quenching.

Key words:
extrusion[挤压]　　　fibrous[纤维性的]　　　anisotropy[各向异性]
heterogeneous[不同种类的]　　　　　　　　preferential[优先的]
consequence[结果]　texture[织构]　　　　dynamic[动态的]
superimpose[重叠]　imparted[给予]　　　critical[临界的]
residual[残余的]

Question:

Do you think extrusions with coarse-grain zones may exhibit

272   *English in Materials Science and Engineering*

higher strength in the direction of extrusion than in the transverse direction?

5.3 Sheet-metal Forming

5.3.1 Bending

U-die bending without pressure pad: As in V-die bending, the process is characterized by different stages of deformation. The punch establishes contact with the sheet and effects elastic bending, which produces a circular arc in the domain of the web due to the constant moment distribution. The legs of the workpiece fold upward, close to the punch, as it moves into the die, and the curvature* of the web is increased. No significant deformation takes place from this point on until the web touches the bottom of the die and coining begins. During coining, the curvature of the web changes from convex* to concave*. Eventually the web is flattened, causing the walls to close tightly against the punch. It should be noted that the displacement of workpiece material from the web into the corners can easily lead to embrittlement there during cold bending.

U-die bending with pressure pad: The pressure pad is intended to keep the web from bending by pressing it against the bottom of the punch throughout the entire bending process. Coining becomes superfluous* as a result. Except for this difference, the bending process is identical to bending without a pressure pad.

Studies with steel sheet show that a pressure pad force having a magnitude of only 0.3 times the force needed to push the workpiece into the die (insertion force) is required if the web is to remain fiat. By contrast, 3 times the insertion force is required for coining when no pressure pad is used. These figures apply to steel sheet at room temperature. Although the smaller force requirements favor bending with a pressure pad, there are serious disadvantages. Equipment is

Forming 273

expensive, and in general the process is limited to small bending lengths.

Key words:
curvature[曲率]   convex[凸起的]   concave[凹入的]
superfluous[多余的]

Question:

What are the advantages and the disadvantages of U-die bending with pressure pad?

5.3.2 Wrinkle* Formation during Deep Drawing*

It was already mentioned that the flange has a tendency to buckle* under the influence of the tangential compressive stresses. The resulting folds are called wrinkles. Wrinkle formation can be prevented by pressing a blankholder with sufficient pressure against the workpiece.

As long as the blank is clamped* rigidly between blankholder* and die, as is the case at the beginning of the draw, buckling cannot occur. During deformation the thickness does not remain constant but increases toward the outside edge of the flange while the center portion near the die radius becomes thinner than the initial thickness so in the early stages of the draw. Since the distance between blankholder and die is determined by the greatest flange thickness, there will be a small gap between blankholder and sheet at places of smaller thickness. This gap offers an opportunity for the initiation of wrinkles. Investigations by Siebel and Beisswdnger have shown that the thickness variations can amount to over 10% of the initial sheet thickness for a drawing ratio 2.0. Thin sheets are especially sensitive to wrinkle formation because their moment of inertia in buckling is small. They require larger blankholder pressures than thick sheets. Thick sheets in general do not tend to form wrinkles because they have a large moment of inertia and

274 *English in Materials Science and Engineering*

thus sufficient resistance against buckling, They can be drawn without a blankholder.

Key words:
deep drawing[深拉延]   flange[法兰]   wrinkle[起皱]
buckle[失稳,起皱]   clamp[夹住]   blankholder[压边圈]

Question:

What is the main function of blankholder during deep drawing process?

5.3.3 Metal spinning *

Spinning can produce workpieces with rotational symmetry of almost any shape. With the aid of special equipment it is also possible to produce elliptical * and oval * components on a spinning lathe *. Bulges * and necks are both possible. To produce bulges or necks, split * chucks * with several segments are used. Workpieces of several meters in diameter can be spun. Typical examples of such parts are bowls, container ends, and reflectors for radar installations *.

When deforming thin sheets of large dimensions, the tendency to form wrinkles is great. In these cases hollow chucks are used in which the blank is clamped along the outside edge. The resulting deformation process resembles * stretching *, that is, drawing with the state of stress of biaxial * tension. This eliminates the possibility of wrinkle formation.

Spinning of cylindrical workpieces is in direct competition with deep drawing. For small components to be produced in large quantities deep drawing is generally more economical because of its shorter cycle times. The opposite is true when large cups, such as drums for commercial washing machines or cool pots for large kitchens, must be produced. These components could possibly be made on deep-drawing presses, but the tooling and machine cost would be very high. These

Forming 275

parts are therefore rather made by spinning. For even larger components, such as radar reflectors, there are no forming processes which can compete with spinning.

All metallic workpiece materials which are available in sheet form can be spun. The most important of these are mild steel, high-temperature steels, stainless steels, nonferrous heavy metals, and light metals. Most of these are spun at room temperature. However, some aluminum-magnesium alloys are heated in order to achieve the necessary formability. Tungsten, titanium, molybdenum, and zirconium alloys are used for rocket and aircraft components as well as for containers for chemical and nuclear industries. They are processed at elevated temperatures. The required temperatures are in the range of the generally used forming temperatures for these metals. Heating is mostly done locally with torches during spinning.

Key words:

spinning[旋压]   elliptical[椭圆的]   oval[卵形的]
lathe[车床]   bulge[凸出部分]   split[分瓣的]
chuck[卡盘]   installation[装置]   resemble[类似]
stretch[拉伸]   biaxial[双向的]

Question:

What kind of workpieces can be produced by spinning?

5.3.4 Rubber Forming

In 1872, Adolph Delkescamp was granted* an American patent concerning the cutting of paper and foil using rubber, and between 1936 and 1940 Henry Guerin of the Douglas Aircraft Company was granted patents on the forming and shearing of sheet metals by means of a confined and pressurized rubber pad hence the Guerin process.

Basically, the technique is relatively simple. A block of rubber is confined in the retainer, when forced upon the piston in a press, the rubber is pressurized rather like a fluid. This produces the results shown by the use of appropriate tooling. Like all processes it has its advantages and disadvantages. The advantages are as follows:

(1) The tooling costs are reduced, often by as much as 90%.

(2) The lead time* is reduced.

(3) Tool modification is simply achieved.

(4) Scoring* during forming is culminated*; so a highly polished sheet will yield a highly polished pressing.

The disadvantages are as follows:

(1) The process entails* a high proportion of trial and error*.

(2) There is poor material utilization. It is advisable to use a large blank to avoid the propagation of flange wrinkles* (formed by generated hoop stresses* into the pressing wall).

(3) A greater press capacity is required for rubber pad than for conventional production, often restricting it to thin sheet(presses used are often about 5 000 ton capacity).

(4) It is generally restricted to shallow parts, for a limitation is the amount to which the rubber itself can be deformed. One aspect, however, of rubber pressing know-how* is the insertion of further blocks or strips of rubber in critical areas to achieve greater depths.

(5) It is often only possible to achieve a general shape; the final part to drawing must be created by subsequent hand work; springback is a problem with high strength materials.

One advance in rubber forming was the substitution of natural rubber by certain synthetic rubbers—the polyurethanes*. These can be made with Shore hardnesses* in the range 5 ~ 95 compared with a maximum of about 65 for natural rubber. These synthetics, even those with the same hardness as rubber, have outstanding abrasion* resistance, toughness and resistance. In short, the loading on the hard polyurethane can be several times greater than on conventional rubber, allowing better shape and smaller radii.

Forming   277

It is clear that this is a low production rate process and it is used today predominantly in the aircraft industry for simple forming of high strength aluminum alloys.

An interesting variation on rubber forming was developed for the manufacture of small foil containers, which generally buckle very easily in the walls during manufacture. Here, a composite punch contains a resilient* element of polyurethane, which grips the blank into the die cavity; space must be allowed for the displaced polyurethane.

With the variables at the tool designers' disposal—shore hardness, insert shape, cavity shape and secondary back up elements wrinkle free cups in 0.1mm sheet can be produced at high speed. All other aspects of tool design remain unchanged.

Key words:
grant[授予]   lead time[研制周期]   score[划痕]
culminate[降到最小] entail[承受]   trial and error[反复试验]
know-how[诀窍]   abrasion[磨损]   polyurethane[聚氨酯]
Shore hardness[肖氏硬度]   hoop stress[周向应力]
resilient[有弹力的]   flange wrinkle[法兰边起皱]

Question:

1) Rubber forming means that the rubber can be formed by pressing. (T/F)

2) The hardness of the rubber used for rubber forming should lower than the product it worked on. (T/F)

3) Rubbers which have a higher hardness and a good elasticity could be used for rubber forming. (T/F)

5.3.5 Explosive Forming

In this method of sheet forming, an underwater explosion generates a shock wave, which in turn deforms a sheet of metal into a female die.

278   *English in Materials Science and Engineering*

Basically the process is simple and employed for small quantity production, where conditions and economics dictate[*]. Many claims[*] were made for this process in its early days, the 1950s, particularly that "unformable" materials acquired formability in this high energy rate process, but these claims have not been clearly substantiated[*]. One important aspect of this process is that the impact of a plane shock wave upon a metal sheet placed above a die will possibly produce a different strain distribution in the formed part from some other forming process. It may be that this is the reason for some of the "anomalous[*]" results.

Nonetheless, the process is useful for the manufacture of one off large parts, such as hemispherical section receivers, which can, with the appropriate expertise[*], be free formed to the correct contours using shaped charges.

Key words:
dictate[注定]   claim[主张]   substantiate[证实]
anomalous[不规则的,反常的]   expertise[专门技术]

Questions:

1) By using explosive forming, very complicated shapes can be achieved. (T/F)

2) If a material is very strong, the method of explosive forming can be selected. (T/F)

5.3.6 Magnetic Forming[*]

This process is related to explosive forming as it is also a high energy rate process. This technique involves the rapid discharge of stored electrical energy from a bank of capacitors[*] to obtain a high current flow through a coil, producing a pulsed magnetic field around the coil windings. As a result, an induced[*] current is caused to flow in the opposite direction through any electrically conductive material

Forming   279

placed near the coil. Current induced in a metal part reacts against the magnetic field around the coil winging and the force produced repels the workpiece from the coil.

If a flat coil is used, a uniform outward force results and so a metal sheet can be forced into a female die, in a similar manner to explosive forming. In broad terms, any sheet metal, of thickness 0.25 ~ 12.0 mm, can be formed with a number of pulses, each of 10 ~ 100 μs duration, the exact conditions depending on the resistivity and thermal properties of the metal in question. Equipment is available which will deliver[*] 6 000 J of energy at 2 seconds intervals, enabling uniform pressures of 350 MPa to be achieved.

This process is used for production of relatively small components, but in some quantity.

Key words:
magnetic forming[电磁成形]   capacitor[电容]
induce[感应]   deliver[释放]

Questions:

1) High electric resistant materials can be worked with magnetic forming. (T/F)

2) The force generated by the coil will apply on the material for 2 seconds. (T/F)

6

Heat Treatment

6.1 Heat Treatment of Steel

We can alter the characteristics of steel in various ways. In the first place, steel which contains very little carbon will be milder than steel which contains a higher percentage of carbon, up to the limit of about 1.5%. [1] Secondly, we can heat the steel above a certain critical temperature, and then allow it to cool at different rates. At this critical temperature, changes begin to take place in the molecular structure of the metal. In the process known as annealing*, we heat the steel above the critical temperature and permit it to cool very slowly. This causes the metal softer than before, and much easier to be machined. Annealing has a second advantage, it helps to relieve any internal stresses which exist in the metal. These stresses are liable to occur through hammering or working the metal, or through rapid cooling. Metal which we cause to cool rapidly contracts more rapidly on the outside than on the inside. This produces unequal contractions, which may give rise to distortion or cracking. Metal which cools slowly is less

Heat Treatment 281

liable to have these internal stresses than metal which cools quickly.

On the other hand, we can make steel harder by rapid cooling. We heat it up beyond the critical temperature, and then quench* it in water or some other liquid. The rapid temperature drop fixes the structural change in the steel and this hardened steel is more liable to fracture than normal steel. We therefore heat it again to a temperature below the critical temperature, and cool it slowly. This treatment is called tempering*. It helps to relieve the internal stresses, and makes the steel less brittle than before. The properties of tempered steel enable us to use it in the manufacture of tools which need a fairly hard steel.[2] High carbon steel is harder than tempered steel, but it is much more difficult to work.

These heat treatments take place during the various shaping operations. We can obtain bars and sheets of steel by rolling the metal through huge rolls in a rolling mill. The roll pressures must be much greater for cold rolling than for hot rolling, but cold rolling enables the operators to produce rolls of great accuracy and uniformity, and with a better surface finish.[3] Other shaping operations include drawing into wire, casting in molds*, and forging*.

Key words:
annealing[退火]   quench[淬火]   tempering[回火]
mold [模具]   forging[锻造]

 Notes:
 [1]首先,在含碳量不超过 1.5%时,含有很少量碳的钢要比高含碳量的钢软一些。
 [2]回火钢的特性使得我们可将其用于高硬工具的制造。
 [3]冷轧压力比热轧压力高得多,但冷轧能够使操作人员生产出高精密且均匀的,表面光洁度更好的产品。

Questions:

1) If a workpiece made of steel is too hard to work, what would

282   *English in Materials Science and Engineering*

you do?

2) Generally speaking, what kind of steel is softer, and what kind is harder?

3) If you want a piece of steel to be harder or softer, what would you do?

6.2   Principle of Heat Treatment of Steel

Theoretical study of heat treatment steel was initiated by the discovery of the critical points in steel made by D. K. Chernov in 1868. Chernov's assumption that the properties of steels are determined by the structure and that the latter depends on the heating temperature and rate of cooling has been generally recognized.[1] During the decades which followed the researchers were engaged in establishing the relationships between the structure and the conditions of its formation (mainly the heating temperature and cooling rate). The principal achievements in the theory of heat treatment were, however, made in 1920's and 1930's.

Metallurgists have gradually come to the conclusion that the type of structure (its texture*, properties, etc.) is determined by the temperature of its formation. It has become clear that the processes occurring in heat treatment can be explained by studying the kinetics* of transformations at various temperatures and the factors affecting the kinetics.

These concepts formed the basis of extensive experimental work undertaken by S. S. Steinberg and coworkers in 1930 ~ 1940. They collected a vast experimental material which has constituted the basis of the modern concepts on transformations in steel and the theory of heat treatment of steel.

Studies in the same direction were started by many researchers in other countries at the same time or somewhat later. Among the pioneers in this field, the names of R. F. Mehl and E. C. Bain (USA), and F. Wever, H. Esser, and H. Hannemann(Germany) should be mentioned first; they carried out numerous and detailed studies into the kinetics of transformations in various steels. The nature of hardened steel could only be examined by using X rays and other methods of physical analysis of metals (electron microscopy*, internal friction*, etc.).[2]

Numerous works of G. V. Kurdymov and his followers, and a number of other foreign metallophysicists have revealed important peculiarities* in the fine structure of steel.

The theory of heat treatment of steel is understood as the analysis of the processes of structure formation (on transformations) and the particularities of structural state of alloys(in non-equilibrium).[3] Here the theory of heat treatment of steel, based on the general theory of phase transformations in undercooled systems will be discussed.

Key words:
texture[织构]　　　kinetics[动力学]　　　microscopy[显微术]
internal friction[内耗]　peculiarity[特性]

Notes:

[1] 契尔诺娃关于钢的性能决定于钢的结构以及后者决定于热处理温度及冷却速度的假说得到了普遍的认可。

[2] 淬火钢的性质只能用 X 射线方法和其他金属物理分析方法进行检测(包括电子显微技术、内耗等)。

[3] 钢的热处理理论被理解为是对结构形成过程(如相变)和合金结构状态特殊性的分析(如非平衡态)。

Questions:

1) Who is the first metallurgist who suggested that the properties of steel were determined by the structure?

2) What are the important factors affecting the structure of steel during heat treatment process?

284   *English in Materials Science and Engineering*

6.2.1 Formation of Austenite

The transformation of pearlite* into austenite can only take place on a very slow heating as follows from the Fe-C constitutional diagram.[1] Under common heating conditions, the transformation is retarded and results in overheating, i. e. occurs at temperatures slightly higher than those indicated in the Fe-C diagram.

When overheated above the critical point, pearlite transforms into austenite, the rate of transformation being dependent on the degree of overheating.

The time of transformation at various temperatures (depending on the degree of overheating) shows that the transformation takes place faster (in a shorter time) at a higher temperature and occurs at a higher temperature on a quicker heating.

For instance, on quick heating and holding at 780℃, the pearlite to austenite transformation is completed in 2 minutes and on holding at 740℃, in 8 minutes.

Irrespective of the heating rate, the transformation occurs immediately after the passage through the equilibrium critical point; the temperature interval on heating determines not the physical beginning and the end of the transformation, but the temperature interval within which the main mass of pearlite changes to austenite.

The end of the transformation is characterized by the formation of austenite and disappearance of pearlite (Ferrite* + Cementite*). This austenite is however inhomogeneous even in the volume of a single grain*.[2] In places earlier occupied by lamellae (or grains) of pearlitic cementite the content of carbon is greater than in places of ferritic lamellae*. This is why the austenite just formed is inhomogeneous.

In order to obtain homogeneous austenite, it is essential in heating not only to pass through the point of the end of pearlite to austenite

Heat Treatment 285

transformation, but also to overheat the steel above that point and to allow a holding time to complete the diffusion processes in Austenitic grains.

The rate of homogenization of austenite appreciably depends on the original structure of the steel, in particular on the dispersity and particle shape of cementite.[3] The transformations described occur more quickly when cementite particles are fine and, therefore, have a large total surface area.

Key words:

pearlite[珠光体]   ferrite[铁素体]   cementite[渗碳体]

grain[晶粒]   lamellae[片]

Notes:

[1] 从铁碳相图可知,只有在缓慢加热时珠光体才能向奥氏体转变。

[2] 该奥式体无论如何是不均匀的, 即便是在一个晶粒内也一样。

[3] 奥氏体均匀化的速率在很大程度上决定于钢的原始组织,特别是渗碳体的弥散程度和颗粒形状。

Questions:

1) There is not diffusion process in the transformation from pearlite to austenite.(T/F)

2) The higher the temperature, the faster the pearlite transforms into austenite.(T/F)

3) Austenite and pearlite are two different phases.(T/F)

4) How to obtain homogeneous austenite?

6.2.2 Coarsening of Austenite Grains

At the beginning of pearlite to austenite transformation, the first grains of austenite form at the boundaries between the ferrite and cementite—the two structural constituents of pearlite.[1] Since these boundaries are very developed, the transformation starts from formation of a multitude of fine grains. Therefore, at the end of the transformation the austenite will be composed of a great multitude of fine grains whose size characterizes what is called the original austenitic grain size.

Further heating (or holding) upon the transformation will cause coarsening of Austenitic grains. The process of grain coarsening is spontaneous, since the total surface area of grains diminishes (the surface energy decreases) and a high temperature can only accelerate the rate of this process.[2]

In that connection, two types of steel are distinguished: inherent fine grained and inherent coarse grained, the former being less liable to grain coarsening than the latter.

The size of grains formed in a steel by heat treatment is called the actual grain size.

Thus, a distinction should be made between: (1) original grain, i. e. the size of austenitic grains immediately after the pearlite to austenite transformation ; (2) inherent (natural) grain, i. e. the liability of austenite to grain coarsening; and (3) actual grain; i. e. the size of austenitic grains under given particular conditions.

The size of pearlitic grains at the same temperature of the austenite to pearlite transformation depends on that of the austenitic grains from which they have formed. Austenitic grains grow only during heating (but are not refined in subsequent cooling), because of which the highest temperature a steel is heated to in the austenitic state and the inherent grain size of that steel determine the final grain size.

Notes:

[1] 在珠光体向奥氏体转变的初始阶段,第一批奥氏体晶粒首先在铁素体和渗碳体(这两者是珠光体的组成部分)的晶界处形成。

[2]因为可以减少晶粒表面积(表面能降低),晶粒的粗化过程是自发的,

提高温度只能够加快粗化过程。

Questions:

1) Where is the austenite nucleus generated?

(a) In ferrite grain.

(b) At the boundary between pearlite and austenite.

(c) At the boundary between ferrite and cementite.

(d) Can not be determined.

2) How is the grain coarsening tendency of inherent coarse grained steel compared with inherent fine grained steel?

3) What is "actual" grain size? Can you describe the factors affecting it?

The properties of a steel are affected only by the actual grain size and not by the inherent grain size. If two steels of the same grade(one inherently coarse grained, the other fine grained) have the same actual grain size upon heat treatment at different temperatures, their properties will also be the same; if otherwise, many properties of the two steels will also be different.

Coarsening of austenitic grain in steels has almost no effect on the statistic characteristics of mechanical properties (hardness, rupture* resistance, yield* limit, elongation), but can appreciably reduce the impact toughness*, especially at a high hardness (low temperature tempering). This is due to the fact that grain coarsening raises the ductile to brittle transition temperature.

Whereas the actual grain size affects the properties of steel, the inherent grain size is decisive for the processes of hot working.

Inherently fine grained steel is insensitive to overheating, i. e. intensive grain coarsening begins at appreciably higher temperatures than in a coarse grained steel.[1] For that reason, the temperature interval of hardening for the former is substantially wider than for the latter.

Inherently fine grained steel can be rolled(or forged) at higher temperature s and the process(rolling or forging) can be finished at a higher temperature without danger of forming a coarse grained structure. As a rule, all grades of killed steel are made inherently fine grained and all rimming steels, inherently coarse grained.

Key words:

rupture[断裂]　　　　yield[屈服]　　　　toughness[韧性]

Note:

[1] 本质细晶粒钢对过热不敏感,也就是说,本质细晶粒钢发生严重晶粒粗化的温度比本质粗晶粒钢的粗化温度高得多。

Questions:

1) What is the key factor affecting the properties of steel?

(a) Inherent grain size.　　(b) Actual grain size.

(c) Austenite grain size.　　(d) Both (b) and (c).

2) Why the coarsening of austenite grain reduces the impact toughness of steel?

3) What is the meaning of "overheating" according to the paragraph above?

4) Which kind of steel has good formability such as hot rolling, hot forging, etc. ?

6.2.3 Decomposition of Austenite

The austenite to pearlite transformation is essentially the decomposition of austenite into almost pure ferrite and cementite.

At the equilibrium temperature, the transformation is impossible, since the free energy of the original austenite is equal to that of the final product, pearlite.

The transformation can only start at a certain undercooling when the free energy of the ferrite carbide mixture (pearlite) is lower than that of austenite.

The lower the transformation temperature, the higher the degree of undercooling and the greater the difference in free energies and the transformation proceeds at a higher rate.

In the pearlite transformation, the new phases sharply differ in their composition from the initial phase; they are ferrite which is almost free of carbon, and cementite which contains 6.67 percent carbon. For that reason the austenite to pearlite transformation is accompanied with the diffusion [*], redistribution of carbon. The rate of diffusion sharply diminishes with decreasing temperature, therefore, the transformation should be retarded at a greater undercooling.

Thus, we have come to an important conclusion that undercooling (lowering the transformation temperature) may have two opposite effects on the rate of transformation.

On one hand, a lower temperature (greater undercooling) gives a greater difference in free energies of austenite and pearlite, thus accelerating the transformation; on the other hand, it diminishes the rate of carbon diffusion, and thus slows down the transformation. The combined effect is that the rate of transformation first increases as undercooling is increased to a certain maximum and then decreases with further undercooling.

At 727°C (A_1) and below 200°C, the rate of transformation is zero, since at 727°C the free energy difference is zero and below 200°C the rate of carbon diffusion is zero (more strictly, too low for the transformation to proceed).

As has been first indicated by I. L. Mirkin in 1939 and then developed by R. F. Mehl in 1941, the formation of pearlite is the process of nucleation of pearlite and growth of pearlitic crystals.

Therefore, the different rate of the pearlite transformation at

290　*English in Materials Science and Engineering*

various degrees of undercooling is due to the fact that undercooling differently affects the rate of nucleation N and the rate of crystal growth G.[1] At temperature A_1 and below 200℃, both parameters of crystallization N and G are equal to zero and have a maximum at an undercooling of 150 ~ 200℃.

It follows from the foregoing that as soon as the conditions are favorable, i. e. austenite is undercooled below A_1, the diffusion of carbon is not zero, centers of crystallization appear, which give rise to crystals. This process occurs with time and can be represented in the form of so called kinetic curve of transformation, which shows the quantity of pearlite that has formed during the time elapsed from the beginning of the transformation.

The initial stage is characterized by a very low rate of transformation; this is what is called the incubation [*] period. The rate of transformation increases with the progress in the transformation. Its maximum approximately corresponds to the moment when roughly 50 percent of austenite has transformed into pearlite. The rate of transformation then diminishes and finally stops.

The rate of transformation depends on undercooling. At low and high degrees of undercooling the transformation proceeds slowly, since N or G are low ; in the former case, owing to a low difference in free energies, and in the latter, due to a low diffusion mobility of atoms. At the maximum rate of transformation the kinetic curves have sharp peaks, and the transformation is finished in a short time interval.

At a high temperature (slight undercooling), the transformation proceeds slowly and the time of the incubation period and the time of the transformation proper are long. At a lower temperature of the transformation, i. e. a deeper undercooling, the rate of transformation is greater, and the time of the incubation period and of the transformation is shorter.

Having determined the time of the beginning of austenite to pearlite transformation(incubation period) and the time of the end of transformation at various degrees of undercooling, we can construct a diagram in which the left hand curve determines the time of the beginning of the transformation, i. e. the time during which austenite still exists in the undercooled state, and the section from the axis of ordinates* to the curve is the measure of its stability. This section is shortest at a temperature of $500 \sim 600°C$, i. e. the transformation begins in a shortest time at that temperature.

The right hand curve shows the time needed to complete the transformation at a given degree of undercooling. This time is the shortest at the same temperature ($500 \sim 600°C$). Note that the abscissa* of the diagram is logarithmic*. This is done for more convenience, since the rates of formation of pearlite appreciably differ (thousands of seconds near the critical point A_1 and only one or two seconds at the bend of the curve).

The horizontal line below the curves in the diagram determines the temperature of the diffusionless martensite transformation. The martensite transformation occurs by a different mechanism and will be discussed later.

Diagrams of the type we discussed are usually called TTT diagrams(time temperature transformation), or C curves, owing to the specific shape of the curves. The structure and properties of the products of austenite decomposition depend on the temperature at which the transformation has taken place.

At high temperatures, i. e. low degrees of undercooling, a coarse grained mixture of ferrite and cementite is formed which is easily distinguished in the microscope. This structure is called pearlite.

At lower temperatures, and therefore, greater degrees of undercooling, more disperse and harder products are formed. The pearlitic structure of this finer type is called sorbite*.

At still lower temperatures (near the end of the C curve), the transformation products are even more disperse, so that the lamellar structure of the ferrite cementite mixture is only distinguishable in the electron microscope.[2] This structure is called troostite*.

Thus, pearlite, sorbite and troostite are the structures of the same nature (ferrite + cementite) but a different dispersity of ferrite and cementite.

Pearlitic structures may be of two types: granular* (in which cementite is present in the form of grains) or lamellar (with cementite platelets).

Homogeneous austenite always transforms into lamellar pearlite. Therefore, heating to a high temperature sets up favorable conditions for the formation of a more homogeneous structure and thus promotes the appearance of lamellar structures. Inhomogeneous austenite produces granular* pearlite at all degrees of undercooling, therefore, heating to a low temperature (below AC_3 for hypereutectoid* steels) results in the formation of granular pearlite on cooling. The formation of granular cementite is probably promoted by the presence of undissolved particles in austenite, which serve as additional crystallization nuclei.

Key words:

diffusion[扩散]　　　　incubation[孕育期]　　　ordinates[纵坐标]

abscissa[横坐标]　　　logarithmic[对数的]　　sorbite[索氏体]

troostite[屈氏体]　　　hypereutectoid[过共析]　granular[粒状的]

Notes:

[1] 因此, 在不同过冷度下珠光体转变速率不同是由于过冷度对晶体成核速率和长大速率的影响不同造成的。

[2] 在更低的温度下(靠近 C 曲线的末端), 转变产物更加弥散, 以至于片状的铁素体和渗碳体只有在电子显微镜下才能分辨出来。

Heat Treatment 293

Questions:

1) At what temperature can the austenite decomposition take place?

(a) Higher than A_1.　　　　(b) Below 200℃.

(c) Between A_1 and 200℃.　(d) Both (a) and (b).

2) Why is the transformation of austenite to pearlite impossible at the equilibrium temperature A_1?

3) Describe the factors affecting N and G.

4) How does undercooling affect the decomposition of austenite?

Initial heating to a temperature up to 900℃ gives lamellar pearlite, with more disperse* structure being obtained at lower temperature.

The structure of the same steel at the same temperature of transformation but upon a low temperature heating (780℃) is granular pearlite. Cementite grains that are formed in the structure are finer at a lower temperature transformation.

Consequently, the size of cementite particles depends on the temperature of austenite transformation and their form depends on the temperature of heating (the temperature of austenitization).

The transformation at temperature above and below the bend of the C curve differ in the kinetics and the shape of decomposition products.

Above the bend of C curve, i. e. at small degrees of undercooling, the transformation begins from a few centers and pearlitic crystals freely grow to interference. Below the bend of C curve there forms an acicular microstructure, since acicular platelets cannot grow freely and the transformation mainly occurs through the formation of new crystals. [1]

As indicated above, the rate of isothermal transformation of austenite is determined by the rate of nucleation and crystal growth, N and G.

The rate of crystal growth is quite sensitive to various changes in the steel structure and can be strongly affected by the metallurgical nature of the steel, the degree of deoxidization, the presence of undissolved particles, the homogeneity of austenite, and the size of austenitic grains. The presence of undissolved particles increases the value of G, since these particles serve as additional nuclei.

The value of G diminishes with increasing size of austenitic grains. Crystallization nuclie appear mainly on grain boundaries, therefore, the conditions for nucleation are worse in coarse grained steel where the extent of grain boundaries is smaller.

The factors mentioned have, however, no effect on the nucleation rate, N. The value of N depends only on steel composition and for a steel of a given composition, is a natural characteristic depending only on the degree of undercooling.

We have discussed the austenite to pearlite transformation in steels whose composition is close to eutectoid* . If the content of carbon in a steel differs from the eutectoid value, the pearlite transformation will be preceded with the precipitation* of ferrite or cementite(as follows from the iron carbon constitutional diagram).

In hypoeutectoid* steels, the transformation of austenite begins with the formation of ferrite and the saturation of the remaining solution with carbon, and in hypereutectoid steels, with the precipitation of cementite and depletion* of the austenite of carbon.[2] Under equilibrium conditions, the decomposition of austenite into ferrite and cementite (pearlite transformation) begins when the content of carbon in austenite, remained upon precipitation of excess ferrite or cementite, corresponds to 0.8% carbon.

The eutectoid which forms from undercooled austenite and has a concentration differing from the eutectoid value is called quasi* - eutectoid. The quasi-eutectoid in hypereutectoid steels contains more than 0.8 percent carbon and that in hypoeutectoid steels, less than 0.8 percent, the deviation from this value being greater at a lower temperature of transformation. Therefore, the lower the temperature of transformation, the less the excess ferrite (or cementite) precipitates before the pearlite transformation begins. At temperatures near the bend of the C curve and at lower temperatures, decomposition of austenite begins without precipitation of excess phases.

Key words:

hypoeutectoid[亚共析]   eutectoid[共析]   precipitation[析出]

depletion[减少]   quasi[伪]   disperse[弥散的]

Notes:

[1] 在 C 曲线的弯曲点以下形成针状显微结构,由于针状物不能自由生长,相变主要是通过形成新的晶粒来进行。

[2] 在亚共析钢中,奥氏体相变开始于铁素体的形成和碳在剩余固溶体中的趋于饱和,而在过共析钢中,奥氏体相变开始于渗碳体的析出和剩余奥氏体含碳量的降低。

Questions:

1) The size of cementite particles depends on the temperature of

_____ .

(a) austenite transformation

(b) austenitization

(c) martensite transformation

2) What is the parameters of G and N, and how are they affected?

3) What is the quasi-eutectoid?

If we take a hypereutectoid steel instead of hypoeutectoid, the decomposition of austenite at small degrees of undercooling will be

296   *English in Materials Science and Engineering*

preceded with precipitation of cementite.

If the cooling rate is higher, the transformation has no time to proceed in the upper temperature range, the austenite will be undercooled to a low temperature and will transform into martensite, such a cooling will result in hardening. Therefore, to harden steel, it should be cooled at a high rate so that austenite has no time to decompose in the upper temperature range.

The lowest cooling rate needed to undercool austenite up to martensite trans formation is called the critical rate of hardening. If a steel is to be hardened, it should be cooled at a rate not less than the critical. The critical rate is lower for steels whose curve of the beginning of transformation passes farther to the right. In other words, with a lower rate of austenite to pearlite transformation, it is easier, to undercool the austenite to the temperature of martensite transformation and the critical rate of hardening will be lower.

If cooling is done at a rate slightly below the critical, the austenite will undergo only a partial transformation in the upper temperature range and the structure will consist of the products of transformation in the upper temperature range (troostite) and martensite.

The critical rate of hardening can be determined from the diagram of isothermal decomposition of austenite.

This analysis shows that a simple superposition[*] of cooling curves on the isothermal diagram of austenitic decomposition can give only an approximate quantitative estimation of a transformation occurring in continuous cooling.

Key words:
superposition[重叠]

Questions:

1) The hardest product of the transformation in steel is

martensite. How can you obtain the martensite?

2) If the cooling speed is not high enough, there may be —— in the microstructure after transformation.

More accurate estimations of the transformations at a continuously varying temperature are made by using the so called thermokinetic, or anisothermal* diagrams of austenite transformations, which characterize the transformation at various cooling rates.

Though isothermal transformation diagrams can give us much knowledge on the nature of transformations, the transformations can only seldom be achieved under isothermal conditions in practice.[1]

With a very quick transformation, the process of decomposition is attained. This is why the isothermal transformation diagrams are quite inaccurate for holding times less than 10s.

When large sections are heat treated, it is impossible to meet another important condition essential for the construction of a diagram, i. e. quick cooling to the given temperature. Isothermal austenite transformation diagrams are of great theoretical significance but are superseded* by anisothermal diagrams in practical cases of selecting heat treatment conditions.

The cooling conditions have been studied quite thoroughly. It is possible in laboratories to imitate the conditions of cooling large massive articles and in various quenchant on small specimens. During cooling of specimens, the points of the beginning and the end of transformations are determined by dilatometric* (by changes in the dimensions of specimens) or magnetic (austenite is non-magnetic and its products are magnetic) method. The experimentally found cooling curves and the points of transformation are then plotted in a temperature time diagram and the sections of like transformations are combined into regions.

298 *English in Materials Science and Engineering*

Up to this point, we have considered only schematic diagrams of austenite transformation. For exhaustive* information on the transformation a particular grade of steel, however, use is made of both types of the diagram and of some additional data: grade and composition of the steel, heating temperature, austenitic grain size, properties (at least hardness) of decomposition products, and proportion of the constituents.

Key words:
anisothermal[非等温的]　　supersede[代替]　　dilatometric [膨胀的]
exhaustive[详尽的]

Note:
[1] 尽管等温相变图能够为我们提供大量有关相变本质的知识,但是事实上等温条件下的相变很难实现。

Questions:

1) According to the paragraph above, the author means that for a large massive articles _____ .

(a) the microstructure of both the surface and center is the same

(b) the transformation products both in surface layer and center are martensite

(c) the surface is martensite and the center the pearlite

(d) the type and size of transformation product depends on cooling rate and thickness of steel

2) Compare the cooling rates of oil quenching with air quenching and water quenching.

6.2.4 Martensite Transformation

If austenite is undercooled to the temperature at which the γ lattice is unstable, despite the presence of dissolved carbon and the rate of diffusion of carbon is so low(owing to the low temperature) that can be neglected, the iron lattice is rearranged without evolution of carbon. This transformation differs in its mechanism and in the nature of transformation products from the eutectoid decomposition of austenite that has been discussed earlier.[1]

As we recall, the austenite to pearlite transformation appreciably relies on diffusion and may be regarded as a diffusion type transformation.

In the austenite to martensite transformation, only the crystal lattice* undergoes arrangement, but the concentration of the reacting phases remains the same. Thus, the transformation is diffusionless. Martensite in steel is a supersaturated solid solution of carbon in α iron of the same concentration as in the original austenite. Since the solubility of carbon in α phase is only 0.01 per cent, martensite is a supersaturated solid solution.

Since the transformation is diffusionless, carbon does not precipitate from the solution, and only iron atoms are rearranged from fcc to bcc lattice.[2]

The crystal structure of martensite is characterized by tetragonality*, i.e. the c/a ratio in the lattice is greater than unity. This tetragonality of martensite is due to the presence of carbon in the solution. And the tetragonality of martensitic lattice is directly proportional to the content of carbon.

Martensite has a specific microstructure. Its crystals are platelets oriented parallel to one another or tilted* at definite angles (60 or 120 degrees).

As has been found, the orientation of martensite platelets is due to the fact that martensite can only form on certain crystal planes and along certain directions in austenite.[3] This oriented* transformation can be regarded as a shear or displacement* of a volume of metal in a definite plane, which occurs simultaneously with the γ to α

300   *English in Materials Science and Engineering*

transformation. The transformation is associated with an appreciable displacement of metal atoms in space, though neither the atoms change places nor the distances between them appreciably change. This oriented displacement of atoms during transformation produces a relieved surface in microsections.[4]

Thus, martensite transformation differs from other phase transformations in the following typical features: (1) it is diffusionless, i. e. is associated only with lattice rearrangement and the composition of the final phase (martensite) is the same as that of the original phase (austenite); (2) it is oriented, i. e. the new phase (martensite) is regularly oriented relative to the old phase (austenite); the shearing effect of the transformation produces relieved surface. Transformations characterized by these two particularities are referred to the class of martensite transformations.

Martensite transformations have been discovered in many metals and alloys. The martensite transformation in steel has the two typical features mentioned above and also some other specific features not found in other alloys. In steels, this transformation is irreversible*, that is, can only proceed in the direction γ Fe to α Fe, but cannot occur in the reverse direction by the same diffusionless mechanism. Further, martensitic crystals form in steel, irrespective of temperature, in an extremely short time interval (of an order of 0. 1 microseconds, i. e. practically instantaneously).

It has been established experimentally that the transformation consists in practically instantaneous formation of a portion of martensitic platelets, rather than of a single platelet (each platelet forms in a time interval of approximately 0. 1 microseconds and the whole portion consisting of hundreds or thousands of crystals, in 1 miliseconds), after which the transformation comes to a stop. With further cooling, the transformation is renewed by the formation of new portions and so on.

The Martensite transformation in cooling starts at point M_s. This point determines the temperature of the beginning of austenite to martensite transformation in a given steel.

The quantity of martensite increases as the temperature is lowered. The end of the transformation is determined by point M_f. At this temperature, a certain quantity of retained austenite remains in the structure. Further cooling below M_f causes no transformation nor changes the quantity of retained austenite.

Carbon appreciably lowers the martensitic points. At a carbon content above 0.5 percent, the temperature range of martensite transformation extends to sub-zero temperatures, i. e. such steels cannot be made fully martensitic by continuous cooling to room temperature.

Some alloying elements also can lower the martensitic point so that certain grades of alloy steel containing a sufficiently high percentage of carbon and alloying elements have their M_s point below 0℃, and common hardening produces a purely austenitic structure in them. It then follows that the temperature of martensite transformation mainly depends on steel composition(composition of austenite).

Key words:
lattice [点阵]   tetragonality[正方度]   tilt[倾斜]
orient[取向的]   displacement[位移]   irreversible[不可逆的]
Notes:

[1] 这种相变在机制上和相变产物的本质上与前面讨论的奥氏体的共析分解不同。

[2] 由于该转变是无扩散的,碳不能从固溶体中析出,而只有铁原子从面心立方点阵向体心立方点阵的重新排列。

[3] 正如所发现的,马氏体片的取向排列是因为马氏体只能在奥式体一定晶面上并沿着奥氏体一定方向形成。

302   *English in Materials Science and Engineering*

〔4〕在相变过程中,原子沿着一定的取向发生位移从而产生微小表面浮凸。

Questions:

1) Is the transformation from martensite to austenite possible?

2) What do M_s and M_f mean? What is retained austenite?

3) What is the effect of carbon content on M_s and M_f?

Let us now discuss some other factors which may affect the martensite transformation.

In the first place, it should be examined how the temperature of martensite transformation is affected by cooling rate.

Experiments with continuous cooling of austenite at various rates (which is roughly 150℃/s for carbon steel) to approximately 10 000℃/s failed to lower the temperature of the beginning of martensite transformation.

It can be concluded therefore that the temperature of the martensite transformation is independent of cooling rate.

Though the cooling rate has no effect on the position of the martensitic point, it can definitely affect the course of the martensite transformation. At temperatures slightly lower than M_s, a slower cooling gives a greater degree of transformation. This is due to the ability of austenite to isothermally transform into martensite at temperatures slightly less than M_s.

If the cooling is interrupted and an isothermal holding is allowed within the martensitic range, a certain, though small, amount of martensite forms during the holding time. This makes it possible to distinguish between athermal* marten site which forms in continuous cooling and isothermal martensite which forms at a constant temperature. The latter differs from the former both in the appearance (microstructure) and the properties (the last circumstance has not been thoroughly studied). In common steels, the formation of isothermal martensite quickly comes to a stop, i. e. only a small quantity of isothermal martensite is formed, so that martensite in real steels is mostly of the athermal type. A holding time in the martensitic range(as also at temperatures 100 ~ 200℃ above M_s) produces the effect of stabilization of austenite which essentially consists in that the austenite to martensite transformation upon the holding time is renewed not immediately but only after a certain undercooling and the final structure contains mo re austenite upon final cooling, i. e. less martensite is formed. [1]

The effect of stabilization can be explained by the relaxation * of the stresses which are essential for realization of the martensite transformation. This is why externally applied stresses cause martensite transformation but if they are eliminated (for instance, by disintegrating * a piece of steel into fine monocrystalline particles), the martensite transformation will not take place.

The structure of martensite in hardened steel is typically acicular *. The austenite which can coexist with martensite at room temperature in the structure is called retained austenite.

The quantity of retained austenite which can be fixed in a steel by hardening depends on the position of the martensitic point, being greater at a lower position of that point. This is why carbon, which lowers the martensitic point, increases the content of retained austenite.

Key words:
athermal[变温的]　　　relaxation[松弛]　　　disintegrate[分解]
acicular[针状的]

Note:

[1] 在马氏体转变温度范围内保温一定时间产生奥氏体稳定化效应,即在继续冷却时不能立即发生马氏体转变,而只有达到一定的过冷度时才能发生转变,并在最后冷却后的组织中含有较多奥氏体,也就是说,得到的马氏

304　*English in Materials Science and Engineering*

体较少。

Questions:

1) The effect of cooling rate on martensite transformation is _____ .

(a) the lower the cooling rate, the lower the martensite transformation temperature

(b) the lower the cooling rate, the higher the martensite transformation temperature

(c) it has no influence on martensite transformation temperature

2) Compare the difference between athermal martensite and isothermal martensite.

3) What is the effect of stress relaxation on the martensite transformation?

4) Why does carbon increase the content of retained austenite?

6.2.5 Bainite Transformation

The bainite transformation of undercooled austenite occurs in a temperature range between the pearlitic and the martensite range and for that reason is often called intermediate transformation. It has features of both the pearlitic and the martensite transformation (therefore it should not be related to the principal types of transformation).

The decisive feature of the bainite transformation is that it occurs in the temperature interval where there is practically no diffusion (self diffusion) of iron, but the diffusion of carbon is quite intensive.

Bainite transformation occurs by the more complicated mechanism than pearlite or martensite transformation.

If austenite is undercooled to a suitable temperature, its carbon is redistributed by diffusion so that some portions of austenite are enriched in carbon and the other are depleted [*] . This inhomogeneity of solution still contains around 0.15 ~ 0.20 percent carbon. The contraction that occurs on further heating is indicative of the complete precipitation of carbon from the solution and of the relaxation of the internal stresses that have appeared owing to the prior transformations which involved volume changes. At the same time, carbides separate from the matrix and form cementite. All these changes characterize what is called the third transformation on tempering.

In other words, the third transformation on tempering involves definite changes which result in stress relaxation and transformations of carbides. The third transformation is finished at 400℃, with the steel structure consisting of ferrite and cementite. A further rise in temperature can cause coagulation* of ferrite and cementite particles, which can be readily seen in microstructures at large magnifications.

Key words:
tempering[回火]   tetragonal[四角的]   specific[比率的]
dissolution[溶解]   radiographic[射线照相术]   sole[惟一的]
coagulation[凝结]   heterogeneous[异质的]

Notes:
[1]正如用X线法和磁热分析法所揭示的那样，低温回火时形成的亚稳碳化物与渗碳体不同.

[2]回火的第一阶段产生回火马氏体,这种回火马氏体是浓度不均匀的过饱和α固溶体和非孤立的碳化物颗粒的混合物。

Questions:

1) What is the purpose of the tempering process?

2) How many stages are there in tempering according to the passage?

3) If heated to 400℃, nearly all the martensite disappear. (T/F)

4) The secondary transformation will be finished at 300℃. (T/F)

which is indicative of certain transformations. As has been detected by X-ray analysis, the parameter c of the martensite lattice gradually diminishes within tempering temperature interval and the c/a ratio tends to unity.

The martensite that forms in this low temperature tempering, in which the c/a ratio is not equal but very close to unity is called temper martensite. Therefore, the first tempering transformation is the transformation of tetragonal martensite into almost cubic temper martensite.

As has been indicated earlier, the sole* cause for the tetragonality of martensite is dissolution* of carbon; thus, a decrease in tetragonality can be explained by precipitation of carbon from the solution.

The high carbon phase that precipitates from the solution is extremely fine carbide platelets which are coherently bonded with the solid solution matrix. As has been established by radiographic* and magnetothermal analysis, the metastable carbide that forms on low temperature tempering differs from cementite.[1]

The first transformation on tempering produces temper martensite which is a heterogeneous* mixture of supersaturated α solution of an inhomogeneous concentration and nonisolated carbide particles.[2]

Heating to a temperature above 200℃ will cause a different transformation resulting in expansion of the steel. This is what is called the second transformation on tempering which is confined to a temperature range from 200 to 300℃. In this interval, the retained austenite changes to a heterogeneous mixture of supersaturated α solution and carbide. In other words, retained austenite transforms into temper martensite. This is diffusion transformation and in its nature resembles the bainite transformation of primary austenite.

At the end of the second transformation, i.e. at 300℃, a solid

保温温度,塑性变形将诱发 γ 以马氏体转变机制向 α 的转变。

[2]由于上述机理对整个贝氏体转变温度区间都有效,所以在此区间内的不同温度将获得非常不同量的贝氏体。

Questions:

1) In what temperature range can the bainite transformation take place?

2) The carbon diffusion for bainite transformation occurs in _____ .

  (a) austenite   (b) α phase
  (c) bainite   (d) martensite

3) What is the key factor which determines the rate of the bainite transformation?

4) What are upper and lower bainites?

6.2.6 Transformation on Tempering*

The transformations occurring during heating of hardened steel have been established quite reliably by studying the microstructure, crystal lattice and the physical and mechanical properties of as tempered steel and of the variation of these properties in the course of tempering. The original structure of hardened steel prior to tempering consists of tetragonal* martensite and austenite. Since martensite is the structure of the highest specific* volume while the austenite is not, the transformations on tempering should be associated with volume changes, i.e. the volume of metal will increase upon martensite transformation (expansion of specimen) and decrease upon austenite transformation (contraction of specimen). The transformation in tempering can be fixed by means of a dilatometric curve. If an annealed specimen is heated in a dilatometer and there are no transformations in the metal, the instrument will generate a horizontal line. While the hardened steel specimen deviates from horizontal line, the concentration causes the appearance of stresses and, since the martensite point of the carbon depleted portions is above the temperature of the isothermal holding, a plastic deformation will induce the γ to α transformation by the martensitic reaction.[1] This γ to α change by the martensite type is the specific feature of the bainite transformation, which is confirmed by the fact that bainite transformation produces a relieved surface on polished microsections.

Thus, though the γ to α change proper in the bainite transformation takes place by the diffusionless mechanism, it is prepared by diffusion processes occurring in the austenite: these diffusion processes determine the rate of the bainite transformation.

The portions of austenite which have been enriched in carbon undergo no changes and remain austenite upon cooling from the temperature of isothermal holding to room temperature (or they may partially undergo the martensite transformation).

Carbide particles which are found in the structure of steel upon bainite transformation precipitate after the γ to α change, which fact indicates that the redistribution of carbon does not result in full depletion of carbon in individual austenite portions.

Whereas the described mechanism is valid for the whole temperature range of bainite transformation, a change of temperature within that range may cause appreciable quantitative differences.[2] At high temperatures, the effect of concentration redistribution is more appreciable than that at lower temperatures. This is why a distinction is made between upper and lower bainite which differ from one another both in microstructure and in properties.

Key words:
deplete[使耗尽,使衰减]

Notes:

[1] 该浓度不均匀导致产生应力,而且因为贫碳区的马氏体相变点高于